# Dates and Meanings of Religious and other Multi-Ethnic Festivals 2002-2005

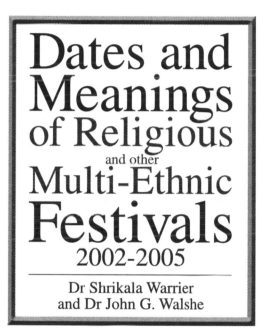

# Dates and Meanings
## of Religious
### and other
## Multi-Ethnic
# Festivals
## 2002-2005

Dr Shrikala Warrier
and Dr John G. Walshe

## foulsham educational

LONDON · NEW YORK · TORONTO · SYDNEY

# foulsham

The Publishing House, Bennetts Close, Cippenham,
Slough, Berkshire, SL1 5AP, England

ISBN 0-572-02659-5

Printed in Great Britain

# CONTENTS

# ACKNOWLEDGEMENTS

*Dates and Meanings of Religious and Other Multi-Ethnic Festivals* has emerged in response to a growing interest among professionals in various statutory agencies and the voluntary sector in the issues of cultural diversity and of providing equitable and appropriate services to clients of different nationalities, religious and ethnic affiliations.

The contents of this book have been gathered from various sources.
However, we particularly wish to acknowledge the help we have received from:

- Pandit Narottam Pandey, Vishva Hindu Mandir, Lady Margaret Road, Southall

- Dr M. Ikbal

- Rev. David Wilson, MA, St Mary's Parish Church, Osterley

- London Beth Din

- Mrs Ammu Warrier, Chinmaya Mission Society, Bangalore, India

- Mrs Joginder Kaur Toor, London and Punjab

- The Buddhist Society

- The Baha'i Centre, London

- The Holocaust Office

We gratefully acknowledge the encouragement and support of Graham Kitchen, Sue Peirce, Wendy Hobson and the editorial team at W. Foulsham and Co. Ltd.

*Shrikala Warrier and John Walshe*

## PUBLISHER'S NOTE
*Every effort has been made through a worldwide spread of advisers to
confirm all the religious and feast days contained in this book.
Many of the celebrations are movable feasts, some based on lunar reckonings,
therefore some of the dates are approximations and others are not yet known by the relevant authorities.
The publisher will be keeping a database of up-to-date information and would welcome
enquiries from schools and others wishing to check any dates.
Please telephone 01753 526769*

# FOREWORD

I feel very honoured to have been asked to write a foreword to this extremely informative work on world religions, rites of passage and festivals by Dr Shrikala Warrier and Dr John Walshe.

In the West, written material on Hinduism and other religions is available in many books. However, it is not easy to assemble all the important aspects of all religions in one book, but this volume by Dr Warrier and Dr Walshe achieves this and is unique for the following reasons:

• It captures the essence of each religion, which is encoded in sacred literature, in lucid and easily accessible language.

• It examines social practice and customs and relates them to the principles of each religion.

In these pages there is a bird's-eye view of a variety of subjects connected with the major religions of the world. The subjects covered are immense. They encompass gods, goddesses, places of worship, philosophical background, literature, rites and rituals.

As I turned these pages, it brought back many vivid memories from my own childhood.

I feel that books such as these are invaluable for educational institutions, statutory agencies and voluntary organisations concerned with issues emerging from cultural diversity. This book is also a wonderful resource for libraries.

I am sure that this beautifully produced book will tempt many people to explore further the meaning of the various world religions, rites of passage and celebrations of festivals.

**Dr M.N. Nandakumara**
Executive Director
Bharatiya Vidya Bhavan UK

# INTRODUCTION

Though we live in an amazingly hi-tech world and exercise considerable control over many facets of our lives, fundamental issues such as those concerning the origin of the universe and our place in it, the crisis of death and what happens in the afterlife, the struggle between good and evil and the why of human suffering, continue to perplex scientists, philosophers, theologians as well as the ordinary person in the street. As Stephen Hawking, the mathematician and theoretical physicist, wrote in his best-seller *A Brief History of Time*, we still do not know 'why ... the universe go[es] to all the bother of existing. ... Does it need a creator, and, if so, ... who created him?'

Our uncertainty about the unknown and our need to have coherent answers to the questions which bewilder us has resulted in the development of systems of belief and related practices charged with strong emotion and pervaded overall by a sense of awe. This aspect of human culture is referred to as 'religion' by anthropologists.

Human societies have, from the earliest times, developed a very clear concept of the 'sacred' to include all those phenomena which are regarded and experienced as extraordinary, supernatural and outside the ambit of everyday events. All organised religions are founded upon a central core of beliefs, which are codified and systematised and handed down from one generation of believers to the next. The term 'theology' is used to refer to the ordered reflections on the nature of God, and the relationship between human beings, the divine being and the universe.

Beliefs frequently rest upon a foundation of myths – sacred tales that relate to the past, to supernatural events and to ultimate reality. Myths have an explanatory, validating and synthesising function in any community of believers and serve as a powerful medium for conveying profound truths and moral principles.

An important dimension of organised religious systems is the artefacts and buildings connected with worship. The traditional architecture of religious buildings is profoundly symbolic and is indicative of their fundamental purpose. Are they places where people come to visit and pay homage to a God residing in a sacred place? Or are they places for a community of believers whose collective act of worship creates a sacred aura?

Closely related to the material artefacts are the verbal symbols and formulae, the prayers and liturgy through which faith is expressed. The primacy of the word and the recognition of the power of sound implies that scrupulous attention is paid to correct enunciation and intonation during the chanting or reciting of prayers and hymns.

For a great many people around the world, religion is woven into their way of life. It is something 'done' and 'lived' rather than a cerebral activity. Rituals express and renew the basic values of a society, especially those concerned with the relationships between people, between humans and nature, and the supernatural world. Festival rituals and celebrations are frequently the mode in which fundamental religious beliefs and values are expressed and reinforced. These calendrical rituals also symbolically link the identity and world view of the participants to events in the cosmic cycle such as the changing of seasons or planetary movements.

Rites of passage or the rituals of social transition, on the other hand, link changes in the individual life cycle to changes in social status and role. The rituals associated with pregnancy, birth, puberty, weddings and funerals serve the important purpose of maintaining social stability and of integrating the individual within society. The ceremonies are usually conducted with the help of ritual specialists or priests. For the participants, the ritual not only proclaims the change in status (from wife to mother, child to adult, or living person to dead ancestor) but is also a necessary factor in bringing about the transition.

This book provides a succinct account of the main living religions of the world. It focuses on their ideational dimension as well as the material artefacts associated with worship and the ritualistic elements including the celebrations of feasts, festivals and high holy days.

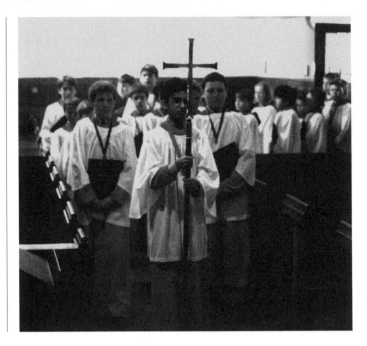

# CALENDARS

The calendar is a method of adjusting the natural divisions of time with respect to one another for both administrative purposes and for the observance of religious festivals. The term 'calendar' is derived from the Latin word *kalendae*, which designated the first day of the month in Roman times.

Celestial bodies provide the fundamental standard for determining the calendar. The basic calendar units are the day, month and year, derived from the movements, or apparent movements, of the earth, the moon and the sun respectively.

## A Day

A day is measured by the rotation of the earth on its axis. The duration of one complete rotation with respect to the stars is called the sidereal day (from the Latin *sidus* which means 'star'), a unit of time that is important in astronomy.

The cycle of night and day has considerable bearing on man's life. Hence, the solar day, or the interval between two passages of the sun across the meridian, is the basis of the civil calendar. The solar day is longer than the sidereal day by approximately four minutes.

## A Week

The week is a calendar unit that is almost universally used. It is an artificial unit of time, although its length of seven days relates it to the phases of the moon. The Hebrews were the first to use it. In most languages the days of the week are named after the seven moving celestial objects that were known in ancient times, namely the Sun, Moon, Mars, Mercury, Jupiter, Venus and Saturn.

## A Month

A lunar month is the time it takes the moon to complete a cycle of phases. It has an average length of 29.5 days.

## A Year

A year corresponds to the cycle of the seasons and is the result of the sun's apparent movement through the constellations as the earth moves around the sun.

The astronomical year is defined as the movement of the sun over the earth's hemisphere. The instant when the centre of the sun's disc crosses the equator is known as the vernal equinox, and the time interval between two vernal equinoxes is known as the seasonal or tropical year. A year averages 365 days.

# TYPES OF CALENDAR

There are three basic types of calendars: the lunar, lunisolar and solar, based on the phases of the moon and the apparent movements of the sun.

## Lunar Calendar

The oldest kind of calendar is the lunar calendar. In this type, the civil month is approximately the same length as the actual lunar month, and the first day of each civil month coincides with the new moon.

To establish agreement between the civil month, composed of a whole number of days, and the lunar month of 29.5306 days, an early solution was to have civil months that were alternately 29 and 30 days long. This made for an average civil month of 29.5 days – a lag of 0.0306 days behind the actual lunar month. Later lunar calendars grouped twelve civil months in a lunar year of 365 days. The year therefore lagged behind the cycle of the moon's phases by 0.3672 days. One way of compensating fairly precisely for this lag was to insert (intercalate) one day in the calendar every three years. Alternative solutions were to intercalate three days over a period of eight years, seven days in nineteen years, or eleven days in thirty years.

## Lunisolar Calendars

Once the significance of the solar year of 365.25 days came to be recognised, an exact relationship was sought between the solar year and the lunar month. One of the first solutions was to add a month to every three years. Alternatively, if three months are added to eight lunar years or seven months to nineteen lunar years, the adjustment closely approximates to eight or nineteen solar years respectively. Both the eight-year (Octennial) cycle and the nineteen-year (Metonic) cycle were used by the ancient Greeks. The Metonic cycle is fairly precise and is still used in Christian ecclesiastical calendar calculations.

## Solar Calendars

In modern times, the lunar month has been largely rejected in many countries in order to ensure better agreement between the civil month and the solar year. The twelve months are retained but are no longer lunar, so that the new moon may fall on any day of the month. Only the value of 365.2422 days as the average length of the year is fundamental to the establishment of the solar calendar.

A year of 365 days came to be used with an additional day intercalated every fourth year. The intercalary year was designated the leap year. This was the solution adopted in the Julian calendar. However, as the fraction to be compensated for is, in fact, 0.2422 days and not 0.25 days, an addition of one day every four years results in an excess of 0.0078 days per year and a cumulative error of about three days every four centuries. The Gregorian reforms that resulted in the modern Western calendar eliminate, to a large extent, this discrepancy.

*The sun at Stonehenge, England*

# The Western Calendar

The Western calendar had its origin in the desire for a solar calendar that kept in step with the seasons and possessed fixed rules of intercalation. With the rise of Christianity, it also had to provide a method of dating movable religious feasts such as Easter, which were based on lunar reckoning. To reconcile the lunar and solar schemes, features of the Roman Republican calendar and the Egyptian calendar were used.

The early Romans used a lunar calendar in which the lengths of the months alternated between 29 and 30 days. The civil year was composed of ten months and therefore of 295 days. The first month in the calendar was March. The seventh, eighth, ninth and tenth months were named September, October, November and December – Latin words indicating the position of these months in the year.

According to legend, it was around 700 BCE that January and February were added as the eleventh and twelfth months of the year. February consisted of only 28 days.

In the course of time, the Roman Republican calendar became increasingly out of step with the seasons. A need therefore arose for a calendar that would allow the months to be based on the phases of the moon and the year to be in line with the seasons.

The reformation of the Roman calendar was undertaken by Julius Caesar in 46 BCE. The lunar calendar was abandoned. Instead, the months were arranged on a seasonal basis and the solar year was used, with its length taken as 365¼ days.

It was also decided that the vernal equinox would fall on 25 March. The civil year was fixed at 365 days and an additional day was intercalated every four years so that the solar year would remain in agreement with the seasons. The extra day was added after 28 February.

The Julian reforms also reinstated 1 January as the first day of the year. January 45 BCE thus inaugurates the Julian calendar. A discrepancy in names was retained, however, in that the months of September to December still had their former names, although they were now the ninth to the twelfth months of the year.

## The Gregorian Calendar

The average length of the year in the Julian calendar, fixed by Julius Caesar in 46 BCE at 365¼ days, is eleven minutes longer than the solar year. There was thus a cumulative error amounting to nearly eight days in the course of 1,000 years, and the calendar became increasingly out of phase with the seasons.

In 1582, Pope Gregory XIII reformed the Julian calendar by shortening the year by ten days to bring the vernal equinox to 21 March. It was further ordained that no centennial years should be leap years unless they were exactly divisible by 400. Thus, 1700, 1800 and 1900 were not leap years although the year 2000 was. The reform measures also laid down the rules for calculating the date of Easter each year.

Easter was – and, of course, still is – the most important feast of the Christian Church and its place in the calendar determined the position of the rest of the Church's movable feasts. Its timing depended on both the moon's phases and the vernal equinox. Church authorities therefore had to seek some way of reconciling the lunar and solar calendars.

Easter was primarily designated a spring festival, and the earliest Christians celebrated it at the same time as the Jewish Passover festival, that is during the night of the first full moon of the first month of spring (14 and 15 Nisan). By the middle of the second century, most Churches had transferred this celebration to the Sunday after the Passover feast. The Council of Nicea observed the feast on a Sunday. Yet many disparities remained in fixing the date of Easter. Today the Eastern Churches follow the Julian calendar and the Western Churches the Gregorian calendar, so that in some years there may be a month's difference in the times of celebration.

The Gregorian calendar was adopted exactly according to the mandate of the Pope in France, Spain, Portugal and Italy in 1582. The Protestant countries, however, were slow to adopt it. In Britain it was not adopted until almost 200 years later in 1752.

# THE EASTERN ORTHODOX CHURCH

In 1054 a split occurred between the four Eastern patriarchates and the Roman (Western) patriarchate. The Orthodox Eastern Church, also known as the Orthodox Church and the Greek Orthodox Church, is the federation of thirteen autocephalous (that is, 'having their own heads') Orthodox Churches chiefly in Greece, Cyprus, Romania, Bulgaria, some of the independent states of the former Soviet Union and the Middle East. Together they comprise about one-sixth of the world's Christian population.

## Slavic Orthodoxy

In the middle of the ninth century two Greek brothers, Constantine and Methodios, were sent to bring Christianity to Slavic lands. Before they began, the scholarly brother, Constantine, translated most of the New Testament and the Orthodox Service books into Slavonic. To do this Constantine developed a new alphabet. When he became a monk, he changed his name to Cyril, so the alphabets to this day used by, for example, Russians, Serbs, Bulgarians and Ukrainians are called Cyrillic.

## Russian Orthodoxy

Towards the end of the tenth century, Vladimir, Prince of Kiev, invited Orthodox missionaries from Constantinople to teach his people. His grandmother, Olga, was a Christian, and he was to marry a Christian princess from Byzantium. The mission met with spectacular success: Greek clergy performed a mass baptism in the river at Kiev in CE 988, and Orthodox Christianity spread rapidly among the people called 'Rus'.

The *Russian Primary Chronicle* gives an account of how Vladimir chose Orthodoxy. He sent envoys to view the various nations at worship. Those who went to the Cathedral of the Holy Wisdom in Constantinople were transfixed by the glory of the service: 'We knew not whether we were in heaven or on earth; but this we know, that God dwells there among them.'

## The Orthodox Church Calendar

The Calendar reform by Pope Gregory XIII in 1582 was rejected by the Orthodox Church who viewed the papal reform as divisive and lacking in due respect for the traditions and oneness of the Church. The enforcement of the Gregorian calendar by several temporal rulers was regarded without enthusiasm.

Since 1923, the Orthodox Church has been divided over the calendar. In that year several churches (mainly Greek) decided to adopt the new calendar for all days except the days that depend on Easter. Easter is still to be reckoned by the old calendar.

Those (mostly Slavic) churches who retain the Julian calendar remain thirteen days behind other Christians in the determining of festival dates. As examples: Christmas falls on 7 January and New Year's Day falls on 14 January in the Gregorian calendar.

# THE HINDU CALENDAR

Whereas the Republic of India has adopted the Gregorian calendar for secular purposes, the religious life of Hindus continues to be governed by the traditional Hindu calendar, which is based primarily on the lunar cycle but adapted to solar reckoning.

The oldest form of the Hindu calendar is known from texts of about 1000 BCE. It divides a solar year of approximately 360 days into twelve lunar months. In order to align it with the solar year of 365 days, a leap month was intercalated every 60 months.

The year was divided into three periods of four months, each of which would be introduced by a special religious rite, the Chaturmasya (four-month rite). Each of these periods was further divided into two parts (seasons or *rtu*):

| Seasons | Hindu Names | Dates |
| --- | --- | --- |
| Spring | *Vasantha* | Mid-February to mid-April |
| Summer | *Grishma* | Mid-April to mid-June |
| Rainy season | *Varsa* | Mid-June to mid-August |
| Autumn | *Sarad* | Mid-August to mid-October |
| Winter | *Hemanta* | Mid-October to mid-December |
| Dewy season | *Sisira* | Mid-December to mid-February |

The month, counted from full moon to full moon, was divided into two parts (*paksha*) of waning (*krsna paksha*) and waxing (*sukla-paksha*) and special rituals were prescribed on the days of the new moon (*amavasya*) and full moon (*purnima*). The lunar day (*tithi*), a thirtieth part of the lunar month, was reckoned to be the basic unit of the calendar. However, as the lunar month is only about 29½ solar days, the tithi does not correspond with the natural day of 24 hours.

The *Jyotisa-Vedanga*, a treatise on time reckoning dated around 100 BCE, adds a larger unit of five years (*yuga*) to these divisions. A further distinction was made between the *uttarayana* (northern course), when the sun rises every morning farther north, and *dakshinayana* (southern course), when it rises progressively south.

The reckoning in general, was mostly dictated by the requirements of rituals, the time of which had to be fixed correctly. When astrology became increasingly important for casting horoscopes and making predictions, zodiacal time measurement was introduced into the calendar.

The year began with the entry of the sun (*sankranti*) in the sign of Aries. The table below indicates the zodiacal signs in the Hindu calendar (rasi) and their Western equivalents.

| Hindu Names | Signs | Western Names |
| --- | --- | --- |
| *Mesa* | Ram | *Aries* |
| *Vrsabha* | Bull | *Taurus* |
| *Mithuna* | Twins | *Gemini* |
| *Karkata* | Crab | *Cancer* |
| *Simha* | Lion | *Leo* |
| *Kanya* | Maiden | *Virgo* |
| *Tula* | Scales | *Libra* |
| *Vrschika* | Scorpion | *Scorpio* |
| *Dhanus* | Archer | *Sagittarius* |
| *Makara* | Goat | *Capricorn* |
| *Kumbha* | Water bearer | *Aquarius* |
| *Mina* | Fish | *Pisces* |

While the solar system has significance for astrology, time for ritual purposes continues to be reckoned by the lunar calendar. The names of the months in this system are:

| Hindu Months | Dates |
| --- | --- |
| *Chaitra* | March–April |
| *Vaisakha* | April–May |
| *Jyaistha* | May–June |
| *Ashada* | June–July |
| *Sravana* | July–August |
| *Bhadrapada* | August–September |
| *Asvina* | September–October |
| *Karthika* | October–November |
| *Margasirsa* | November–December |
| *Pausa* | December–January |
| *Magha* | January–February |
| *Phalguna* | February–March |

In the course of time, India also adopted the seven-day week (saptaha) and the days were named after the corresponding planets.

| Western Names | Hindu Names | Planets |
| --- | --- | --- |
| Sunday | *Ravivara* | Sun |
| Monday | *Somavara* | Moon |
| Tuesday | *Mangalvara* | Mars |
| Wednesday | *Budhvara* | Mercury |
| Thursday | *Brihspativara* | Jupiter |
| Friday | *Sukravara* | Venus |
| Saturday | *Sanivara* | Saturn |

## The Eras

The years of events were recorded in well-defined eras from the first century BCE.

Among those which have remained influential are the Vikrama Era (begun in 58 BCE), the Saka Era (from CE 78), the Gupta Era (from CE 320) and the Harsha Era (from CE 606). All these were dated from some significant historical event, though the first two are the most commonly used.

In the Hindu calendar, the date of an event takes the following form: month, fortnight (either waxing or waning moon), name (usually the number) of the *tithi* in that fortnight, and the year of the particular era that the writer follows. Important Hindu festivals are usually based on the lunar calendar. However, the sun's entry into the sign of Aries, marking the beginning of the astrological year, and the sun's entry into the sign of Capricorn (*makara sankranti*) are also regarded as important days in the calendar. The latter coincides with a harvest festival, which in the southern Indian state of Tamil Nadu is widely celebrated as the Pongal Festival.

# THE MUSLIM CALENDAR

The Muslim Era starts in the year of Hegira (CE 622) – the migration of the Prophet Mohammed and his followers from Mecca to Medina. The second caliph, Omar I, who reigned CE 634–644, set the first day of the month Muharram as the beginning of the year.

The Muslim calendar is based on the lunar cycle and consists of twelve months alternating 30 and 29 days each. The first day of each month is determined by the sighting of the new moon. The year is reckoned to have 354 days, but the last month, Zul-Hijja (*Dhu-al-hijjah*), sometimes has an intercalated day, bringing it up to 30 days and a total of 355 days for that year. The Muslim calendar is therefore eleven days shorter than the Gregorian calendar year. Although the Christian Era may be in official use, people in Muslim countries tend to use the Muslim Era for non-official purposes. To calculate conversions from the Muslim to the Gregorian calendar, the following formula is used:

$$G = H + 622 - \frac{H}{33}$$

$$H = G - 622 + \frac{G - 622}{32}$$

G = Gregorian calendar
H = Hegira

The names of the months in the Muslim calendar and the number of days in each are listed below.

| Names | Length |
| --- | --- |
| Muharram | 30 days |
| Safar | 29 days |
| Rabee ul-Awwal | 30 days |
| Rabee ul-Thani | 29 days |
| Jumadi ul-Awwal | 30 days |
| Jumadi ul-Thani | 29 days |
| Rajab | 30 days |
| Shaban | 29 days |
| Ramadhan | 30 days |
| Shawwal | 29 days |
| Zul-Qeda | 30 days |
| Zul-Hijja | 29 days |

The first month (Muharram), the seventh (Rajab) and the last two (Zul-Qeda and Zul-Hijja) are considered sacred months. Ramadhan, the ninth month of the Muslim calendar, is observed throughout the Muslim world as a period of fasting. According to the Qur'an, Muslims must see the new moon with the naked eye before they can begin their fast. Should the new moon prove difficult to sight then the month Shaban, immediately preceding Ramadhan, will be reckoned to have 30 days and the fast will commence on the day following the last day of Shaban.

'The number of months with Allah has been twelve by Allah's ordinance since the day he created the heavens and the earth. Of these, four are known as sacred.'
(The Qur'an 9:36)

'They ask thee, O Prophet, concerning the phases of the moon. Tell them: these alterations are a means of determining time for regulation of people's affairs and for the pilgrimage.'
(The Qur'an 2:190)

The solar system of reckoning time is used as the basis for the five daily prayers as well as for determining the beginning and breaking of the fast during Ramadhan. When worship is to be completed within a particular month or part of a month, the lunar system is used, as in the determination of the month of fasting or fixing the time of Haj, the pilgrimage. Islamic festivals, however, are based on lunar sightings rather than lunar reckonings. It is therefore not possible to have the exact dates of these festivals very much in advance.

# THE JEWISH CALENDAR

The Jewish calendar in use today is lunisolar, the years being solar and the month lunar. The year consists of twelve months, which are alternately 29 and 30 days in length. In order to celebrate the festivals in their proper season, the difference between the lunar year (354 days) and the solar year (365½ days) is made up by intercalating a thirteenth month of 30 days in the third, sixth, eighth, eleventh, fourteenth, seventeenth and nineteenth years of a nineteen-year cycle. The month so added is called Adar Sheni (second Adar) and the year, a leap year. The intercalary year can contain 383, 384 or 385 days, whereas ordinary years contain 353, 354 or 355 days.

The year commences at the new moon of Tishri (September to October) but its beginning may be shifted by a day for various reasons, among them the rule that the Day of Atonement must not fall on a Friday or Sunday, the seventh day of Tabernacles or a Sabbath.

The months are counted (following a biblical custom) starting from Nisan. Only a few biblical month names are known. The present ones are of Babylonian origin. The Jewish Era in use today is dated from the supposed year of the creation, calculated on biblical data to coincide with 3761 BCE. In giving Hebrew dates, it is customary to use Hebrew letters for numbers and to omit the thousands from the year number.

The Hebrews can be considered to have established the week as a unit of time. The pivot of the week is the Sabbath, or day of rest, which corresponds to Saturday in the modern calendar.

For practical purposes, for example, for reckoning the commencement of the Sabbath, the day begins at sunset. The calendar day of 24 hours, however, always begins at 6 p.m.

The names of the months in the Hebrew calendar and the number of days in each are listed below.

| Hebrew Names | Babylonian Names | Length |
| --- | --- | --- |
| Nisan | Nisannu | 30 days |
| Iyyar | Ayaru | 29 days |
| Sivan | Shimanu | 30 days |
| Tammuz | Du'uzu | 29 days |
| Av | Abu | 30 days |
| Ellul | Ululu | 29 days |
| Tishri | Tashretu | 30 days |
| Marheshvan (Heshvan) | Arakshanana | 29/30 days |
| Kislev | Kishnuu | 29/30 days |
| Tevet | Tabetu | 29/30 days |
| Shevat | Shabatu | 30 days |
| Adar | Addaru | 29 days (30 days in leap year) |

The New Year can be said to begin on the 1st of Nisan (Leviticus 23:5) or on Rosh Hashanah, at 1 a.m., which was Monday 7 September 3760 in the Gregorian calendar, or Monday 7 October 3761 BCE in the Julian. The day begins at sunset and is generally taken to be 24 hours long. For religious purposes, however, it is reckoned that the day begins at sunset, but ends when the stars become visible on the following day.

# THE SIKH CALENDAR

Until 13 March 1998, the Sikhs used the Hindu lunar calendar to determine their feast days and festivals. They now use their own Nanakshahi calendar, which aligns with the Gregorian calendar as follows:

| Sikh Months | Gregorian starts |
| --- | --- |
| Chet | 14 March |
| Vaisakh | 14 April |
| Jeth | 15 May |
| Harh | 15 June |
| Sawan | 16 July |
| Bhadon | 16 August |
| Asu | 15 September |
| Katik | 15 October |
| Maghar | 14 November |
| Poh | 14 December |
| Magh | 13 January |
| Phagan | 12 February |

The Nanakshahi calendar is used to determine all the *gurpurabs* or festivals marking events in the lives of the Sikh Gurus except the birthday of Guru Nanak, which continues to be celebrated according to the Hindu lunar calendar on Karthik Poornamashi.

The celebrations of the gurpurabs commence three weeks in advance of the actual date. They include the Akhand Path and the Prabhat Pheris or early morning religious processions, which are headed by five armed guards carrying the Nishan Sahib. Devotees offer tea and sweets to the marchers. On the actual festival day, the Guru Granth Sahib (holy scriptures) is carried in procession on a float decorated with flowers. Sikhs visit *gurdwaras* (Sikh places of worship) where special services are arranged. Sweets and food are also served to all visitors irrespective of their religious faith.

# THE BUDDHIST CALENDAR

The Buddhist calendar combines solar and lunar elements. The year is solar, usually consisting of twelve months, with the inclusion of an additional month every four or five years. All religious festivals, however, follow the lunar calendar.

The full moon days in each month are important to Buddhists and many of them are celebrated with colourful ceremonies. The full moon day in the month of Vesakha (Vaisakha) is particularly significant in Theravada Buddhist countries such as Sri Lanka and Thailand, as it commemorates the birth, enlightenment and death of the Buddha. Followers of the Mahayana and Zen traditions normally celebrate each of these events on separate days.

The Buddhist calendar tends to vary from one country to another, and from one school of Buddhism to another. In Sri Lanka, Nepal and south-east Asian countries such as Thailand, the year begins on a fixed date in April. The Chinese and Tibetan New Year's Day, however, falls at a new moon. Chinese New Year is usually celebrated in the second half of January or the first half of February. The Tibetan New Year, Losar, usually falls in February. The exact date varies from year to year.

In Pali, the ancient North Indian language, the names of the Buddhist months are:

**Buddhist Months**

*Citta*
*Vesakha*
*Jettha*
*Asalha*
*Savana*
*Potthabada*
*Assayuja*
*Kattika*
*Maggasira*
*Pussa*
*Maga*
*Phagguna*

The additional or thirteenth month is called *Adhivesaka*.

# THE BAHA'I CALENDAR

The Baha'i Era dates from 1844. The calendar year consists of nineteen months each of nineteen days duration, adding up to 361 days, with four intercalary days between the eighteenth and nineteenth months. The leap year has five intercalary days.

The names of the nineteen months represent various sublime attributes, and the avoidance of references to old pagan feasts and Roman holidays emphasises the arrival of a new era. The months are:

| Arabic Names | Translation | First Days |
| --- | --- | --- |
| *Bahá* | Splendour | 21 March |
| *Jalál* | Glory | 9 April |
| *Jamál* | Beauty | 28 April |
| *'Azamat* | Grandeur | 17 May |
| *Núr* | Light | 5 June |
| *Rahmet* | Mercy | 24 June |
| *Kalimát* | Words | 13 July |
| *Kamál* | Perfection | 1 August |
| *Asmá'* | Names | 20 August |
| *'Izzat* | Might | 8 September |
| *Mash'yyat* | Will | 27 September |
| *'Ilm* | Knowledge | 16 October |
| *Quadrat* | Power | 4 November |
| *Qawl* | Speech | 23 November |
| *Masá'il* | Questions | 12 December |
| *Sharaf* | Honour | 31 December |
| *Sultan* | Sovereignty | 19 January |
| *Mulk* | Dominion | 7 February |
| *'Alá* | Loftiness | 2 March |

The cycle of the year ends with nineteen days of fasting to prepare for the coming of the New Year (Naw-Ruz). The Baha'i day starts and ends at sunset. The dates of the celebration of feasts are adjusted to conform to the Baha'i calendar time.

These are the important anniversaries and festivals observed by the Baha'is.

| Festival | Dates |
| --- | --- |
| Festival of Ridvan (Declaration of Baha'u'llah) | 21 April–2 May |
| Declaration of the Bab | 23 May |
| Ascension of Baha'u'llah | 29 May |
| Martyrdom of the Bab | 9 July |
| Birth of the Bab | 20 October |
| Birth of Baha'u'llah | 12 November |
| Day of the Covenant | 26 November |
| Ascension of Abdu'l-Baha | 28 November |
| Period of the Fast | 19 days beginning 2 March |
| Feast of Naw-Ruz (Baha'i New Year) | 21 March |

(If the vernal equinox falls on 21 March before sunset, Naw-Ruz is celebrated on that day. If at any time after sunset, the New Year will then fall on 22 March.)

Baha'i law forbids work on Nine Holy Days.

## Holy Days

1  The first day of Ridvan
2  The anniversary of the declaration of the Bab
3  The ninth day of Ridvan
4  The anniversary of the birth of Baha'u'llah
5  The twelfth day of Ridvan
6  The anniversary of the birth of the Bab
7  The feast of Naw-Ruz
8  The anniversary of the ascension of Baha'u'llah
9  The anniversary of the martyrdom of the Bab

# THE CHINESE CALENDAR

Evidence from the Shang oracle bone inscriptions shows that, as early as the fourteenth century BCE, the Shang Chinese had established the solar year at 365¼ days and lunations (the time between new moons) at 29½ days. The ancient Chinese calendar was lunisolar and the ordinary year contained twelve lunar months. As this was shorter than the solar year, in seven years out of every nineteen a thirteenth intercalary month was inserted during the year to bring the calendar back in step with the seasons. Because of this, and the need for accurate dates for agriculture, there was an underlying solar year which was divided into 24 sections. These have colourful names such as the Waking of Insects, Grain in the Ear and White Dew. Although most festivals are fixed by the lunar calendar some, such as Qingming, are fixed in the solar cycle.

The Chinese New Year begins with the first new moon after the sun enters Aquarius, that is the second new moon after the winter solstice. Thus New Year's Day falls any time between 21 January and 20 February.

The years in the Chinese calendar are named after twelve animals, which follow one another in rotation. According to one version of the legend, these animals quarrelled one day as to who was to head the cycle of years. When asked to decide, the gods suggested a contest. Whoever was to reach the bank of a certain river first would head the cycle, and the rest of the animals would be grouped accordingly. All the animals assembled at the river and the ox plunged in.

Unknown to him, the rat jumped on his back and stepped ashore. Thus the cycle starts with the rat.

These are the animals, in order, with their equivalent Chinese names.

| Chinese Names | Animals |
| --- | --- |
| *Shu* | Rat |
| *Niu* | Ox |
| *Hu* | Tiger |
| *Tu* | Hare |
| *Long* | Dragon |
| *She* | Snake |
| *Ma* | Horse |
| *Yang* | Goat |
| *Hou* | Monkey |
| *Ji* | Cock |
| *Gou* | Dog |
| *Zhu* | Pig |

Chinese horoscopes are based on the characteristics of the animal sign for the year of a person's birth, rather than on the month as for Western horoscopes. All Chinese know their animal sign, and from it one can easily guess a person's age (to a multiple of twelve years).

Nowadays in China the Western calendar is used for all administrative purposes, but the lunar calendar is still the basis for reckoning most festivals, religious activities and for birthdays.

# ORIGINS AND BELIEFS OF THE MAJOR RELIGIONS

This section deals with all the major religions of the world: Hinduism, Judaism, Christianity, Islam, Sikhism, Buddhism, Jainism and Baha'i. It provides not only an understanding of how they originated and became established, but it also aims to impart an understanding of the fundamental belief systems on which they are based.

Each section also looks at the major festivals and holy days linked to each religion and explains the background to and the meaning of the celebrations. The text explores the major life stages, or rites of passage, which are important to the members of that culture, to aid a fuller understanding of their view of life and its meaning.

# HINDUISM

## AN INTRODUCTION TO HINDUISM

Hinduism is one of the world's oldest living faiths in which complex rituals and practices co-exist with highly developed philosophical systems and metaphysics. Attempts to capture the essence of Hinduism encounter innumerable difficulties since there is no single founder or book which is acknowledged by all Hindus to be the source of their faith. The roots of this religion go far back into India's ancient past. In the course of several thousands of years, a multiplicity of different strands of belief and practice have been assimilated into the Hindu fold. In view of this diversity, it is often said that Hinduism is more a way of life rather than a religious system which requires its followers to adhere to a specific set of beliefs. Hindus themselves refer to their faith as *sanatana dharma* or eternal law.

The term 'Hindu', according to the noted philosopher-statesman, S. Radhakrishnan, has territorial rather than credal significance, since it originally referred to the culture that developed and flourished in the region drained by the River Indus (*Sindhu*) and its tributaries. Archaeological evidence suggests that the protagonists of the Indus Valley civilisation subscribed to a religion dominated by a powerful male deity and a mother goddess as well as various fertility symbols. These elements have been incorporated into Hindu worship.

The civilisation in the Indus Valley disappeared around 2500 BCE and was replaced by the culture of nomadic horsemen from the Central Asian steppes. These invaders called themselves Arya and their religion was a form of animism in which the forces of nature, which could not be understood or controlled, were invested with divinity. The principal deities were Surya (the sun god), Indra (the god of war) and Yama (the god of death). The domestic hearth was dominated by Agni, the god of fire. The cosmos was also believed to be populated by a variety of celestial beings. Hymns were composed in Sanskrit in honour of these various divinities and these are contained in the *Rig Veda*, the oldest and most sacred literature of the Hindus.

The central feature of Aryan religious practice was the conduct of large-scale sacrifices in order to sustain order (*rta*) in the universe. The corpus of revealed sacred Hindu literature (the Vedas) includes the Sama Veda, a collection of hymns from the Rig Veda, which were chanted at sacrifices, the Yajur Veda, a collection of prose utterances recited by the priests who officiated at these ceremonies and the Atharva Veda, which consists mainly of prayers for achieving specific results such as victory in war or curing illness. The Atharva Veda is the source of Ayurveda, the traditional medical system of India. Some of the Rig Vedic hymns expound a theory that souls were born to happiness or sorrow according to their conduct in a previous life. This idea was to evolve into the doctrine of *karma*, one of the core elements of the Hindu world view.

The mystical and esoteric aspects of Hinduism were developed more fully in the *Upanishads*. These speculative treatises, dated around 600 BCE, were primarily concerned with the nature of reality, the origins of the universe and the meaning of human existence. The Upanishads emphasise the unity of the individual soul (*atman*) with the impersonal and absolute Universal Soul (the *Brahman*). The words, *Tat tvam asi* – 'that art thou' (Chandogya Upanishad) provide insight into a belief which lies at the heart of Hinduism.

*Surya, the sun god*

## The Fundamental Ideas of Hinduism

Hinduism is distinguished from the other major religions of the world in that, at no stage, has there developed any clear concept of a God who is the creator of the universe or is an essentially moral being who must be obeyed. In fact, at the higher levels of philosophical speculation, the very existence of a God is denied, with the emphasis instead being placed on achieving salvation through the achievement of knowledge and spiritual insight.

There are six orthodox schools of Hindu philosophy which accept the Vedas as revelation but offer different perspectives (*darshana*) on the nature of the world, the meaning of human existence and the means of acquiring true knowledge. The Samkhya recognises two final eternal realities, *purusha* (non-matter or pure spirit) and *prakriti*, an all-pervasive force which consists of three contrasting qualities or *gunas*. When prakriti which is always changing, is united with purusha, the result is the creation of the full conscious human being. Samkhya denies the existence of a divine being and sees the cosmos as being ruled by natural and moral law (*dharma*).

The Yoga school is closely allied to that of Samkhya. Its main ideas were first set out in systematic form in the writings of Patanjali (1st century CE). Earthly existence is believed to be full of sorrow because of the separation of the individual soul from the Absolute Brahman. Patanjali set out eight steps for achieving self-control, concentration and deep meditation in order to reach an attachment-free state which leads to salvation.

According to the *Nyaya* school, suffering is the result of ignorance. The means of acquiring true knowledge are fourfold, namely, perception (*pratyaksha*), inference (*anumana*), comparison (*upama*) and verbal testimony from an authoritative source (*aptavakya*).

Closely allied to Nyaya, is the Vaisheshika school, which also teaches that the external world can be studied by the application of logic. According to this system, the world is constructed of nine atoms which include the four elements: earth, water, fire and air, three all pervasive entities, namely ether, time and space and the non-physical entities of *atman* (individual soul) and *manas* (mind).

The Vedanta school gave a systematic form to the teachings of the Upanishads, concentrating mainly on the attainment of liberation through knowledge of the unity of the Brahman and atman. The theistic interpretations of its leading exponents greatly encouraged the development of *bhakti*, or devotion, as the means of achieving personal salvation.

The Purva Mimamsa school teaches that the four Vedas are uncreated and eternal. Belief in the existence of a God is unimportant; on the other hand, correct ritual action as laid down in the Vedas leads to liberation.

Hindu religious belief begins with the assumption that all living beings have a soul, which passes through successive cycles of birth and rebirth (*samsara*). Whether the individual soul is reborn as a human being, animal, insect or plant depends upon the sum total of its actions (*karma*) in a previous life. Thus all living beings are equal, being differentiated only by their karma.

The concept of karma relates to the principle of causality. Every good thought, word and action is believed to produce a positive reaction, whereas every bad thought, word and deed results in a negative reaction. Karma has several different aspects. Hindus believe that while some things, such as the family in which one is born, are predetermined by the sum total of acts performed in a previous existence and therefore unchangeable, individual characteristics and aptitudes, also a product of karma, are more amenable to change. The course of the future can also be influenced by thoughts, words and deeds performed by someone in the present existence.

From the time of the Upanishads, reincarnation has been regarded as undesirable and the major preoccupation of the religious-minded is to transcend the cycle of transmigration through closer identification with the undifferentiated source of the universe – the Brahman. Once this unity is achieved, the whole of the external world will be seen to be an illusion (*maya*).

*Moksha*, or liberation from the endless cycle of births, can be achieved in several ways. The ascetic path to personal liberation is strongly advocated in the Hindu tradition. Men and women frequently withdraw from the cares and demands of every day existence to meditate and contemplate upon the nature of the Brahman and subject themselves to rigorous forms of mental and physical training (*yoga*) to induce mystical experiences.

However, it has always been understood that the path of contemplation and asceticism is not suitable for all. The majority of Hindus seek to attain salvation through the path of action (*karma marga*) or the path of devotion (*bhakti marga*). The former advocates the conscientious observance of duties relevant to one's station in life. All work, however humble it may be, can, according to this school of thought, become an act of creation and thereby a means of liberation. On the other hand, the path of devotion assumes that escape from the cycle of birth, death and rebirth can be achieved through devotion to the various deities in the Hindu pantheon.

In the higher levels of metaphysical thinking, Hinduism is essentially monotheistic because all differences are reduced to a single entity or principle – the Brahman. However, at the level of popular Hinduism, there are a multiplicity of deities and divinities, each of whom has been attributed distinctive individual characteristics and special powers.

Hindus, it has been said, recognise godhead in everything around them. Natural features such as mountains and hills, rivers and trees are all regarded as the abodes of gods and goddesses or may themselves be personified as deities. Animals are worshipped either as vehicles of the gods or as their representatives. Harmony with natural phenomena is a pervasive element in classical Hindu belief and ritual observance, because the differences between human beings and animals, between animate and inanimate nature, are interpreted as differences of degree rather than of kind.

# HINDU GODS AND GODDESSES

## Brahma

The power regarded in the Upanishads as being universal and the elemental matter from which everything (including the gods themselves) originally emerged became fully personalised under the name of *Brahman*. In later texts, Brahma is regarded as one of the Holy Trinity (*Trimurthi*) of Hinduism and closely associated with the creation and control of the universe. From the 6th century CE onwards,

however, the worship of Brahma gradually declined and there is only one temple in India (Pushkar in the state of Rajasthan) that is dedicated to Brahma.

Hindu iconography usually portrays Brahma with four heads and four arms that hold a variety of objects including the Vedas, a rosary, a bow and a water pitcher. His vehicle is a white swan (*hansa*), the symbol of knowledge.

## Vishnu

The Vedas refer to Vishnu as one of twelve sun gods. However, as Hinduism evolved, Vishnu acquired the characteristics of many of the Vedic Aryan gods as well various folk deities.

Images of Vishnu show him in many poses. He is usually painted blue and dressed in yellow garments, holding in his four hands, a conch shell (*shankh*), a discus or wheel (*chakra*), a mace (*gada*) and a lotus (*padma*). Symbolism forms an important aspect of Hindu iconography and conveys many of the characteristics associated with the deity. Thus, the blue colour of Vishnu's body represents infinity, whereas the yellow garments symbolise majesty. The wheel represents time as well as the powers of creation and destruction. The conch shell is associated with the origin of existence through its spiral form and its connection with water and sound. The mace represents authority and the lotus indicates perfection and purity.

In the Hindu myth of creation, the world is believed to pass through cycles within cycles through all eternity. These cycles are related to the life of Vishnu. Between each cycle of creation, Vishnu, in the mythology, lies asleep on the coils of the many-headed serpent king – Shesha, who represents time as well as the condition of the universe before its manifest creation. However, in his intense concern for the world, he descends from time to time from *Vaikuntha*, the heaven over which he presides, as an *avatar* or incarnation.

Hindus believe that there have been nine full incarnations of Vishnu so far, with one more yet to come. In the first three incarnations – the fish (*matsya*), tortoise (*kurma*) and boar (*varaha*) – Vishnu appeared in the form of an animal to save the world and the Vedas from a great flood. In the fourth and fifth incarnations – man-lion (*narasimha*) and dwarf (*vamana*) – he saved the world from demons. In the sixth incarnation – Parasurama – he took on a human form and established the supremacy of the priests (Brahmins) within the social order.

The seventh and eighth incarnations as Rama and Krishna, have great religious significance, for it is in these forms that Vishnu is chiefly worshipped by Hindus.

Rama is the hero of the great Hindu epic, the Ramayana, and epitomises honour, filial piety and nobility of character. Images of Rama in Hindu temples usually depict him accompanied by his wife Sita and his brother Lakshman, and Hanuman, the monkey leader.

Krishna is probably the most popular figure in the Hindu pantheon and the hero of the Hindu romantic literary tradition. He is often worshipped as an infant holding a ball of butter in his hand, or as the youthful flautist who dwelt among cowherds and charmed the hearts of women of all ages. Images of him in temples usually show him accompanied by Radha, a simple cowherd's wife. The Radha-Krishna romantic theme symbolises the worshipper's desire for union with the Brahman or the Absolute.

Krishna also figures as the leading character in the epic Mahabharata. In many Hindu temples, there are images or paintings of him as the divine charioteer of Arjuna, one of the main protagonists, to whom he preached what many Hindus believe to be the essence of the faith. The advice given on the battlefield to Arjuna is contained in the sacred text, the Bhagavad Gita.

In the famous Guruvayoor temple in the southern Indian state of Kerala, the daily ritual is symbolic of the lifecycle of Krishna. In the first service (*puja*) conducted just after

dawn, the main focus of devotion is the infant Krishna (Balakrishna). The next puja is directed towards Venugopala, the adolescent flute-playing Krishna who enjoyed life amidst the cowherds in Vrindavan. Later in the day, devotions are addressed to Krishna, the charioteer of Arjuna (Parthasarathy). The last *puja,* conducted just after sunset, is a grand occasion marked by bright burning oil lamps, the rhythm of drums and flutes and a procession of caparisoned elephants, to honour Krishna, the King of Dwaraka.

The ninth incarnation of Vishnu is Buddha. It is believed that the purpose of this incarnation was to put an end to the animal sacrifices that formed an integral part of religious rituals in the early history of Hinduism.

The final incarnation of Kalki is yet to come. In the sacred texts, Vishnu will appear riding on a white horse and holding a flaming sword, to put an end to the immorality and corruption existing in society.

Besides the nine full incarnations, Hindus also believe that there have been several partial avatars of Vishnu so far. One of these is Dhanwantari, the deity associated with the traditional Hindu medical system of Ayurveda.

## Shiva

The worship of Shiva reaches far back into the history of Hinduism. Archaeological evidence from the Indus Valley points to the worship of a fertility god known as Pasupati, who shares many characteristics with the later Shiva. The Vedic Aryan god Rudra, the god of storms and natural elements, is also believed to be a prototype of Shiva.

Whereas Vishnu is perceived as a benevolent protector, Shiva combines the powers of creation, preservation and destruction, and the trident he holds represents these three forces. Images of Shiva in Hindu temples frequently depict him as a great ascetic, engrossed in meditation in his abode Mount Kailasha, high up in the Himalayan mountain ranges. He is usually shown with a knot of matted hair (symbolising stored up ascetic power) in which the crescent moon (symbol of creation) is fixed and from which the sacred River Ganges flows. In this pose he is usually shown dressed in a tiger skin with a snake (representing time) draped around his neck like a garland. The third eye in the middle of his forehead (from which his destructive powers are unleashed) is usually closed. The universe is maintained by his meditation and thus, for his devotees, he takes over the preserving function of Vishnu.

Shiva is also frequently depicted in a dancing pose with his body smeared with ashes from the cremation grounds and wearing a garland of skulls. In one hand he is shown holding an hourglass-shaped drum which regulates the rhythm of the dance, and, in the other, the ashes of the fire with which he destroyed the universe.

In some Shiva temples, the focal point of worship may be the *linga* (a phallic symbol) in conjunction with the *yoni*, which symbolises the female principle. Devotees worship the icon with lights, flowers, milk and other offerings. Shiva and his consort Parvati represent the ideal of marital bliss and many Hindu women observe a fast on Mondays to ensure a peaceful and prosperous married life.

## Ganesha

One of the most popular deities in the Hindu pantheon is Shiva's son, Ganesha. Also known as Ganapati, (lord of all beings), Vinayaka (the supreme leader) and Vighneshwara (remover of all obstacles), he is propitiated by Hindus before the commencement of any auspicious ritual or at the start of a journey or enterprise. As the god of wisdom, he is also invoked by students and seekers of knowledge.

Ganesha is usually described as having a human form with an elephant's head, and Hindu mythology is replete with explanations for this. In one account, Ganesha, while guarding his mother Parvati's door, refused to admit Shiva, who in anger cut off his son's head. Later, in order to placate his distressed wife, Shiva offered to replace Ganesha's severed head with that of the first living thing that came along. This happened to be an elephant.

Images of Ganesha in temples usually represent him with a conspicuously large stomach, sitting with one leg tucked under him and the other resting on the ground. A variety of food is arranged at his feet. He is usually depicted with four arms in which he holds an axe, a rope, a sweet rice cake (*modaka*) and a lotus. His vehicle is a rat. Painted images of Ganesha are usually red or yellow.

All aspects of Ganesha's form are rich in symbolism. His obesity contains the whole universe and his trunk is bent to remove obstacles. The foot resting on the ground represents his concern for the world, whereas the other symbolises his concentration upon the supreme reality (Brahman). The food laid out before him represents material wealth, power and prosperity.

The axe he holds in one hand symbolises his destruction of all desires and attachments. The rope is meant to pull the devotee from worldly entanglements. The rice cake represents the rewards of spiritual searching and the lotus symbolises perfection, the goal of human endeavour. The elephant-headed god riding on a rat illustrates the different ways in which obstacles can be removed to achieve spiritual goals; for, while the elephant has the strength to trample down any barriers, the rat can creep through cracks to achieve the same goal.

## Hanuman

Hanuman, the monkey god, is a popular deity and there are many Hindu temples dedicated to his worship. He is one of the main characters in the great epic, the Ramayana, and for Hindus he epitomises devotion and unswerving loyalty.

Hanuman (literally meaning *one with the broken chin*) is believed to be the son of Vayu, the god of wind and Anjana Devi, the monkey princess. Legend has it that as a young child he once attempted to capture the sun, mistaking it to be a ripe fruit. Indra, the chief among the gods, came to the rescue of the endangered sun and struck a severe blow on the baby Hanuman's chin, rendering him unconscious. The distressed father, Vayu, fled with his injured son into a cave, leaving the world breathless and at a standstill.

The sages and gods petitioned Brahma, the creator, for help. Brahma responded by approaching Vayu and granting his son two gifts: immortality and unlimited wisdom.

Hanuman's image is found in many forms, often kneeling in homage before Rama or flying through the air holding aloft the mountain of medicinal herbs needed to revive Rama's brother Lakshmana, who was seriously wounded in battle. He is also often shown grouped along with Rama, Sita and Lakshmana, standing a little to one side of the others with his hands joined together in prayer. In many Hindu temples, special prayers are offered to Hanuman on Tuesdays and Saturdays.

## Female Deities

Worship of female deities has always been part of folk religion in India, although their importance within the classical Hindu tradition has tended to vary from time to time and in different parts of the country. Some of the earliest ritual objects discovered in the Indus Valley are terracotta female figures representing the Mother Goddess who is generally associated with fertility and prosperity. As Hinduism evolved, the status of female deities changed from being merely secondary divinities and the consorts of male gods to being the active power (*shakti*) of the impersonal Absolute Brahma. As a personification of creative energy, goddesses are worshipped in their own right, also offering the devotee the possibility of approaching the male deity indirectly through his shakti.

## Parvati

The consort of Shiva occupies an important place in the Hindu pantheon. Known in her benign aspect as Parvati or Uma and in her fierce aspect as Durga or Kali, she is often referred to simply as 'the Mother', and her images are found in nearly all Hindu temples along with Shiva. She is worshipped as a secondary deity by most orthodox Hindus and as the major divinity by followers of the Shakti cult, who regard her as more accessible than Shiva and as a powerful force in her own right. Parvati is also referred to as 'Annapurna, the provider of food'.

Besides worshipping the goddess for securing favours, she is also invoked for her active assistance against terrors and disasters. In Hindu iconography, Durga or Kali is usually depicted as an awesome figure, clothed in garments of red and gold, mounted on a lion and holding in her eight hands a trident, sword, arrow and lotus (right hands); discus, bow, shield and skull (left hands). Many sculptures and pictures also show her wearing a garland of skulls and trampling on the demon Mahisha, who took the form of a buffalo and persecuted the gods.

Special prayers and ritualistic offerings to Durga are an important part of the Dassera festival celebrations.

## Lakshmi

Lakshmi, the wife of Vishnu, is regarded by Hindus as the goddess of good fortune, beauty and success, and she is worshipped in every Hindu household and temple on all important occasions. Lakshmi is said to have had several rebirths, in each one as the consort of the Vishnu incarnation. Thus, when Vishnu came to earth as Rama, Lakshmi was Sita; when he came as the dwarf, she was a lotus (Padma).

In sculptural representations, Lakshmi may have four arms when worshipped on her own, but is usually shown with two when she is with Vishnu. She may hold a lotus flower in her hand or may be shown seated on a lotus. Lakshmi is especially venerated during the Hindu festival of Diwali.

## Saraswati

Saraswati, the consort of Brahma, is worshipped as the goddess of wisdom, learning and eloquence as well as the patron deity of music and the arts. Some of her names reflect these aspects of her activities; others are related to her association with Brahma. The deification of speech is evidence of the high regard in which the spiritual power of the spoken word is held by Hindus as well as the importance attached to knowledge and learning.

Treatises on ritual art usually describe Saraswati as dressed in white and gold garments, holding in her four hands a lotus, the sacred scriptures (the Vedas) and playing the *veena* (a plucked string instrument).

During the nine-day festival of Dassera, the goddess Kali (Durga), Lakshmi and Saraswati are worshipped. On the ninth day (Mahanawami) it is customary to place books, musical instruments and all the implements necessary for one's work in front of the Goddess Saraswati. Prayers are offered on the tenth day (Vidhyarambha) to Saraswati for enlightenment, wisdom and spiritual awakening.

For Hindus, divinity inheres in almost every aspect of nature. India's most sacred river, the Ganges, is personified as a goddess. Legend has it that the river rushed down from its source in the Himalayas as a mighty torrent that would have flooded the earth had not Shiva allowed it to flow through his matted locks and so broken its fall.

The banyan is regarded as the most sacred tree while the fig tree is associated with spiritual understanding. It was under its branches that the Buddha received enlightenment. The *tulasi (Occimum sanctum)* is associated with Vishnu, and many Hindu homes have tulasi plants in their gardens.

Among animals, the cow is revered because it is believed to be the representative of Mother Earth (Bhumidevi). Similarly monkeys, considered to be the representatives of Hanuman, are never killed, even though they may do great damage to crops.

The planets – Sun, Moon, Mars, Mercury, Venus, Jupiter, Saturn and the two mythical planets, Rahu and Ketu – are also worshipped, because it is believed that at various periods in an individual's life these planets exert either beneficial or malevolent influence. In many southern Indian temples, the nine planets (*navagrah*) have a special shrine dedicated to themselves.

Images of Nandin the bull, are frequently found in Siva temples. There are several accounts in the sacred literature of the way in which he achieved divine or semi-divine status. According to one interpretation, Nandin is another form of Siva.

In most Siva temples, Nandin has a shrine to himself and, because of his association with fertility, is worshipped by devotees to the temple.

## SACRED LITERATURE

Hindu sacred literature can be divided into two categories: *shruti* (literally 'hearing') and *smriti* ( memory or recollection). The former consists of the four Vedas, the eternal wisdom that was 'heard by' or revealed to the sages at the beginning of creation.

The Rig Veda is the oldest literary work in the world. It consists of 1028 hymns, composed in Sanskrit, which are dedicated to the various Vedic deities. The Purusha sukta hymn also describes how the whole world emerged out of the great sacrifice of a cosmic person (*purusha*), whose ritual dismemberment created all realities including the four castes. The *Brahmins* (priestly caste) are said to have emerged from Purusha's mouth; the *Kshatriyas* (warriors) from his arms and trunk; the *Vaishyas* (the merchant and agricultural caste) from his thighs; and the *Sudras* (workers and artisans whose duty is to serve the other castes) from his feet.

The Sama and Yajur Vedas are collections of hymns relating to sacrificial rites. The Atharva Veda includes magical incantations, knowledge about medicinal herbs and plants and mantras (sacred formulae) for healing purposes.

The transmission of the Vedas was for many centuries entirely oral. Sound was sacred and great emphasis was placed on correct pronunciation and recitation. Only the Brahmins were allowed to recite the Vedas. The Kshatriyas and Vaishyas were permitted to hear them being recited, but the Sudras were denied access to this sacred knowledge.

Each of the four Vedas had, as appendices, two types of writing of a different character: the Brahmanas, written in prose and containing the formulae for sacrificial rituals and the Upanishads, which are philosophical texts that probe deeply into the nature of the universe and of human beings within it. As many as 108 Upanishads are known. The two earliest are the Brihadaranyaka and the Chandyoga Upanishad, dating back to 600 BCE or earlier.

Texts that have been remembered from generation to generation are known as smriti. The best known of these are the two epics, the Ramayana and the Mahabharata. The former was composed around the fourth century BCE, and it illustrates some of the highest moral values. The continuous reading of the Ramayana is considered by Hindus to be an act of great religious merit.

The Mahabharata is the longest epic in the world. It consists of 100,000 Sanskrit verses, grouped into 18 major sections and subdivided into many chapters. One of the most important components is the Bhagavad Gita (700 verses divided into 18 chapters), which is a general philosophical debate about the nature of self, Brahman and the different paths to moksha. The Gita emphasises the discipline of knowledge (*jnanayoga*), action (*karma yoga*) and devotion (*bhakti*).

The Puranas are collections of Hindu myths concerned with five major themes: creation, periodic re-creation, genealogy of the gods and sages, descriptions of the different eras and the feats of particular dynasties. There are 18 great Puranas, of which the Bhagavata Purana, dating from tenth century CE is the most popular. It is divided into 12 books and the 10th, which details the life of Krishna, is the best known.

The Tantras, divided along sectarian lines, reflect the religious beliefs and practices of Hindus in medieval times. The various Tantras deal with subjects such as philosophy, yoga and concentration techniques, as well as the conduct of religious worship, ritual art and architecture.

In addition to the classical Sanskrit literature, there is a rich collection of religious writing in prose and verse, in various Indian vernacular languages. They tend to emphasise devotion in contrast to the abstract metaphysics of the Upanishads.

*Ritual purification at Varkala*

## HINDUISM IN PRACTICE

Hinduism, as pointed out earlier, is more a way of life than a religion. It is possible to be a devout Hindu without ever having visited a temple or read the sacred scriptures. Nor is it of great concern if a person believes in one god or several. What is of significance, however, is the need to uphold *dharma*, the natural law of the universe and the social and moral order which is maintained within the family and the community in which one lives.

In most Hindu homes a small shrine may be set up in the corner of any room in the house, and great care is taken to maintain it in a state of ritual purity. Despite the multiplicity of gods and goddesses in the Hindu pantheon, each family and even each individual member may have their own 'chosen deity' (*ishtadevata*), whose images or pictures are placed in the household shrine and to whom homage is paid.

Daily rituals include the greeting of the sun in the morning with prescribed *mantras* or sacred formulae, and the *Sandhya* prayers recited as dusk falls when small oil lamps and incense sticks are lit in every traditional home. Offerings of fruit, flowers, milk or grain may be made daily and these are distributed as *prasad* (blessings) to all the family members. On important festival days, elaborate rituals are performed in which the entire family, including young children, participate.

Though women are subject to forms of 'temporary pollution' such as menstruation, they nevertheless have an important role to play in the regular rituals and ceremonies performed in a Hindu household. The responsibility for getting the house cleaned and purified, securing the many diverse ingredients needed for the ritual, and preparing the elaborate meals that are served on auspicious days, is usually assumed by the female members of the family. Fasts (*vrata*) are also observed on certain days in the week or the year to ensure the health and well-being of the family.

## THE HINDU TEMPLE

Archaeological evidence suggests that worship in ancient Vedic times took place in the open air, and that the principal ritual was the conduct of large-scale sacrifices to propitiate the various forces of nature. The development of temple architecture is historically associated with the mass devotional cults that sprang up as the influence of Buddhism generally declined in India.

Many of the great temples in India were built for royal patrons and, as Hinduism evolved, a parallel was established between the life of gods and the life of kings; and the daily and seasonal rituals conducted in temples came to resemble the personal services rendered by subjects to the king.

Though any building may serve the purpose of a temple, whether it be a simple mud shelter housing a clay or stone image or a converted terraced house in an English suburb, the traditional temple is an imposing structure built according to the elaborate and precise details laid down in the ancient treatises on architecture (*vaastu shastra*) or ritual art (*shilpa shastra*). Most temples are surrounded by walls, which separate the sanctified space of the temple from the everyday world outside. To enter the temple, it is necessary to pass through a gateway, which can be a simple door or an ornately carved and towering structure. The entrance to the temple usually faces east.

In Hindu mythology, the gods are usually said to live in the mountains. The architectural plan of a traditional temple replicates the gods' mountain abode. Inside the walls there may be several small shrines as well as the main temple. There may also be a tank, a well or a tap where worshippers can cleanse themselves before they enter the temple. Footwear is always left outside the main gateway to the temple or in a room specially set aside for this purpose.

There is usually a bell at the entrance to the main temple which is rung by devotees. This produces the sound, 'Om', the primordial sound of the universe and has the effect of creating an auspicious ambience that helps the worshippers to focus their minds on the deity.

Leading to the heart of a traditional temple are several pillared hallways containing statues of various gods and goddesses. The chamber in which the main image is installed, the *garbha griha*, is usually situated at the very back of the temple and illuminated only by oil lamps. Access to this chamber is restricted to the priests. A small passage is left around the chamber so the devotees can walk round the deity (*pradakshana*) as a sign of reverence.

Most temples have a tall tower rising above the spot where the main icon stands. The tower and walls of the temple are usually intricately carved with images of various gods, goddesses and other celestial beings as well as sacred plants and animals.

The installation of a stone, marble or metal image in a home or a temple is an important event and this is followed shortly after by a special consecration ceremony, *prana pratishtha*, wherein life is infused into the idol. Thereafter, it is necessary to treat the image as a living entity and to ensure that it is fed, washed, clothed and rested every day.

## THE SIXTEEN STEPS OF PUJA

Ceremonial worship in a Hindu temple or home is an elaborate process consisting of a number of steps, which follow each other in precise detail. These represent the invocation, reception and the hospitality accorded to a god as a royal personage or an honoured guest in one's home.

The puja begins with an invocation to Ganesha to ensure its successful completion. This is followed by prayers to Saraswati. The *Kalasha puja* (sanctification of the water) is next, followed by the *Dravya puja*, the consecration of the materials to be offered to the deity. An *Atma puja* is also done for the purification of one's self, when the person conducting the puja places a flower on their own head.

After these preparatory rituals are carried out, the *Sodasa Upachara* or sixteen steps of the puja commence. The deity is first welcomed with a prayer (*avahana*), offered a seat (*asana*), and water for washing and drinking.

After this, the deity is bathed (*snana*) to the accompaniment of appropriate prayers, dressed in new garments, decked out with ornaments and anointed with sandalwood paste and red kumkum powder. Offerings of incense (*dhupa*), lights (*deepa*) and freshly cooked food (*naivedya*) are also made.

The puja is concluded by the *arati*, the waving of an oil lamp or burning camphor in a special receptacle in front of the deity. This is then passed among the other participants of the puja as an act of purification and sanctification.

The food offered to the deity becomes *prasada* (blessing) and it is distributed among all the worshippers. As a final act of homage, devotees either bow to the deity or prostrate full length on the floor in a gesture of complete submission. Each person receives a spoonful of the sanctified water used in the puja and some kumkum or sandalwood paste, which is applied on the forehead.

# RITES OF PASSAGE

The sacred scriptures stipulate forty sacraments (*samskaras*) which an orthodox Hindu should perform or have performed on his or her behalf at various stages of their life. No less than three rites are prescribed before conception takes place and during a woman's pregnancy. These are *garbhadhana* to ensure that conception takes place; *pumsavana* which is performed in the third month of pregnancy to ensure the birth of a son; and *simantonnayana*, a ceremony which takes place in the seventh month of pregnancy. The expectant mother returns to her parental home and a female relative who has given birth to a healthy male child pours rice into her lap. She may also stick a few rice grains on the pregnant woman's forehead with sandalwood paste. The mother-to-be receives gifts of clothes and jewellery from her parents, and gifts are also presented to close female relatives of her husband. After this ceremony, which is nowadays only performed on the occasion of the first pregnancy, the woman stays on at her parental home for her confinement.

Immediately after birth, a short ceremony, *janmajata*, is performed before the umbilical cord is cut. The act of giving birth renders the mother impure and the pollution extends to the new-born infant. It is only after a special ceremony, usually performed ten days later (*jata karma*), that the baby and the mother cease to be ritually impure.

The naming of the child (*namakarana*) takes place at any time within three months. The exact time of birth is given to an astrologer who then selects an initial appropriate to the constellation in the ascendant at the time of the birth. The infant is conferred with a name beginning with that letter. The name is usually chosen with great care, to ensure longevity, happiness and prosperity, and may be that of a god or goddess or having some religious or spiritual significance.

The baby's first sight of the rising sun and the first feeding with solid food (*annaprasana*) are usually ceremonially observed, as is the ritual tonsure or shaving of the head (*chooda karan*). The last ritual was only performed for boys, usually when they were three years old. Nowadays, it is observed only in very traditional families.

The ear-piercing ceremony (*karna bheda*) was also performed for children of both sexes in orthodox Hindu families. Unlike the other rituals, which require the services of a Brahmin priest, *karna bheda* was usually performed by the goldsmith with a very fine gold wire.

## Initiation Ceremonies

According to the Hindu world view, an individual's life may be divided into four stages or *ashramas*. These are *brahmacharya*, the period of intellectual, physical and spiritual discipline which prepared an individual for the stage of *grhstha* or the life of a householder, during which men and women discharge their duties and obligations to their ancestors, their descendants and to society in general. With advancement in age, the householder and his wife were expected to prepare themselves for total detachment from all worldly preoccupations and to spend more time in prayer and contemplation. This is the third stage of *vanaprastha*, which leads to the fourth and final stage of *sanyasa* when the individual should be mainly concerned with the realisation of *moksha* or liberation from the cycle of birth and death.

Of the various rites of passage, the *upanayana* or initiation ceremonies are particularly important. This ceremony was traditionally performed for boys from the three highest castes, namely Brahmin, Kshatriya and Vaishya. The age of the initiates may vary from eight to twelve, and the chief feature of the ceremony is the donning of the sacred thread, which is made of three strands of white cotton for Brahmins, hemp for Kshatriyas and wool for Vaishyas. This sacred thread is hung over the left shoulder and the right ear.

The sacred thread (*janeo*) symbolises a spiritual birth and consequently these three castes are also referred to as the 'twice born'. At this ceremony, which is conducted at an auspicious time determined by an astrologer, the young boy is taught the *Gayatri mantra*, from the Rig Veda which is thought to be particularly sacred.

According to ancient tradition, the upanayana marked the transition from childhood to the first stage of brahmacharya. The initiate was expected to leave home to undertake a long course of study under the guidance of a *guru* who was well versed in the Vedas and the other sacred scriptures. During this period he was committed to a life of austerity, celibacy and service to his teacher.

On completing his studies, the young man was expected to marry and start the next stage of life. The wedding ceremony (vivaha) is one of the most solemn and complex rites of Hinduism and marks a major transition in the ritual and social status of the bride and groom.

# HINDU MARRIAGE CUSTOMS

According to classical Hindu philosophy there are four major aims in life, namely *dharma, artha, kama* and *moksha*. The ultimate goal for every human being is supposed to be moksha or freedom from the cycle of birth and death. Artha (which refers to the satisfaction of the acquisitive instinct in man) and kama (to the emotional, aesthetic and creative urge) together represent worldly interest, and spiritual aspirations are maintained by dharma or moral duty.

The theory of the four-fold aims in life is given concrete expression in the scheme of ashramas, according to which life is divided into four stages. Brahmacharya is the period of intellectual, physical and spiritual discipline. It comes soon after the performance of initiation rites, and prepares a person for the stage of grhstha, the life of a married man and householder, during which he is expected to perform his duties towards the gods, his ancestors, to succeeding generations and towards society in general.

As he grows older, the householder is expected to prepare himself for total detachment form all worldly matters. Elders are supposed to withdraw from the active management of the household and to spend more time in prayer and contemplation during the third stage *vanaprastha*. This leads to the fourth and final stage of sanyasa when the individual's main concern ought to be with the realisation of spirituality.

To a Hindu, marriage is an important event and a necessary step in the path to spiritual progress. It is also a social duty towards the family and the community, and a wedding is one of the most important rituals or samskaras in the life of a Hindu. The largest number of relatives and friends assemble on this occasion and the wedding feast serves as the reaffirmation of a network of relationships to which individuals and families are bound.

## Aims of Marriage

The aims of marriage according to the ancient scriptures are said to be *dharma* (duty), *praja* (progeny) and *rati* (pleasure).

Marriage is considered to be a necessary step in the life of an individual in order to obtain a partner for the fulfilment of various religious duties. These obligations cease only on the death of the male head of the household.

Another important aim of marriage is procreation, and one of the blessings bestowed upon a newly married couple is *Bahuputravan/vatee-bhava* or 'may you have many sons'. Procreation is considered to be both a moral and social duty. However, the scriptures also advise that there should be a proper balance between dharma, artha and kama, so that the eventual aim of moksha can be achieved.

In the past, contraception was practised only by abstinence and by avoiding ovulation periods. Abortion as a method of family planning is condemned by the Hindu *sastras* (sacred writings) and at certain periods of history was considered to be a heinous offence. The Manusmriti (the laws of Manu) equated abortion with *Brahmahatya* (the killing of a live god) and recommended death as a suitable punishment for a woman who deliberately aborted her baby or performed one on another.

## Polygamy

In ideal terms, marriage was looked upon by the Hindus as a legal union between two persons of opposite sex.

Polygamy was tolerated only when no male child was born to the first wife within the first few years of marriage. Even in such cases, however, considerable sanctity was attributed to the first marriage and the consent of the first wife had to be obtained before subsequent marriages could be contracted.

Though rarer and more selective in their geographical distribution, polyandrous marriages are also known to have been in existence among Hindus. However, in later times the right to contract polygamous marriages was questioned, and considerable pressure was exerted by social reformers during the mid-nineteenth century onwards to ban the practice. Bigamy was abolished by the Hindu Marriage Act 1955 and has since been made a criminal offence.

## Age at Marriage

Marriage for a female was equated with initiation ceremonies for a man. As such it represented an important stage in her life cycle. From very early times, girls, particularly those from the upper castes and the wealthier sections of society, were married before they attained puberty, although cohabitation was delayed for several months and even years. Pre-pubertal marriages gradually filtered down to all sections of society and became a characteristic feature of marriage among Hindus throughout India until the early decades of the twentieth century, when a number of liberal, progressive thinkers campaigned vigorously against it.

The Child Marriage Restraint Act was passed in India in 1929, and the minimum legal age for the marriage of girls was fixed at 15 years. With the spread of education among girls, particularly in urban areas, the age at marriage has since risen.

## Dowry and Other Forms of Gift-giving

Within the patrilineal structure of the Hindu family, daughters could not inherit immovable property except in the absence of sons. Convention decreed that they receive their share of the patrimony in the form of a dowry at the time of marriage. It was only with the passing of the Hindu Succession Act, 1956, that daughters, widows and mothers could inherit immovable property, such as land, on equal terms with male heirs.

The dowry given to a girl at the time of marriage usually consists of three elements: household goods and equipment to be used by the young couple when they set up an independent household; gifts of jewellery and clothes for the husband and his kin; and a trousseau consisting of jewellery and clothes for the bride herself. These gifts are made in public at the time of the girl's departure from her parental home and they are usually displayed later at the groom's house.

The property gifted as dowry is often given directly to the groom's parents who may then re-distribute it to a wider circle of kin. The only items that are handed to the girl herself are the gifts made to her by the groom's family. These usually consist of clothes and ornaments. The jewellery with which parents adorn their daughter at her wedding are also regarded as her personal property, a category of *stridhana* or female wealth, which in many families is handed down from mother to daughter.

The value of a girl's dowry depends primarily on the wealth and social circumstances of her parents and upon the expectations and demands of the bridegroom's family. It is also frequently correlated with the educational qualifications and earning potential of the bridegroom.

The wedding of a daughter is usually an expensive undertaking and parents often save for it from the moment of her birth. The practice of giving dowry has been frequently condemned as a social evil, and several attempts have been made to prohibit it by law. However, it continues to be fairly widespread in India as well as among expatriate Hindu communities, and its value has kept pace with inflation.

The marriage of a daughter inaugurates a gift-giving relationship between her parents and her in-laws which continues long after the wedding. A woman's parents are expected to give her clothes and jewellery on important religious festivals such as Diwali and Dussera and to bear the expenses of her first confinement. The birth of her first child, particularly if it is a boy, is an occasion when the most expensive gifts are given.

Weddings usually involve the entire extended kin network, and certain categories of kin have specific duties to perform on this occasion. The close, affectionate tie between a man and his sister's children, for instance, becomes particularly evident at the time of their marriage. Over much of northern India, the wedding garments of the bride and groom are gifts from their respective maternal uncles. The man is also obliged to bring gifts for his sister (the mother of the bride or the bridegroom), his brother-in-law and the other children in the family. If his financial situation permits, these gifts would include items of jewellery for the bride, her mother and sisters.

## Arranging a Marriage

When a young person reaches marriageable age, steps are taken by the elders of the family to arrange a suitable match. The initiative is usually taken by the girl's father, although, very often, discreet enquiries may also be made by the boy's family when they consider him ready for marriage. The initial negotiations are generally conducted by the most important male members of both families. Women rarely participate in direct discussions, although they may exert considerable influence behind the scenes.

In the past, young people were never consulted in the choice of a mate, nor did they get an opportunity to see each other before their wedding ceremony. Nowadays, however, photographs of the girl and boy are exchanged, and in many families a proposal is accepted only after the boy and girl have met and expressed their mutual liking.

The selection of marriage partners for a son or daughter is guided by both proscriptive and prescriptive rules. Two basic requirements are sub-caste endogamy and regional and linguistic endogamy.

Hindu society was traditionally divided into four castes: Brahmins (priests), Kshatriyas (rulers and warriors), Vaishyas (agriculturalists and traders) and Sudras (menial workers). Each caste was further divided into numerous sub-castes. Endogamy was believed to be the minimum criterion for the maintenance of the caste system and each sub-caste had more or less institutionalised a set of rules which ensured that the social ties of kinship and affinity did not extend outside its boundaries.

Within some of the larger sub-castes in any particular region, a system of differential ranking also operated, which had considerable significance in marriage arrangements. A typical example is that of the 'marriage circles' of the Patidars (members of the sub-caste usually bear the surname Patel) of central Gujerat. These 'circles' are associations formed by a varying number of member villages, within which there are agreements to exchange children in marriage.

The marriage circles are arranged in a hierarchy, and within each the constituent villages are considered to be of a higher or lower status. Whereas hypergamy (the practice of marrying one's daughter to a person of superior status) is tolerated and even encouraged, its converse, marrying one's daughter to a status inferior, is looked upon with extreme disfavour. Patidars living in Britain today continue to be mindful of their relative status within the caste, and the custom of arranging marriages within a particular circle still continues.

Under modern Hindu law, a breach of the endogamous boundary between sub-castes does not invalidate a marriage, although the rules of *gotra* (clan) and *sapinda* exogamy continue to be effective.

Among North Indian Hindus, the traditional rules prohibit marriage between two people if any pair of the following four clans are common: the boy's and girl's natal clans, their mothers' natal clans and both their maternal and paternal grandmothers' natal clans.

In South India, the four-gotra rule does not apply with the same rigidity. Marriage between a man and his sister's daughter and between cross cousins are preferred as they not only avoid the pain of marrying off daughters to strangers, but also conserve property within the family.

Besides the four-clan rule, a wide circle of kin is also forbidden to a prospective bride or groom. The *sapinda* rule prohibits marriage between people who can trace a common ancestor to the seventh inclusive generation on the male side and to the fifth inclusive generation on the female side. In practice, this rule is interpreted as barring marriage to anyone known to be a blood relative.

Throughout much of northern India, marriages which result in the exchange of women between kin groups meet with strong disapproval as they contradict the asymmetrical relationship between bride-givers and bide-takers, the latter in any transaction being considered superior in status. There is no bar to the marriage of a pair of brothers to a pair of sisters, as in such cases no exchange of women is involved. However, such marriages are generally not preferred.

The search for suitable marriage partners is usually confined to a region but outside the boundaries of one's own village.

Two reasons are usually advanced to justify the practice of village exogamy. Firstly, there is the belief that the inhabitants of a village are related by a fictive genealogy – so they are regarded as relations even though not related by blood. Hence marriage within one's village is equivalent to incest and must be avoided. Secondly, there is the notion that the tensions inherent in the relationship between in-laws can best be managed through living apart from each other, so a partner is sought from beyond the home village.

Within the framework of customary marriage rules, great variation may exist in the individual standards by which marriage partners are selected. Considerable weight is attached to the ancestry (khandan) and local reputation of prospective in-laws, and marriages are usually arranged between families of more or less equal social and financial standing. Personal attributes such as beauty, charm and modesty in a girl, and the educational qualifications of a boy, are also important criteria.

A Sanskrit verse that is commonly quoted illustrates the complex nature of the selection process:

> *The girl counts beauty;*
> *the mother riches;*
> *the father knowledge;*
> *relatives, good lineage;*
> *other people, sumptuous marriage feasts.*

## Engagement and Pre-nuptial Ceremonies

When a suitable proposal has been accepted by both parties, a short ceremony is performed at which cash and other gifts are presented to the prospective groom and to members of his family. This is called *rokna* in Punjab and symbolises the formal 'reservation of the boy'. In the western Indian state of Gujerat, it is customary for the father of the girl, her maternal uncles and other senior male relatives to visit the groom's house to view the boy before the marriage is actually settled. They take with them cash and other gifts, which are exchanged with the immediate kin of the boy. This is the giving of *chanalo,* which commits both parties to the agreement.

The next day or soon after, the female members of the boy's family visit the girl and give her cash gifts, which vary in value according to their financial situation. In turn, they receive gifts from the girl's father, which are usually slightly higher in value than those he received at their house the previous day.

In the past, formal engagements were entered into long before the marriage, and, in the intervening period, the girl's family were obliged to keep up a steady flow of gifts to the boy's family on important religious and ceremonial occasions. Nowadays, however, marriage usually follows shortly after the betrothal.

## Wedding Ceremonies

Hindu marriage is a sacrament and the sacred literature or the *Dharma-sastras* deal elaborately with the various rites and ceremonies that must be performed on this occasion. The main rites are *Kanyadaan, Panigrahan, Vivaha-homa,* and *Saptapadi.* The rituals are usually performed by a Brahmin in the presence of the sacred fire and are accompanied by the chanting of Vedic mantras.

According to modern Hindu law, a marriage can be validated by:

a)  performing the religious rituals and ceremonies recognised by Hindu law.

or

b)  by observing the customary formalities that prevail in the caste, community or tribe to which one (or both) of the parties belong.

Of the various rituals that have been prescribed, the performance of the Saptapadi before the sacred fire is obligatory, although the chanting of mantras is not.

Weddings are usually celebrated on an auspicious date chosen by an astrologer after the horoscopes of the boy and girl have been compared. The most popular months for a wedding coincide with the period when agricultural work is finished for the season. Once the harvest has been gathered, there are sufficient resources to defray the expenses of a wedding.

Preparations for the wedding commence soon after the date has been fixed. The bride's trousseau is prepared, gifts for close kin of the bride and the groom are purchased, and a large store is laid in of rice, wheat flour, ghee (clarified butter) and other food stuff to feed the numerous relatives and friends who are expected to attend the ceremony.

A few days before the wedding, the *pandal* (marquee) is erected outside the bride's house. An image of Ganesha, the elephant-headed god, is installed there, and a *puja* (prayer service) is performed to ensure that the celebrations proceed without hindrance.

Pre-nuptial ceremonies vary in formality and content according to local custom and the wealth of the parties concerned. In many parts of India, the bride is rubbed with a mixture of flour, turmeric and oil (*maiyan*), which has purificatory and cosmetic effects. This ritual takes place in a convivial atmosphere, and various female relatives take turns at applying this mixture and presenting her with gifts. A similar ritual also takes place in the bridegroom's house.

On the eve of the wedding, female relatives and friends in both families take part in singing sessions. The songs are either an explanation of the various rituals or else in praise of various deities, and they also express heartfelt wishes for the future happiness of the couple.

An important aspect of pre-wedding preparations is the 'showing' of the dowry. The contents are put on display in a room, and neighbours, friends and relatives come to inspect, admire and compare. Later they are displayed and inspected at the groom's house, and judgements are passed by his relatives and friends about its value. Because the status of the bride's family and her own future happiness often rest upon the value of the dowry she has received, great efforts are made by her parents to ensure that it is very impressive.

In the southern Indian state of Kerala, an important ritual conducted on the eve of the wedding is the preparation of the 1001 cotton wicks that will be used to light the sacred fire before which the marriage is consecrated. Female relatives and friends of the bride gather together at her house to take part in this ceremony to the accompaniment of music, singing and some gentle teasing of the bride. The wicks are prepared from clean, unbleached, cotton cloth.

The crucial rites of the wedding start with the arrival of the bridegroom and his entourage. This is usually an occasion for conspicuous display. In the north, the bridegroom often arrives on horseback, richly garlanded with flowers and accompanied by a professional band. He may be dressed in the traditional costume of *churidar-achkan*, a long silk or brocade tunic and tight trousers, or a Western-style suit.

In the south, the traditional wedding clothes for a man are a gold-bordered, white or cream-coloured *dhoti* (a long piece of silk or fine cotton material which is draped around the waist) with a shawl of similar material.

On arrival at the bride's house, the groom and his party are treated to lavish hospitality. It is customary for a young male relative of the bride to wash the feet of the groom. The welcoming party would also include women, bearing small silver trays on which are placed a small lamp, flowers, little pots of *kumkum* (red powder which is applied to the forehead), sandalwood paste and rose water, which is sprinkled on all the guests.

After the groom has been served with refreshments and seated in the *mandap* (raised platform on which the marriage rituals will be conducted) the bride is led out from the house. She is usually accompanied by a group of young female friends. In northern India, the bride is traditionally dressed in either a gold-embroidered silk sari or *shalwar-kameez* (a long tunic worn over trousers) or a *gharara kameez* (a long tunic worn over flowing trousers). The end of the sari or scarf may be draped over her head, partially concealing her face. She is adorned with gold jewellery, which includes items such as earrings, bracelets, necklaces, rings and ornaments for the hair.

The southern Indian bride is usually dressed in a rich gold-embroidered silk sari and is similarly adorned with jewellery and garlands of flowers. However, it is not customary for the bride to be veiled.

Throughout India, the bridal garments are usually in shades of red or pink. Gold, white and cream are also considered to be auspicious colours.

The wedding ceremonies commence with an invocation to Ganesha. Prayers are also offered in the presence of the sacred fire to Brahma, Vishnu and Shiva and the other gods in the Hindu pantheon as well as the nine planets – Venus, Jupiter, Mercury, Mars, Saturn, Sun, Moon and the two mythical planets of Rahu and Ketu. Once the fire has been lit, care is taken to ensure that it does not go out until the ceremonies are completed; otherwise it would be considered an ill omen.

In southern India, especially in the state of Tamil Nadu, the invocation to the deities is followed by the ritual of *Kashi Yatra*. The bridegroom simulates the various preparations required for a pilgrimage to the holy city of Varanasi (also known as Kashi). He leaves the venue of the marriage accompanied by his married female relatives singing in chorus, his parents and friends. Further along the road, he is met by the bride's father who entreats him to return and marry his daughter. The pilgrim accepts the proposal and returns with his escort to the marriage pandal.

Then follows the important ceremony of *Kanya daan*, the gift of the virgin. It is usually performed by the bride's father or her brother, who places her hand in that of her future husband along with the token gift of betel leaves. The tying of the *tali* or *mangalyasutra* symbolises the bridegroom's acceptance of the gift. This is a gold ornament that all married Hindu women wear around their necks. It is strung on a cord consisting of 108 strands of fine cotton, tightly twisted together and dyed yellow with saffron or turmeric powder. The bridegroom places it around the bride's neck while reciting some Vedic *slokas* (prayers) and one of her female friends secures it with three knots. The tali/mangalyasutra is usually threaded on to a gold chain after the wedding.

The bridegroom then takes hold of his bride's hand (*panigrahana*),and together they perform various rituals such as *laja homa* or the offering of grains to the fire, and circumambulations of the sacred fire to the chants of Vedic *slokas*. The *saptapadi* (seven steps) is one of the most essential features of the Hindu marriage ceremony. It is symbolic of a solemn promise, because as the couple take the seven steps together they are supposed to recite in Sanskrit the following verse from the Atharva Veda (one of the four Vedas, which are the oldest and most sacred literature of the Hindus).

> *Walk with me four steps and three,*
> *I seek thy hand; let me not*
> *Break from thee; nor thou from me,*
> *Let us swear, in joy and strength,*
> *One in thought and deed, one within.*

Each of the rituals which have been described are highly symbolic. *Kanya daan* signifies the renunciation of parental authority over a daughter. The *saptapadi* and circumambulation are a mutual ratification of the marriage contract in the presence of the sacred fire which Hindus regard as the purest of the five elements. The *laja homa* or the offering of grains to the fire, on the other hand, is believed to be a fertility rite.

Once the religious and ritualistic part of the ceremony is over, the guests are treated to a grand feast. Male members of the bridegroom's party are generally served first. Close relatives of the bride sit down to eat only after they have ensured that all their guests have partaken of the meal.

Custom requires the bride to move out of her parental home at marriage to join the household of her husband. Consequently, all married women have two homes, and in most of the Indian languages there are specific terms to designate natal kin and kin through marriage.

The groom's departure with the bride is usually a highly emotional occasion and the tears of the bride, her mother and other female relatives heighten the trauma of separation. At the husband's home, several rituals are performed that symbolise her incorporation into his family and household.

For the first few months of her married life, the young bride is very much on display. Friends and relatives of the bridegroom visit the house to inspect her and the dowry she has received from her parents.

Married women generally returned to their parental home for their first confinement. The expenses for this event were usually borne by her father and/or brothers. The birth of a child, especially a son, is an important occasion, which is marked by ritualistic gift-giving.

## Divorce

Marriage, according to the Vedic ideal, was a sacrament and hence indissoluble. However, in the religious texts of a later period there are references to marriage as a contract which could be dissolved under certain circumstances.

According to the customary law of Hindus, a divorce could be obtained for either of the following reasons:

• Renunciation, abandonment or repudiation

• Immorality, adultery or conversion to another religion.

Barrenness in either spouse was never considered to be reasonable justification for seeking the dissolution of a marriage. Nor did Hindu law stipulate that it was a wife's duty to produce a son or prescribe penalties for default. In practice, however, a second marriage was permissible for a man if his wife failed to bear a male child within eight to twelve years of marriage.

The Hindu Marriage Act, 1955 was an important milestone in legal history, because it provides for a formal divorce procedure which could be initiated by either the husband or the wife after at least three years of marriage. Divorce is permitted if the spouse is:

• Living in adultery
• Has converted to another religion
• Has renounced the world
• Has disappeared for seven or more years
• Has failed to resume cohabitation two years after a decree of restitution of conjugal rights
• If either spouse has contracted a bigamous marriage.

Divorce by mutual consent is recognised by Hindus. The wife is entitled to maintenance and she also has the right to the matrimonial home. Both partners are free to remarry once the divorce is granted.

# HINDU FUNERAL CUSTOMS AND DEATH-RELATED RITUALS

Hindus believe implicitly in the law of *karma* which stipulates that each individual passes through a series of lives until, depending upon the actions of their previous existences, the state of *moksha*, liberation from the cycle of birth and rebirth, is attained. Death is not the end of the process, but is viewed merely as a stage in a long chain of transitions. It is this continuity, which endures beyond the limits of any single lifetime, that is enhanced and focused upon during the elaborate mortuary rituals performed by Hindus.

When death is imminent, the person is lifted from the cot and laid on the floor so that the soul's free passage into the next life is not obstructed. *Gangajal* (water from the holy River Ganges) is given to the dying person and a *tulasi*

(*Ocimum sanctum*) leaf is placed in the mouth. This plant is associated with Lord Vishnu, one of the Holy Trinity and the Preserver of the Universe. It also has many medicinal, particularly disinfectant, properties.

The dead body is washed and dressed, preferably in new clothes. Married women are clothed in pink or red saris and adorned with jewellery. *Kumkum* (red powder), is placed in the parting of the hair and a red spot or *tilak* is applied on the forehead.

The customary mode of disposal of a dead body by Hindus is cremation, although very young children are buried. In villages in India, the dead body is placed on a bier made of bamboo poles and carried on the shoulders of male kinsmen to the cremation grounds. The funeral is attended by all the relatives living in the village and by other members of the sub-caste. When an elderly and highly respected man dies, even his genealogically and geographically distant kin would make it a point to attend the funeral.

The nearest male relatives of the deceased are generally forbidden to shave or cut their hair and nails for thirteen days following the death. This custom, however, varies among different groups. In Punjab, male mourners are required to shave their heads and beards on the eleventh day. In Gujarat and some other parts of western India the nearest male relatives of the deceased are required to shave their heads on the day of the death.

At the cremation grounds, the body is placed on a pyre of wood with the head pointing north in the direction of Mount Kailasha (in the Himalayas), the abode of Siva. If the deceased was from an affluent family, this pyre may be of expensive, exotic varieties of wood such as sandalwood. *Ghee* (clarified butter) is poured on the pyre to help it burn. The wood is then set alight by the son of the deceased (or son's son, daughter's son, brother or brother's son in this order of preference). Other mourners will then throw fruit, flowers, incense and fragrant spices into the fire. Mourners traditionally wait until the body has been consumed by fire. In the final stages of this long process, the chief mourner (that is, the male relative who first lit the pyre) would break the skull with a long pole to allow the soul to escape. This rite is known as *kapol kriya*. On the fourth day (in certain parts of India this may take place on the third day), the ashes are collected by the chief mourner and the place of cremation cleared. The ashes are then traditionally immersed in a river, preferably the Ganges. After this ceremony (*chautha*) has been performed, the mourners gather together in the deceased's house and offer prayers. Food is then distributed among them. This is usually *kitcheree* or a mixture of boiled rice and dal (lentils).

In Britain, the dead body is transported in a coffin to the local crematorium. The funeral director can arrange to have the ashes collected and scattered in the crematorium's Garden of Remembrance or stored in an urn until such time as the relatives of the deceased can arrange to have it transported to India.

Among the Hindus, in India as well as in Britain, the ceremonies following the death normally last for thirteen days, but the ritual pollution incurred by the close kinsmen is terminated on the eleventh day. The chief mourner performs a rite aided by a Brahmin priest and the male relatives present shave their hair and beards. Throughout this crucial part of the 40-day official mourning period, the relatives are required to sit on the floor, eat only simple vegetarian food, and generally lead a secluded life. Friends and distant relatives visit to mourn the deceased person.

On the thirteenth day, Hindus in northern and western India perform the *pugri* ceremony, which quite simply means the tying of a turban on the eldest son of the deceased to mark his formal acceptance of family responsibilities. In the case of a married man, this turban is presented by his wife's father, brother or an equivalent relative. After the pugri rite, it is customary to provide a feast for all the relatives who are present.

Various memorial ceremonies for the dead are conducted by Hindus. The main rite (*shradh*) occurs in the month of *Kuwar*, when for a fortnight there is remembrance of the recently dead and also a propitiation of all ancestors. It is customary to put out food (usually a mixture of rice and curds) for crows, which are regarded to be inauspicious birds, proverbially associated with death.

# HINDU FESTIVALS

All Hindu festivals have a deep spiritual import, besides commemorating certain historical and mythological events. As most festivals are based on the lunar calendar, the dates vary from year to year. Traditional ways of celebrating them also vary in different parts of India, among expatriate Indian communities and between different sects and castes. Festivals may be celebrated in the home, in the presence of the family deities, or by the worshipping community, congregated in a temple.

On festival days, temple rituals commence with the elaborate ritual cleansing of the image of the deity who is the particular focus of worship on that day, with recitations from the sacred texts and congregational singing. In the home, the occasion may be observed by the ceremonial cleansing of the house, decorating the entrance with pictures and patterns drawn with coloured powder (*rangoli*), an elaborate feast, the exchange of gifts, and fireworks. Certain festivals are also marked in a more austere manner, by fasting and spending time in prayer and meditation.

## Lohri

Lohri is the winter festival of the Punjab and is celebrated by Hindus and Sikhs (see page 112).

## Makara Sankrant

Makara Sankrant is observed by Hindus all over India as the Winter Solstice Festival. The day is spent in prayer and, in the state of Maharashtra, a special sweet made of sesame seeds (symbolising life) is distributed to friends and relatives.

## Pongal

Hindus in the southern Indian states of Tamil Nadu, Andhra Pradesh and Karnataka celebrate the Pongal-Sankranti festival to coincide with the winter solstice or the sun's entry into the sign of Capricorn. It is an important harvest festival and the celebrations extend over three days.

The first day is called Bhogi Pongal and is observed as a family feast. The main feature of the second day's celebrations is the worship of Surya (the sun god). The third day, Mattu Pongal, is the most important and is observed as the day for the worship of cattle. Cows and oxen are bathed and decorated with garlands of flowers and worshipped. *Pongal,* a sweet dish made of rice, is offered to the household deity and then distributed to family members, as well as given to the cattle to eat.

## Vasanta Panchami

The festival of Vasanta Panchami is celebrated by all Hindus in the month of Magha (January–February), mainly in honour of Saraswati, the goddess of learning, wisdom and fine arts.

Saraswati is an exceptionally charming goddess who plays on the musical instrument called a vina. Her mount is a white swan. In every part of India, Hindu children start their education by writing the alphabet in front of the image of Saraswati. She bestows success on her worshippers, and without her grace none can attain proficiency in poetry, music or fine arts. Saraswati is mainly a deity for personal worship rather than community adoration. The worship of Saraswati is particularly popular among Hindus in Bengal.

## Kumbh Mela

This festival takes place once every twelve years when there is a confluence of the moon, the sun and the planet Jupiter, and was last celebrated in January 2001. Millions of Hindus congregate in the holy city of Prayag (Allahabad) at the meeting point of three rivers: the Ganges, Yamuna and the mythical Saraswati. Devotees take a dip in the sacred waters and then gather together in large or small groups to offer worship, listen to discourses, participate in devotional singing or recitations from the scriptures, and to enjoy the various attractions of the big fair that is organised in the town to mark the event. Holy men, mendicants and the *sadhus,* or those who have renounced the world and all material interests, also leave their mountain retreats to converge on Prayag at this time to participate in the great festival. The celebrations continue for a month. Religious fervour intensifies on the days of Makara Sankranti, Basant Panchami, Maha Sivaratri, Chaitra, Amavasya, Ram Navami and Baisakhi.

According to legend, the gods and demons wanting immortality joined forces to churn the mythical ocean of milk in order to extract amrit, or nectar. Various wondrous objects emerged from the ocean as a result of the churning, including ucoha sraiva and airavata, the horse and elephant commandeered by Indra, the lord of the gods; Kamadhenu, the bountiful cow; the moon; the goddess Lakshmi; bows and arrows; and the gemstone Koustubham. Finally, Lord Dhanwantari, a partial incarnation of Vishnu, emerged out of the ocean bearing the pot of nectar. As the demons and gods rushed to grab it, the pot was borne away to safety by Garuda, the eagle and vehicle of Vishnu. Drops of nectar are believed to have fallen in four places: the towns of Allahabad (Prayag), Hardwar, Nasik and Ujjain. A minor Kumbh Mela is celebrated once every three years in the last three towns.

## Mahasivaratri

Mahasivaratri is celebrated in honour of the marriage of Lord Siva to Parvati. Devotees observe a strict fast on this day and keep vigil all night. Congregational worship in Hindu temples consists of hymns in praise of Lord Siva and sacred chanting.

The festival normally falls on the thirteenth or fourteenth day of the month of Phalguna (February–March) in the Hindu calendar.

## Holi

Holi is the most colourful of Hindu festivals. It is a spring festival celebrated on the full moon day of the month of Phalguna (February–March). It occurs when the season is neither hot nor cold, and the trees bloom with different kinds of flowers.

According to legend, a mighty king named Hiranya Kashipu once ruled on the earth. His arrogance grew to such an extent that he declared himself to be a god and ordered his people to worship him. But Prahlad, the king's only son, refused to accept him as a god, as he had firm belief only in Rama. To punish his son, the King took various severe measures and even tried to kill him, but all the time Prahlad was saved as he uttered the name of Vishnu. At last, Prahlad's aunt, Holika, claiming that she was fire-proof, took the child in her lap and sat in the fire to burn him alive. When the flames died down, the King found the child was safe but his aunt had perished in the fire.

Another legend associated with Holi is about the destruction of the handsome Kama, the god of love, by Shiva. In southern India, the songs sung during Holi include the lamentations of Rati, Kama's wife.

According to another account, the festival of Holi was instituted to commemorate the destruction of a female demon called Putana by Krishna. When Krishna was a baby, his uncle Kansa, the King of Mathura, ordered a general massacre of all children in order to destroy him. One of Kansa's agents was a female fiend named Putana, who assumed human form and went about the country sucking to death every child she found; but the infant Krishna, knowing her to be a fiend, sucked her blood and thus destroyed her. Those who attribute the origin of all festivals to seasonal cycles maintain that Putana represents winter; and her death and cremation, the cessation of winter.

The festival is observed for two days. On the first day, a bonfire is lit either in the evening or during the night. The effigy of Holika is placed in the centre of the pile and a Brahmin recites verses in the worship of Holi before setting it on fire. People then return to their homes.

On the second day, from early morning till noon, people, irrespective of caste and creed, amuse themselves by throwing handfuls of coloured powder on their friends and relatives; or they spray coloured water. The damage to people's clothes is taken in good spirit. The same evening, people exchange sweetmeats, and friends embrace and wish each other good luck. Children and young people touch the feet of their elders to express their respect.

## Ramnavami

The festival of Ramnavami is celebrated throughout India to commemorate the birth of Shri Rama, who was born to King Dasharatha of Ayodhya on the ninth lunar day in the bright fortnight of Chaitra (March–April). It is observed with sanctity and fasting. On this day, temples are decorated, religious discourses are held, and the Ramayana (the life story of Rama) is recited in most Hindu homes. Thousands of devotees visit to temples to have *darshana* (visualisation of the deity) of the beautiful images of Rama which are enshrined there.

## Vishu – The Malayalam New Year

Vishu is celebrated by Hindus in Kerala (a state in southwest India) as the New Year. This festival coincides with spring and the beginning of the zodiacal cycle, when the sun enters the sign of Aries.

Preparations for this festival start the day before, when the house is cleaned, and an artistic arrangement of beautiful and auspicious objects is created in the room (or area) where the family deities are enshrined. The items used in this arrangement include flowers (especially yellow laburnum); fruit (especially the yellow citrus variety); vegetables such as pumpkins, coconuts and rice; polished brass and bronze lamps; a small mirror; a gold ornament; and silver coins.

Children do not participate in the preparations and are

generally not allowed to see the display until the next day, when they are awakened at dawn and led with their eyes closed to the *puja* room. Thus, the first sight to greet their eyes on New Year's Day is this beautiful arrangement. They are then presented with new clothes and gifts of money.

A feast, to which friends and relatives are invited, is an essential element in the day's festivities.

## Rakshabandhan

The Rakshabandhan festival is celebrated throughout northern India in the month of Sravana (July–August). The word *raksha* signifies protection. The festival is also called Saluno.

Girls and married women tie a *rakhi*, made of twisted golden or simple yellow threads, on the right wrist of their brothers, for their welfare and also for protection from any evil influence, and in return they receive cash and gifts. This is an age-old festival, which strengthens the bond of love between brothers and sisters.

On this day, members of a Hindu family bathe very early and go to market to purchase rakhi and sweets from the colourful stalls that spring up everywhere. The men, dressed in their best, and women in their colourful costumes, first offer a prayer to their favourite deity. A man considers it a privilege to be chosen as a brother by a woman who ties a rakhi on his wrist. If the brother is not at hand, the rakhi is sent to him by post or passed on to him by someone. In some parts of India, women also tie a rakhi for close friends and neighbours.

The Brahmins also tie a rakhi for their *yajamanas* (patrons and clients), recite hymns for their safety, and receive a gift in cash or kind from them.

The rakhi festival has a special appeal in India which extends to other non-Hindu communities. One story tells of a beautiful Hindu queen called Padmini, who sought protection from the Mughal Emperor by sending him a rakhi. When Padmini was threatened by another Muslim king who had determined to marry her when he saw her reflection in the mirror, the Queen was defended against his invasion by the Mughal Emperor in response to the rakhi. To this day, a rakhi from a woman is honoured even when the man is not a Hindu.

## Janmashtami

The popular festival of Janmashtami is observed throughout India at midnight, on the night of the new moon during the month of Bhadrapada (August–September). It is joyously celebrated in honour of Lord Krishna, who was born on this day, at Mathura in Uttar Pradesh.

On the festival day, all temples and many Hindu homes are beautifully and tastefully decorated to welcome the birth of the divine chief, Krishna. His image is placed on a swing, in a decorated *mandapa* (small pavilion). Every member of the family, including children, observes a fast for the whole day, which is only broken when the moon is visible at midnight. At this time the image of an infant Krishna is first bathed in *charnamrita* (curd mixed with milk, dry fruits and leaves of the *tulasi* plant) and then the *arati* is performed. (Arati is the veneration and supplication accompanied by circular movements of the lamp and by the throwing of flower petals.) The *prasada* is distributed to all present and the day-long fast is broken. (Prasada is symbolic communion in food and is usually made of semolina, sugar and water.)

## Ganesh Chaturthi

Ganesha, the elephant-headed god in the Hindu pantheon, is worshipped all over India as the remover of obstacles. His blessings are especially invoked before the start of any important enterprise. On this day, prayers are offered to the god along with specially prepared foods.

In the city of Bombay and in other parts of the State of Maharashtra, this festival has always been closely associated with a strong feeling of patriotism and is celebrated in a particularly dramatic manner. Gaily coloured and garlanded statues of the god are taken out in procession through city streets and are finally immersed in the sea to the accompaniment of loud chanting and music. Prasada is then distributed to the gathering of devotees.

In parts of southern India, devotees of Ganesha believe that it is unlucky and inauspicious to look at the moon on this day. The belief has its origins in a myth referring to the god and his love of good food, especially *laddus* (sweetmeats) and coconut. Thus, it is said, that when Ganesha was returning from a celestial banquet, he saw a reflection of the new moon in a pool of water. Mistaking it for a sliver of coconut, he stooped down from his mouse-drawn carriage to pick it up. Seeing this, the moon laughed loudly and Ganesha, highly offended, cursed her and all those who saw her on this day.

## Dassera

Dassera, one of the most popular festivals in India, is celebrated all over the country for ten days in the month of Asvina (September–October). The festival is focused on the worship of the goddesses Durga, Lakshmi and Saraswati during Navaratri (Nine Nights), the Ram-Lila pageant.

Among the Hindu festivals, Durga Puja is unique. The festival starts on the first night of the Hindu month of Asvina. Durga is worshipped as Divine Mother or as Kumari, the virgin goddess. The Saktas, who consider the goddess as the supreme deity, worship a manifestation of the goddess on each of the Navaratri nights. Usually, the images of the goddess are installed in people's homes or, in the case of community worship, in public places, and worshipped by the performance of *puja* (worship), by *katha* and religious music. Katha is story-telling, and it is a favourite form of devotion among Hindus. A *pandit*, a person well versed in ancient lore, reads passages from a text extolling the deity. He explains it to the audience with comments enlivened by anecdotes and parables.

In the Punjab, the first seven nights of Navaratri are considered to be a period of fast. According to a legend, malicious demons who ruled the Punjab forbade the people from eating anything, all the available food being consumed by the voracious brood. On this day, the people prayed to the goddess Durga who appeared in her warlike form and fought the demons for seven days and put them to flight.

On the eighth, the goddess went among the people and asked them to celebrate with feasts. In memory of this, the people of Punjab observe the first seven days of Navaratri as a period of austerity but, on the eighth, ample amends are made by enjoying feasts.

In Gujerat, the celebration of Navaratri is marked by *garba*, a dance performed by women. They joyfully dance around an earthen lamp placed on a stand, singing and clapping hands in rhythmic movements. In Tamil Nadu, the first three days of the festival are dedicated to the goddess Durga, the next three days to the goddess Lakshmi, and the last three days to the goddess Saraswati. Durga worship is especially popular in Bengal. Both Hindus and non-Hindus worship her in the form of Kali. After nine nights (Navaratri) of fasting and worship, the images of Durga/Kali are taken out in procession and immersed in a tank, river or in the sea.

The main feature of Dassera, especially in northern India, is the Ram-Lila based on the epic story of Ramayana. During this week, dramatic troupes perform plays based on the Ramayana.

On Vijayadasmi Day, which is the last day of the Dassera festival, the worship of gods, especially Lord Rama, is done with fervour, and prayers are offered in every home. Poor people and Brahmins carrying *navratras* (small fresh offshoots of barley plants, which are sown in every house on the first day of the festival), go to wealthy people to offer them stalks of navratras and receive alms in return.

Though celebrated all over India by rich and poor alike, Dassera is chiefly a royal festival beloved of the ruling classes. With independence and the disappearance of the princes from the Indian political scene, the ancient state rituals and pageants are dying out, and the festival is becoming more democratic.

## Karva Chauth

According to legend, a princess observed a fast for a whole day. When she broke the fast at dusk, she received news about her husband's death. As she made her way to her husband's dead body, Parvati, the consort of the Lord Siva, met her and blessed her. She gave the princess some blood out of her finger with which she was asked to annoint her dead husband. The man immediately sprang to life. Hence, on this day, married women observe a fast for the whole day, for the welfare, prosperity and longevity of their husbands.

Prayers are offered to the god Siva and his consort, Parvati. At dusk upon sighting the moon, water and flowers are offered to the household deity. An elderly woman usually recites the story of Karva Chauth to a gathering of married women, and the fast is broken.

On this occasion, mothers bless their married daughters and present them with jewellery, garments and sweetmeats.

## Diwali (Deepawali)

Diwali or Deepawali is the festival of lights. It is celebrated on the new moon day (Amavasya) of the month of Karthika in the Hindu calendar, and generally falls sometime in late October/early November. It is a five-day festival which includes the last two days of the month of Asvina and the first three days of Karthika.

As with most Hindu festivals, Diwali has great religious significance. The celebrations consist of prayers and meditation upon Lakshmi, the goddess of prosperity and her consort Vishnu; Durga, the goddess of primal energy (Sakti); and Saraswati, the goddess of learning. Rama and Krishna, incarnations of Vishnu, are also worshipped during this festival.

Hindus associate the five-day festival with a number of historical and religious events. Dhan Trayodashi is the day to buy new clothes and gifts to commence the festivities. The Puranic story associated with the celebrations on this day is that of the legendary churning of the ocean for *amrit*, the life-giving elixir, by the gods and the demons. Dhanvantary, the god of health, is believed to have emerged from the ocean bearing the pot containing the amrit on this particular day.

On Narak Chaturdashi, Krishna is worshipped. According to popular belief in Gujerat and the west coast of India, Krishna killed the demon Narakasura on this day and liberated several thousand innocent women who were held captive.

On Mahalakshmi Amavasya, businessmen offer prayers and dedicate their account books to the goddess Lakshmi. According to a legend which has wide currency, Lakshmi promises to visit and bless those houses where she is welcomed by lights.

Govardhan Anakuta is the day to worship Krishna who is believed to have saved thousands of cows and cowherds from torrential rains by lifting Mount Govardhana and holding it over them like a giant umbrella.

On Bhratri Dwitiya, sisters remind their brothers of their pledge to protect them from any danger. Girls and women tie a cotton thread on the right wrist of their brothers, followed by the application of a *tilak*, or red mark, on their forehead and the offering of sweets. Brothers, in turn, give gifts of jewellery, clothes or money to their sisters.

Diwali is celebrated as the coronation day of Lord Rama who, after fourteen years of exile and vanquishing the demon king, Ravana, returned in triumph to his capital, Ayodhya. It is also associated with the coronation of the Emperor Vikramaditya who started the new Hindu Era, the Vikram Samvat.

Diwali is a harvest festival which marks the end of the monsoon season and the beginning of winter. Houses are cleaned and decorated, lit with candles and small oil lamps (*diva*). Gifts and sweets are exchanged among friends and relatives and businessmen open their account books for the new year.

There is a pervading spirit of joy and happiness to mark the beginning of the new year, and celebrate the triumph of good over evil.

# JUDAISM

## AN INTRODUCTION TO JUDAISM

Judaism has its roots in the Hebrew Bible. This collection of books, written over a period of nearly 1,000 years, is basically a record of the Jewish people's aspirations to understand God and His ways in relation to the natural world and to humanity. The formation of the Jewish people may be traced back to the exodus of the Hebrews from Egypt and it is closely bound up with a divine revelation and with the commitment of the people to obedience to God's will. The history of Judaism is intimately bound up with the history of the Jewish people and it is this close connection between religion, ethnicity and a sense of history which gives Judaism its unique character.

As a religion centring around the Jewish people, Judaism has been influenced by the cultural, social and political conditions under which its adherents have lived. Consequently, there are various interpretations of some of the beliefs and practices. At times, over its long history, tensions have arisen between rationalism and faith, this-worldliness and other-worldliness, loyalty to the tradition and the desire for change and reform. At all times, however, the Bible has been the source of authority and inspiration for the way in which Jewish people have conducted their lives in different lands.

## THE FUNDAMENTAL BELIEFS OF JUDAISM

At the centre of Jewish belief lies the faith in one God, who is the creator of the natural order, including humanity. One of the most important prayers of the Jews, the Shema, encapsulates the oneness and uniqueness of God.

*Hear, O Israel, the Lord our God, the Lord is One.*
(Deuteronomy 6:4)

There are several names for God in the Hebrew Bible such as, Yahweh, Jehovah, Adonai and Elohim. One of His names is also 'the Eternal', signifying His omnipresence. The Jews believe that God is not only the Creator but also the saviour at the end of time.

The God of the Bible is on the one hand a remote, transcendent being, demanding absolute obedience under the sanction of severe penalties; on the other hand, a loving and compassionate figure who has a close personal relationship with His true believers. In all aspects of the religion portrayed in the Bible, there is an overriding consciousness of the central religious purpose of the Hebrew people.

History provides the Jewish people with evidence of two important kinds, namely a disclosure of God's purpose and a manifestation of human inability to live in accordance with God's purpose. The biblical stories of the Fall from Paradise, the Flood and the Tower of Babel, all point to the rebellious nature of man. Abraham is identified from among all humanity or 'chosen' by God for a specific divine purpose, namely, the establishment of peace and wellbeing in the world and among mankind. The Jews believe that as the descendants of Abraham, they stand in a unique relationship to God, a relationship confirmed by a special covenant between God and Abraham.

Under the terms of this covenant, people are not simply passive objects of divine grace but have to work at their salvation by meeting God's requirements. The covenant is therefore not only a reward for the faith of Abraham and his descendents but also a burden and an obligation.

The doctrine of the close relationship that existed

between God and the Hebrews was the main message of prophetic exhortations. Various prophets, starting with Abraham, appeared in particular historical situations to proclaim and recall God's promises and commands to the Jewish people.

In the prophetic tradition, Moses takes pride of place, as the leader of his people from bondage to the Pharaoh in Egypt and as the bearer of God's commandments. Many traditional Jewish stories centre around the life of Moses, and his prophecy is recorded in the five books referred to as the Pentateuch.

There is no concept of original sin in Judaism. People, it is believed, have the possibility and the capacity to make choices. They also have the power of reasoning, the ability to understand the ethical order of the world and to act in accordance with God's moral laws.

Sin is viewed as rebellion against God and the divine and ethical order. The Jews also believe sin to be a degradation of the true nature of humanity. The purpose of punishment is therefore not retribution but to remind the transgressor of the true nature of man's involvement in maintaining the moral order. The problem of evil in creation is generally approached through the idea that, so far as human beings are concerned, evil must exist in the universe for it to be an arena in which mankind must struggle in order to merit the grace of God.

The search for the essence of Judaism has engaged the minds of many Jewish thinkers. It was not until the Middle Ages that a more or less authoritative list of fundamental beliefs was drawn up by the Jewish thinker Moses Maimonides (1135–1204 CE). His Thirteen Principles of the Faith are widely accepted by all sections of the Jewish community.

### The Thirteen Principles of the Faith

- Belief in the existence of a creator and of providence
- Belief in His unity
- Belief in His incorporeality
- Belief in His eternity
- Belief that worship is due to Him alone
- Belief in the words of the prophets
- Belief that Moses was the greatest of all the prophets
- Belief in the revelation of the Torah to Moses at Sinai
- Belief in the unchangeable nature of the revealed Law
- Belief that God is omniscient
- Belief in retribution in this world and in the hereafter
- Belief in the coming of the Messiah
- Belief in the resurrection of the dead.

### Moral Freedom

The concept of suffering is central to Judaism. It is a consequence of the belief in man's moral freedom and his capacity to choose between right and wrong. Jews believe that suffering may be experienced in three ways: as a punishment, as a test or as a means of atonement of the righteous. It is in the last sense that the collective suffering experienced by the Jewish people at various periods in history has been frequently interpreted. There is also a belief in a compensatory and retributional justice, which arises out of the faith in a just God. Life in the Promised Land is one of the enduring and sustaining beliefs in the midst of suffering.

In Jewish eschatological writings, there are repeated references to the coming of a Messiah who would establish a kingdom of peace, love and justice. Although there is a general belief that the righteous will be resurrected, Jewish thinkers have been divided over the issue of eternal punishment in Hell for the most wicked. From the nineteenth century, Jewish messianic hopes began to be expressed in secular terms as in Zionism and the establishment of the State of Israel.

## JEWISH SACRED LITERATURE

The Torah consists of the first five books of the Hebrew Bible (the Pentateuch), which are regarded as having been revealed by God directly to Moses. They contain a traditional history of the world until the death of Moses, the law as given by God to Moses on Mount Sinai and a variety of rules and regulations concerning religious ritual, diet, justice, social intercourse and administration. It is through their strict adherence to the teachings of the Torah that the Jews, it is believed, fulfil their part of the covenant with God. The language of the Torah is Hebrew.

Every synagogue has a set of parchment scrolls on which the Torah is handwritten, and there is a Torah reading set for every Sabbath in the year to ensure a complete reading in the course of the year. The study of the Torah is deemed to be a religious obligation for all Jews and, in many synagogues, classes may be held by a *rabbi* or teacher for both adults and children. One of the most important occasions in a Jewish male's life is when at the age of thirteen he becomes *Bar-Mitzvah* – or a 'son of the commandment' and reads from the Torah scrolls for the first time in public.

## Mishnah

According to Orthodox Jews, the written Torah was not the only law revealed to Moses. God is also believed to have revealed supplementary laws, which were passed on by oral tradition until they were committed to writing at the beginning of the third century CE. These are called the Mishnah. It comprises six sections (*sedarim*), each of which is subdivided into a number of tractates on individual subjects. The six sections are as follows: agriculture, festivals, women, civil law, sacred things and ritual cleanliness. Together with the Gemara, or completion, it forms the basis of the Talmud.

The Talmud refers to the rabbinical teachings compiled between the destruction of Jerusalem (70 BCE) and the end of the fifth century. It is regarded as the highest legal authority by Jewish people after the Pentateuch.

The Talmud consists of interpretations of scripture, rules of hygiene, diet and conduct, as well as legal decisions and regulations for synagogue services for changing circumstances and sermons, folklore and legends.

# JEWISH SECTS

One of the major consequences of the Jewish diaspora is the rich diversity of traditions which find expression in the ways in which Jewish communities in various parts of the world express their faith and their Jewish identity. The majority of Jews today are descendants of either the Ashkenazim or the Sephardim. The former were originally from central Europe, notably Germany, while the latter were from Spain and the Mediterranean countries. There are distinctive cultural differences between the two. The Ashkenazim developed Yiddish as the medium for a rich literary and artistic cultural heritage; whereas the Sephardim produced a unique culture as a consequence of their close contact with the Islamic world.

Contemporary Judaism is firmly rooted in its biblical traditions. Nonetheless, sectarian differences in beliefs and practices have become accentuated in recent times.

Orthodox Jews are the staunchest adherents of the Torah, the sacred eternal Law revealed to Moses by God on Mount Sinai. All aspects of life are governed by the commandments, including the strict observance of the Sabbath and the laws of kashrut. The rabbi are venerated as the teachers and interpreters of the divine law, and great emphasis is placed on daily prayer and the study of the Torah. Men and women sit separately during synagogue services and women may not be ordained as rabbi. Marriages to non-Jews or non-Orthodox Jews are frowned upon.

Reform Judaism developed in Germany in the wake of intellectual and social movements which emphasised the primacy of reason, scientific enquiry, secularism and the rights of the individual. Jews who were influenced by these new ideas adopted a critical stance to the Torah and a more liberal interpretation of dietary rules. Synagogue services were shortened, and prayers were translated from Hebrew into local languages. Women were ordained as rabbis and the segregation of the sexes in the synagogue was discontinued.

Conservative Judaism emerged at the end of the nineteenth century as a compromise between the Orthodox and Reform schools of thought and practice. Conservatism stresses the need for commitment to traditional law but accepts that beliefs and practices must be interpreted in the light of contemporary needs and experiences. In the main, religious services and ceremonies are closer to Orthodox than to Reform practice, although men and women sit together during worship in the synagogue, and prayers are recited in Hebrew as well as the local language.

# JEWISH MYSTICISM

Until recently it was believed that the whole of Judaism was founded upon the mystical encounters of the patriachs and prophets with God. However, modern scholars distinguish between revelation and mystical experience. The former refers to God's contact with humanity for the purpose of imparting some knowledge of the divine reality and the divine will, whereas the latter refers to man's attempts to penetrate the divine domain.

The three main elements within the mystical tradition are knowledge of God, love of God and communion or reunion with God.

The kabbalists agreed that God Himself is beyond the range of human comprehension. The mystic, however, responds to this challenge by reaching out passionately towards God. Prayer was the main vehicle for the Jewish mystics to reach out and comprehend the divine reality. The kabbalists developed a system of meditation that focused on the secret meanings of each prayer. Worship was also transformed from a public activity to an essentially private and personal communion with God.

Mysticism in Judaism was largely a scholarly tradition, well grounded in the sacred scriptures and their interpretation. The study of the Torah is central in Kabbalah, which was given to man by the creator and is a precise description of the interwoven nature of spiritual and physical reality and how to attain worthy goals and gain happiness within that reality; but the aim is to find hidden, sacred meanings.

Mystical movements such as Hasidism, which arose in Poland in the eighteenth century, gave hope to the Jews living in the ghettos. The key figure in this movement, which emphasised devotion and emotion, was Israel Baal Sheri Tor (1700–60 approx), a dynamic, charismatic leader who preached a passionate devotion to God, expressed in ecstatic prayer, singing and dancing.

Hasidism met with strong opposition from other sections of the Jewish community. The movement came to be accepted only in the mid-eighteenth century. The Hasidim has many sects around the world, each led by its own *rebbe* who acts as an intermediary between his followers and God.

The kabbalists and Hasidim tend, on the whole, to be isolated from the mainstream of modern Jewish life. Nevertheless the influence of the mystical tradition continues to endure in the liturgy of the synagogue.

## Zionism

Zionism is a political movement to establish a national homeland for the Jewish people. Founded by Theodore Herzl in the nineteenth century, as a response to the widespread oppression and persecution of Jews in eastern Europe, this secular movement gained greater momentum as the rising tide of anti-Semitism in Nazi Germany resulted in the horrors of the Holocaust. The creation of the independent State of Israel in 1948 was, for many Jews, a vindication of the prophetic message delivered through the ages that the Jews would recover their Promised Land.

# THE SYNAGOGUE

In Jewish tradition, the synagogue has functioned as the house of prayer (*Bet ha-tefilah*), the house of study (*Bet ha-midrash*) and as the house of assembly (*Bet ha-knesset*). The date of its origin is unknown, but there is sufficient historical evidence to show that with the destruction of the Temple at Jerusalem in 70 BCE, the synagogue emerged as the centre of Jewish socio-cultural and religious life.

There is no prescribed form for a synagogue. Consequently the architectural style and external ornamentation usually reflect the local environment.

The most sacred object in a synagogue is the Sefer Torah. This contains the Hebrew text of the Pentateuch handwritten on strips of parchment, which are sewn together and attached to wooden rollers. The scrolls are kept in a container called the Holy Ark. In Jewish tradition, the congregation is supposed to face Jerusalem during the prayers. To facilitate this, in Western countries, the Ark is usually built against the east wall.

An important feature of every synagogue is the Eternal Light (*Ner Tamid*) burning in front of the Ark, in memory of the perpetual fire in the Temple at Jerusalem as well as symbolising the endurance of the faith. The service is conducted from a raised platform know as the *bimah* which may be either in the centre of the synagogue or immediately in front of the Ark.

Seating for the worshippers varies according to the cultural milieu, from rugs and cushions in Oriental synagogues to pews and standing desks in European ones. In the Orthodox synagogue, men and women are seated apart, some synagogues having separate galleries for women. In Liberal synagogues, it is more usual for male and female worshippers to sit together.

According to Jewish law, prayers may be recited in any language, and in ancient times vernacular languages were used extensively. However, in the course of time, Hebrew became the language of Jewish public worship and it continues to be the practice in Orthodox synagogues. Liberal synagogues, however, use both Hebrew and vernacular languages in communal worship.

Congregational service traditionally required the presence of at least ten males above the age of thirteen. Liberal synagogues, however, do not exclude women from the *minyan* or quorum. The Orthodox service is generally led by the chazan or cantor, but any Jewish male with the requisite knowledge may act in this capacity. In Liberal synagogues, the service is read by the rabbi, sometimes alone, sometimes in unison or responsively with the congregation.

As a mark of mourning for the destruction of the Temple, all instrumental music was traditionally banned from the synagogue. The Jewish Reform Movement introduced the organ in the nineteenth century. Orthodox synagogues have an all-male choir and there is no instrumental music except on special occasions such as weddings. In Liberal synagogues mixed choirs are accompanied by an organ.

Three daily services are held in the synagogue, coinciding with the ancient tradition of the three daily sacrifices in the Temple at Jerusalem. Each of the services consists principally of a series of benedictions known collectively as the Tefillah. The morning and evening services also include the recitation of the Shema ('Hear, O Israel, the Lord is our God, the Lord is one.'). The Shema is preceded and followed by other benedictions.

The reading of the Torah takes place mainly on Monday and Thursday mornings, Sabbath and festival mornings and afternoons, and on the afternoon of the Day of Atonement. For this purpose, the Torah is divided into weekly portions. On the Sabbath and the morning service on high holy days and on the afternoon of the Day of Atonement, the reading of the Torah is followed by a reading from the prophets.

To conclude the service, there are a number of prayers and hymns. One of these is the Kaddish, which expresses a fervent longing and belief in the coming of the Messianic Age. Of the concluding hymns, the best known is the Adan Olan (Eternal Lord), which epitomises the Jewish conception of God.

From its very inception, the synagogue has functioned as a community centre offering cultural, educational and social as well as religious facilities. This tradition has continued into modern times.

## WORSHIP IN JUDAISM

Prayer is regarded as one of the most solemn and holy observances in Judaism. It is termed as mitzvah in Hebrew and it encompasses all religious and secular activity. One of the fundamental beliefs of Judaism is that divine–human communication is possible. Prayer is essentially an attempt to realise man's relationship with God and a means to keep open the channels of communication and influence of God upon the worshipper.

Judaism has, over the years, acquired an extensive liturgy. Prayers include those of praise, confession, supplication and thanksgiving. Some of the prayers refer to God in the third person. Many, however, address God in the second person and express man's I–Thou relationship with the divine presence. Besides verbalised prayers, there is also a tradition of silent meditation and the joyful form of worship in song and dance of the Hasidim.

Three orders of daily prayers are prescribed. According to tradition, the *Shacharith* (morning service) and the *Mincha* (noon service) represent the early morning sacrifice and the noon offering brought daily to the Temple at Jerusalem. After the destruction of the Temple in 70 BCE, these two services continued to be held in the synagogue and served as reminders of the sacrificial ritual that was at the heart of Temple worship. The *Ma'ariv* (evening service), on the other hand, has no connection with the sacrificial cult. On the Sabbath, new moon and festival days, the *Musaf* service is recited in the synagogue as a reminder of the additional sacrifice brought to the Temple on holy days.

Besides the three daily services, there are also prayers to be recited at meal times, on holy days and at other stipulated times and occasions. Formal prayers are justified on the grounds that they embody the values and aspirations of a unified community. The repetition of prescribed prayers is also believed to correspond to the eternal cycle of nature, always the same, but constantly renewed.

The formal posture for prayer is the standing position. However, as the synagogue service grew longer, only the most important prayers were recited while standing. What is today called the Silent Devotion or the Eighteen Benedictions (the *Tefila* in Talmudic times) was the longest prayer said while standing. When a nineteenth Benediction was added at a later date, it became known as the *Amida* or the standing prayer.

Bowing and kneeling were an integral feature of worship in the Temple at Jerusalem. They were, however, prohibited in the synagogues by the rabbi. The only exception is on Yom Kippur, when an account of the ancient Temple service is read and the cantor and the congregation kneel and prostrate themselves.

The first mention of waving in Jewish worship is found in connection with the sacrificial system. At the Feast of Tabernacles (Succoth), it is customary to wave a branch of the date palm and a citron in various directions. The act of waving was believed to bring the person offering the sacrifice closer to God. Some Talmudic scholars, however, believed that waving kept away evil spirits that threatened the performance of Temple ritual.

The custom of swaying while reciting prayers has also been the subject of much conjecture. Today, most authorities consider it to be no more than the body keeping time to the rhythm of the prayer.

A unique feature of Jewish worship is that it is performed in association with several external symbols such as the *tallith, tefillin, mezuzah* and *yarmulka*.

The *tallith* is a prayer shawl decorated with tassels or fringes on all four corners. It is usually made of white wool, with black or purple stripes crossing it. The top of the shawl is decorated with an ornamental fringe of silver or gold thread called the *atarah*. It is worn by Conservative and Orthodox male worshippers during daytime prayers at home or at the synagogue.

The source of the law requiring the wearing of the tallith is the Bible, wherein Moses reminded the Children of Israel to observe God's commandments and thereby achieve holiness.

The tefillin or *phylacteries* consist of two small leather boxes containing four Biblical selections (Deuteronomy 6:4–9; Deuteronomy 11: 13–20; Exodus 13: 1–10; Exodus 13: 11–16). These are strapped to the arm (in line with the heart) and forehead (near the mind) by male worshippers during weekday morning services, in accordance with the biblical injunction to 'bind the words of God between your eyes and upon the arm' (Deuteronomy 6: 8). Jewish women in ancient times were permitted to wear the tefillin but this was banned in the sixteenth century, possibly as a result of the growing belief that religious objects should not be worn by women when they were in a state of ritual impurity as during the time of their menstrual periods.

The tefillin are not worn on the Sabbath or on the occasion of festivals, because such days in themselves purify and focus devotion to God. They are also not worn from the day a Jewish person learns of the death of a close relative until after the funeral.

A *mezuzah* is a small parchment scroll encased in wood, metal or glass, which is fixed at an angle on each of the doorposts (except bathrooms and toilets) of Jewish homes and offices. The parchment is inscribed with the most commonly recited verse from the *Shema* and any of the other biblical selections enclosed in the teffilin. The inscriptions are usually handwritten by scribes who use a quill taken from a kosher fowl and indelible ink specially prepared from vegetable ingredients. The mezuzah is a constant reminder for Jewish people, as they enter or leave their home or office that they are guided by God's presence.

The earliest Jewish reference to a head covering may be found in Exodus 28:4. The Talmud associates the wearing of headgear with the concept of reverence to God and respect (for men of stature). Most Orthodox Jewish men wear a skull cap or *yarmulka* (*kipah* in Hebrew) at all times. Conservative male Jews cover their heads only during acts of worship. In many Reform congregations, covering the head during prayer is entirely optional.

In Biblical and Talmudic times, it was customary for women to cover their heads with scarves or veils as a sign of chastity and modesty. Towards the end of the eighteenth century, the *sheitel* (wig) was introduced as a head-covering for women. Today, only women from the Orthodox Jewish tradition cover their head at all times. Conservative Jewish women generally keep their heads covered when they offer prayers at the synagogue. In Reform synagogues, this practice is rarely adhered to.

## ICONOGRAPHY IN JUDAISM

Jewish monotheism is firmly based on the idea that God alone is sovereign and may not be worshipped in any way other than according to His revealed will in His law and, secondly, that idols are useless in a universe controlled by a single omnipotent God of all creation.

The second of the Ten Commandments explicitly prohibits the making and worship of images:

> *Thou shalt not make unto thee any*
> *Graven image, or any likeness of any thing*
> *That is in heaven above, or that is in the earth beneath,*
> *Or that is in the water under the earth:*
> *Thou shalt not bow down thyself to them, nor serve them.*
> (Exodus 20:1–17)

It is evident from the biblical record, however, that within Israel certain ancient practices persisted as a sort of folk religion alongside the aniconic worship of Yahweh. The household gods (*teraphim*) appear in this category of tacitly accepted images. Even in the official temple worship there were representations of cherubim, winged guardian figures facing one another on the 'mercy seat' above the sacred Ark of the Covenant and also on the tabernacle curtains and the veil of the temple.

Symbolism, verbal or visual, became an established feature of Judaism after the ancient period. Though synagogue buildings tended to be modest and functional in the medieval period, they were embellished with ornamentation and inscriptions. Since the Talmud encouraged the use of fine arts to glorify God in the instruments of worship, there were beautiful works of ritual art such as Torah scrolls, breastplates, lamps, plates and cups.

The seven-branched menorah, an important symbol since ancient times as the light in the temple, was later interpreted as the tree of life and a symbol of the seven days in the week. Guardian lions in sculptured forms were sometimes placed in synagogues, representing the Lion of Judah. The modern Jewish symbol – the Star of David – may have originated as a magic hexagon but it has no biblical or rabbinic warrant.

The use of paintings in the decorations of synagogues goes back to at least 3 CE. The art of making and decorating books became important for Jews, and the Renaissance period saw the appearance of beautifully decorated scrolls, illuminated manuscripts and *kettubot* (marriage contracts).

Literature has throughout history been the major arena of Jewish artistic and intellectual activity. The Hebrew Bible is considered to be a work of great examples of historical narrative poetry, exhibiting grandeur of form and language. Yiddish, the Jewish form of Middle High German, became a highly developed language in the nineteenth century. During the same period, Hebrew also developed into a literary language. It has become the basis of the spoken vernacular of the State of Israel and a flourishing literature has developed.

# THE SABBATH

The Sabbath is considered to be the most important day in the Jewish calendar. It is observed on Saturday, the seventh day of the week.

The term 'Sabbath' is derived from the Hebrew word *Shabbath* meaning 'to rest' from labour. According to biblical tradition, it symbolises the original seventh day on which God rested after completing the creation of the universe. A further justification for its observation is that the Sabbath commemorates the deliverance of the Jewish people from Egyptian bondage.

On this day, conforming Jews refrain from all kinds of work or secular activity and observe the Sabbath at home and in the synagogue through worship, study and leisure. The importance attached to the Sabbath in Jewish culture is attested to by the severity of the punishment, namely death, recommended in the Bible for those who desecrate it.

In the Talmud, 34 categories of activities have been clearly defined as 'work' and hence to be avoided on the Sabbath. These include shopping and preparations for it, which therefore have to be done beforehand. As the Bible specifically prohibits kindling of fire on the Sabbath, cooking is also forbidden on this day. Certain Orthodox Jewish communities also consider electricity to be a form of fire and hence refrain from switching on lights or using electrical appliances on the Sabbath.

In the Jewish calendar, all days begin at nightfall and extend for 24 hours. Hence the Sabbath commences just before sundown on Friday and comes to an end late on Saturday evening. Special rituals mark the beginning and ending of the Sabbath.

In a Jewish home, the Sabbath is welcomed by the woman of the house lighting two special candles and saying a blessing over them. This is followed by the *Kiddush* – a blessing pronounced by the male head of the household over wine and bread. The family then sit down to eat the first of the three special meals prescribed by tradition as the appropriate number to be eaten on the Sabbath. The second meal is eaten on the Sabbath after the morning service in the synagogue and the third, late in the afternoon, usually after the *Mincha* service.

An important component of the Sabbath meal are the two braided loaves (*challoth*), which serve as a reminder of the double portion of manna which God provided for the Israelites in the desert. Special songs are sung during the meal, which ends with a thanksgiving.

Orthodox Jewish men usually usher in the Sabbath by attending synagogue services on Friday evening before dinner. Certain Conservative and Reform Jews attend a later evening service. For all three groups, however, Saturday is a day for communal worship in the synagogue, and the entire family attends the special services.

Starting with the Book of Genesis, a portion of the Torah is read aloud every Sabbath during worship, and the entire Torah is read within the span of the annual Jewish calendar. During the service, seven people are 'called up' (aliya) to follow the reader of the Torah. An eighth person then reads a selection from the Prophetic Books, and the service is concluded with an interpretation or a sermon based on the Torah. Families then return home for a festive meal.

The rest of the Sabbath may be spent either attending special study sessions in the synagogue, or in social activities such as visiting friends and relatives or simply resting after the week's work.

Jewish Law forbids leisure – time activities such as dancing, swimming or playing ball games. However, certain authorities permit such activities within reasonable limits, as they add joy to the Sabbath Day. Some Orthodox Jews do not drive a car or travel in a bus or train on the Sabbath. However, Reform and Conservative Jewish communities find it acceptable to use a car for social purposes.

The departure of the Sabbath is marked by a special ceremony, the *Havdalah*, which emphasises the difference between the holiness of the Sabbath and the rest of the week. A blessing is said over wine and a lighted candle – the latter symbolising the approach of a new week as well as a reminder that God created light on the first day. A spice box containing sweet-smelling spices is passed around – again symbolising the sweetness of the Sabbath and the hope that this quality will endure through the week.

The final act is to extinguish the candle with some of the blessed wine, and for everyone present to wish each other a good week.

## JEWISH DIETARY LAWS

Central to the lives of Orthodox Jews and to a lesser extent, Reform and Conservative Jews, are a comprehensive set of laws that regulate diet and the preparation of food. The basic principles are stated in the Bible (the Book of Leviticus). The rationale for these laws, however, is not elucidated.

The general term for permissible food is *kosher* or kasher. The Hebrew word *terayfa* has been extended to include all forbidden foods as well as food that has not been prepared in accordance with *kashrut* (the system of dietary laws). It is generally agreed by Jewish writers and scholars that observance of kashrut has helped to unify the Jewish people throughout their history, and continually serves to remind them of their distinctive culture.

Fruit and vegetables of all kinds are permitted, but only the meat of animals that chew the cud as well as have a cloven hoof, such as cattle, sheep, goats and deer, may be eaten. Fish that have fins and scales are considered to be kosher, but all other seafood is forbidden. Birds are permitted if there is any reliable evidence to suggest that they were eaten by Jewish people in the past. Different Jewish communities, however, have their own views with regard to these customs and traditions.

The preparation of food must also comply with kashrut. Animals and birds must be ritually slaughtered by a specialist *(shoket)* who is trained in Jewish law. A sharp knife is used to sever the jugular vein so that the animal dies instantaneously and the maximum amount of blood drains away.

According to the traditional dietary laws, it is forbidden to eat the flesh of an animal which has died naturally or been killed through other methods. A slaughtered animal is carefully examined for signs of disease. The fat of domesticated and non-domesticated animals must be removed, as must the sciatic nerve. The laws also specify that the major arteries must be excised.

The Bible repeatedly reiterates that blood should not be consumed, because it symbolises the very essence of life (Leviticus 3:17; Deuteronomy 13:23–25). Hence, before cooking, the meat of all animals is washed and soaked in salt to remove traces of congealed blood.

In accordance with the biblical law against boiling a kid in its mother's milk, three further conditions on the consumption of meat and dairy products are adhered to, namely, they may not be eaten together, cooked together or served in any kind of combination. A time interval ranging from one hour in some communities, to six in others, is usually maintained between eating meat and dairy products. To segregate these products even further, a kosher home is equipped with two sets of kitchenware, crockery, cutlery and washing-up facilities. The Passover feast requires separate sets of dishes for meat and dairy products as well as one set which is untainted by any kind of fermented or leavened food.

This special Seder plate is used to contain the six symbols of the Passover Seder: maror (bitter herbs), karpas (vegetable), chazeret (bitter vegetable), charoset (apple, nut, spice and wine mixture), zeroa (shankbone) and beitzah (egg).

# JEWISH LIFECYCLE RITUALS

## Birth

On the eighth day after birth, a Jewish male child is circumcised by a *mohel*, a specialist in the act of ritual circumcision. This is an important rite of passage as it is symbolic of the child entering into the covenant that God made with Abraham and his descendants. It is traditional to schedule the ceremony as early in the day as possible. The baby is brought into the room by the godparent (*sandek*), who sits, holding the child, in a chair that is designated as Elijah's Chair. According to tradition, the chair derives its name for two reasons: firstly because one of the Prophet Elijah's main complaints against the Hebrews was that they had ceased circumcising their children; hence Jewish parents demonstrate to Elijah that they are fulfilling the covenant. The second reason is because tradition teaches that Elijah will return to earth to herald the coming of the Messiah and, when a baby is born, there is a hope that he could be the Messiah, and so he is welcomed by being held in Elijah's Chair. After this ceremony a boy receives his Hebrew name, which will be used on the occasion of his *Bar-Mitzvah*, his wedding and on his gravestone. Ashkenazi Jews generally name their children after deceased relatives, whereas Sephardic Jews often name their children after living relatives. The ritual is followed by a festive meal.

The only traditional rite recognising the birth of a daughter is naming. Her father would be called for an *aliyah* following her birth, and prayers are said for the child's and mother's health. The baby's name would be announced publicly in the synagogue.

In the past two decades or so, ceremonies are conducted which welcome girls into the Jewish covenant. *Brit Rechitzah* involves washing the child's feet as a sign of welcome, based on the account in Genesis, in which Abraham washes the feet of angels as a gesture of welcome and hospitality.

Within a Jewish family, great importance is placed on the religious education of children. They are taught to recite the Shema at a very young age and most synagogues have facilities for conducting religious education classes for young people.

## Initiation Ceremonies

At the age of thirteen, a boy is formally initiated into the ways of the Jewish faith. The ceremony takes place on the Sabbath after his birthday. For the first time, he wears the *tallith* or prayer shawl, and the *tephillin* or *phylacteries* (the leather boxes containing biblical texts which are worn on the left arm and the forehead). He reads publicly in Hebrew from the scrolls of the Torah and accepts the commandments of the faith. As a *Bar-Mitzvah* or 'Son of the Commandment', he is recognised to be a responsible member of the religious community and may count as one of the ten adult men who are required to make a quorum for public prayer (*minyan*).

The Bar-Mitzvah marks an important turning point in the life of a Jewish male and it is an occasion for joyful celebration. It also has considerable religious and symbolic significance for the community as it reaffirms belief in the fundamental principles of Judaism and ensures continuity of the Jewish way of life. The young boy prepares for this event under the guidance of a *rabbi*.

A Jewish girl automatically comes of age at twelve years and is known as a *Bat-Mitzvah* or 'Daughter of the Commandment'. In Reform and Liberal Jewish communities, this event is marked by a ceremony similar to the Bar-Mitzvah.

# JEWISH WEDDING RITUALS

The home and the family are of central importance in Judaism, since it is here that the values underpinning the Jewish way of life are inculcated, developed and nurtured. The Jewish family is based upon the sanctity of the marriage tie. The term *kiddushin* or sanctification reflects the essence of marriage in Judaism.

The importance of the wedding rituals must be understood with reference to the Old Testament and the principles enshrined in the Talmud. Despite the adjustments that have been made to changing social and historical circumstances, there is a clearly definable thread of continuity that reaches back for several centuries.

An examination of Jewish wedding customs reveals considerable agreement among all sections of the community as to the basic procedures that must be followed. These include:

- The *huppah* or canopy
- The *erushin* or *kiddushin* (betrothal)
- The *nissu'in* (marriage)
- The reading of the *ketubah* (marriage contract)
- The Seven Benedictions
- The shattering of a glass.

## The Aims of Marriage

Asceticism and celibacy are not upheld as ideals in Judaism. On the other hand, it is obligatory for every person to marry and to continue the human race in accordance with the commandment:

> *Be fruitful, multiply, fill the earth and conquer it.*
> (Genesis 1:28).

The object of marriage in Talmudic teaching is the promotion of chastity and purity of life. The basis of the marriage relationship rests not only upon fidelity but also unity in aim and purpose.

Monogamy has always been the ideal, and in ancient times marriages were generally arranged between members of the same tribe. The Shulchan Aruch, a synopsis of Jewish law that was first printed in 1565, stated that it was: 'mandatory for one to marry his niece, whether the daughter of his sister or his brother'. If nieces were not available, then it was desirable to marry a cousin.'

The practice of marrying within a limited circle probably arose from the Jewish people's need to preserve their religious and ethnic identity in the face of at times seemingly overwhelming odds.

Marriages were traditionally arranged by parents with the help of professional matchmakers, known as shadchan. These matchmakers were originally learned scholars, well versed in the scriptures and customs. Gradually, however, the shadchan became more of a business person working on a commission basis, and Jewish folklore is rich in the tales of matchmakers who attempted to oversell the qualities of the young woman or man on whose behalf they were negotiating. Nowadays it is more usual for young people to select their own marriage partners.

## Selecting the Day

In the Jewish tradition, marriages may be solemnised on any day except Friday and on the Sabbath. Weddings may be celebrated throughout the year except during part of the period between Passover and the Pentecost. The three weeks in July–August, which commemorate the Destruction of the Temple, are also considered to be inauspicious for weddings.

## The Wedding Ceremony

Jewish weddings are usually conducted during the daylight hours. The ceremonies are always conducted under a canopy (*huppah*) in the synagogue, although some Jewish communities prefer the more traditional wedding conducted under a canopy in the open air. The canopy is a symbol of the vault of Heaven and signifies that the marriage is consecrated in the presence of God. Jewish weddings are usually conducted by a rabbi, together with the cantor of the synagogue. A marriage between a Jew and a Gentile may not be solemnised in a synagogue.

The Jewish bride is usually dressed in white with a veil draped over her head. The bridegroom may be dressed in formal morning dress.

In Talmudic times, there were two distinct stages in the ceremony: betrothal and marriage. Betrothal (*erussin* or

kiddushin) was the ceremony whereby a woman was promised to a man. This ceremony took place before witnesses, and the man either gave the woman a nominal sum of money as a token of betrothal or else confirmed the betrothal in writing. The ceremony was performed by the man but had no validity unless the woman gave her consent.

The second stage of the marriage ceremony was the *nissu'in* or the act of bringing the bride into her marital home. When socio-political factors forced the dispersal of the Jewish people, and uncertain living conditions made the waiting period between betrothal and marriage difficult, the two ceremonies were merged into a single service with two parts, which followed each other immediately.

The first part of the accepted modern Jewish wedding ceremony consists of the *Benediction of Betrothal,* which is in praise of God and the institution of marriage. It is recited over a cup of wine. This is followed by the rite of *Kiddushin,* in which the bridegroom places a ring upon the forefinger of the right hand of the bride with the declaration:

*Behold, thou art sanctified unto me by this ring according to the law of Moses.*

The betrothal ceremony is conducted in the presence of two witnesses who are usually the officiating rabbi and his assistant.

Jewish law decrees that no marriage may be performed unless the bridegroom has first drawn up a document providing his wife-to-be with some safeguards in her future married life. This document, known as the *Ketubbah,* is read out immediately after the ring ceremony and includes among other clauses, a promise made by the bridegroom to his bride that:

*I work for thee, I will honour thee, I will support and maintain thee, as it beseemeth a Jewish husband to do.*

The second part of the ceremony consists of the recital of the Seven Benedictions of Nuptial over a cup of wine. These include praise to God for the creation of man and woman to be companions to each other, praise for the joys of matrimonial bliss, a prayer for the happiness of the bride and bridegroom, and a blessing linking the hopes cherished on behalf of the couple with the hopes of the Jewish people.

The cup of wine over which the Benedictions have been recited are drunk by the couple to indicate their resolve to share their future joys and sorrows. The wedding ceremony ends with shattering of a glass under the foot of the bridegroom. There are several explanations for this custom. The most widely accepted one is that this symbolic act is a reminder of the Destruction of the Temple of Jerusalem, a theme that is continually reiterated in Jewish prayers.

The bride and groom usually fast on the day of the wedding in preparation for the consecration of their marriage. Immediately after the wedding ceremony, they go into a separate room where they eat together. It was customary to prepare a marriage feast for each day of the following week during which the Seven Benedictions were repeated at the table. Nowadays, this practice is only observed by some Orthodox Jewish families.

The officiating rabbi is authorised to sign the religious marriage certificate. However, the Registrar of Marriages must be notified before the wedding so that a civil licence may be issued.

The primary objective of marriage is procreation. According to Orthodox Jewish law, a Jew is one who is born of a Jewish mother. Children not only ensure the continuity of the family but they also guarantee the survival of Judaism. Consequently contraception and the termination of pregnancy are disapproved of by the religion except on medical grounds.

## Divorce

A marriage that has been consecrated and solemnised in the presence of religious witnesses is expected to endure. However, if the relationship has irretrievably broken down, the Talmud provides for divorce (*get*), which gives both the wife and the husband the freedom to remarry. A religious divorce is necessary if either partner wishes to contract a second marriage and if it is to be solemnised in a synagogue.

Petitions for a religious divorce are made to the *Bet Din* (court of law). Each group within the Jewish community has its own Bet Din. A religious court consisting of three rabbis meets to decide about divorce petitions. Usually a religious divorce is granted automatically once a civil divorce has been obtained.

# RITUALS ASSOCIATED WITH DEATH, BURIAL AND MOURNING

Death is defined in Judaism as the cessation of respiration. The last words uttered by religious Jews or said on their behalf, are the words of the *Shema*: 'Hear, O Israel, the Lord our God is one Lord...' Orthodox Jewish tradition prescribes that funerals should take place within 24 hours of death. The deceased person is dressed in a white shroud (*kittel*) and prayer shawl (*tallith*) with its tassels cut off and then placed in a plain wooden coffin.

There is a belief that while the body of the deceased person is in the house it should not be left unattended. Candles are lit at the head and the foot of the coffin and the sons or other close kin of the dead person maintain a constant vigil. If no relatives are present, professional mourners are called in.

All arrangements for the funeral are made through the synagogue. The rabbi is sent for as soon as death occurs, and he returns to the house of mourning an hour or so before the funeral to offer special prayers in the home of the deceased. Close relatives of the dead person gather at the house and make a small tear in their clothes as a mark of mourning. This torn garment is worn throughout the seven days of intense mourning (*shiveh*).

The coffin is carried out of the house after the prayers, and the mourners usually proceed to the cemetery on foot. The use of transport is permitted if the burial ground is not within walking distance, although many Orthodox Jews insist on covering at least part of the way on foot. Jewish tradition prescribes that burial should take place in consecrated ground.

At the cemetery, the coffin is taken to a special room. The male mourners stand on the left and the women on the right of the coffin. Prayers and psalms are recited and the rabbi makes a special mention of the dead person's virtues. Flowers and music are conspicuous by their absence at Jewish burials.

The mourners then follow the coffin to the grave. The sons and brothers of the deceased shovel some earth on to the coffin. It is customary to throw some earth from the Land of Israel on to the coffin as a symbolic recognition of the Jewish belief in the resurrection, which will take place in the Holy Land. After the burial the kaddish, or special prayer in praise of God, is recited by the male relatives of the deceased. A meal consisting of eggs, salt-herrings and bagels is served to the mourners. Peas or lentils are also considered as suitable foods to be served after a funeral as, according to Jewish belief, roundness is symbolic of life.

During the seven days of intense mourning, close relatives of the dead person are required to sit on low mourning stools, unwashed and unshaven, wearing torn garments and special slippers which are not made of leather. Prayers are said throughout the day, and friends and neighbours visit to offer condolences and help.

The mourning ritual prescribed for women ends on the seventh day. Male relatives, however, are forbidden to cut their hair or shave for 30 days. In the 11 months following a death, the sons and other close male relatives are required to go twice a day to the synagogue to recite kaddish. The gravestone is erected after 11 months and this symbolises the end of the official period of mourning.

Four times a year prayers for the dead are recited at the synagogue and, on every death anniversary, the grave is visited and prayers are recited in which the names of all surviving relatives and descendants are mentioned. Memorial lights are also lit in the home and in the synagogue.

# JEWISH HOLY DAYS AND OTHER FESTIVALS

Jewish holy days always commence immediately before dusk and terminate at nightfall the following day – a 25-hour period. If there are two consecutive holy days, the laws relating to the festival continue over both days, terminating at nightfall on the second day.

According to Jewish law, work of any sort, including creative activity, travelling, engaging in commercial transactions and operating equipment, even telephones, is strictly prohibited on holy days. A 'dispensation' cannot be given by a rabbi from these restrictions and obligations. However, individuals are free to decide on their own level of observance.

The two most important festivals in the Jewish calendar are Rosh Hashanah (the Jewish New Year) and Yom Kippur (the Day of Atonement). These high holy days are unique because they are the only Jewish festivals that have neither a historical nor an agricultural basis.

## Purim

This marks the deliverance of the Jews of Persia from the persecution of Haman, the Prime Minister of King Ahaseurus, and his followers, mainly because Haman hated the wise Jew Mordecai. Providentially, the tables were turned on him when Mordecai's niece Esther was chosen by King Ahaseurus as his new queen. She pleaded for her people and saved them from destruction.

School may be attended, but the day is usually celebrated with much jollity, including fancy dress.

## Pesach or Passover

This celebrates the deliverance of the Children of Israel from Egypt where they were held as slaves. The festival lasts for eight days, during which no bread, cakes or similar foodstuffs may be eaten, and matzoh (unleavened bread) is substituted for these.

The first two and last two days are particularly holy, and Jewish children do not attend school on these days.

On the eve of the first two days, special celebrations, called the Seder, are held in Jewish homes when families gather together for a festive meal, preceded by recounting the story of the Exodus from Egypt.

## Lag B'Omer

On the second day of Passover in ancient Israel, the first sheaf was cut of the barley harvest and offered up in the Temple. This started the counting of the omer (a measure of the grain) leading to Shavuot. The Jewish people were commanded to count the 49 days between the second night of Passover and the festival of Pentecost. The 12th day is Holocaust Remembrance Day and the 33rd day is Lag B'omer, a popular day for weddings.

At the end of the second day, a service is held, throughout which the congregation stands. At the end, the shofar (a ram's horn) is blown to signal the end of fasting. The congregation responds with a fervent wish, 'Next year in Jerusalem'.

School may be attended.

## Shavuot

This is the Jewish feast to celebrate the giving of the Ten Commandments on Mount Sinai. The festival is also connected with agriculture, and synagogues are usually adorned with flowers and plants. A portion of the law, including the Ten Commandments, is read in synagogues, and children should not attend school on these two days.

## Tish B'av

The ninth day of the Jewish month of Av is a solemn, sombre occasion which commemorates the destruction of the first temple in Jerusalem by Nebuchadnezzar, King of Babylon, in 586 BCE and of the second temple by the Romans in 70 CE. Other tragic events associated with this day are the expulsion of the Jews from Spain in 1492, the beginning of World War I and the holocaust.

Tish B'av is observed with prayers and fasting. No greetings are exchanged, and mourning restrictions apply. Shaving and the wearing of leather are banned. All ornaments are removed from the synagogue and the lights are dimmed. The Book of Lamentations, written by the prophet Jeremiah after the destruction of the first temple, is read at the evening service. In Israel, it is customary for mourners to congregate at the Western Wall, the last vestige of the second temple, to recite elegies (kinot).

## Rosh Hashanah

On the two days marking the New Year, the Jewish people are symbolically judged by God in Heaven, and the ram's horn, the shofar, is blown to awaken the people to repentance.

The two-day festival is observed by all Jewish people and children should not attend school. Most Jews, wherever they happen to be, will attend synagogue.

## Yom Kippur

The Day of Atonement falls on the tenth day from Rosh Hashanah. A fast is observed from the eve of the day to nightfall on the day itself. During these 25 hours or so, no food or drink touches the lips of Jews, and most Jewish people remain in the synagogue throughout the day in worship and contemplation.

## Succoth or Tabernacles

Succoth or Feast of Tabernacles. This is a nine-day (eight days in Israel) festival commemorating the divine protection given to the Israelites during their wanderings through the wilderness. Temporary dwelling places (*succoth*) are erected in the synagogue and meals are taken there. Palm and myrtle branches are waved, symbolic of God's universal presence. Seven circuits of the synagogue are made. The first, second, eighth and ninth are especially holy days, and the eighth involves prayers for rain, and recalls the former temple ceremonies of drawing water.

On the first two and the last two days of the festival, Jewish children should not attend school.

## Simchath Torah

This is the ninth and last day of Succoth on which the cycle of the reading of the law in synagogues is completed for the year with the reading of the last section of the Book of Deuteronomy. Another scroll is unwound from which is read the beginning of the Book of Genesis, to demonstrate that the study of the Torah is an everlasting and continuous process. There is much festivity to celebrate this event, and children play a prominent part in it.

The privilege of reading the last portion of the law and beginning again is given to members of the synagogue who have been active on behalf of the community.

## First Day of Chanucah

Chanucah commemorates the heroic efforts of the Maccabean brothers to lead the war to oust the Syrian/Greek invaders, who not only ruled Israel at the time but also passed laws proscribing the practice of Judaism, and desecrated the Temple by offering sacrifices of unclean animals.

When in 165 BCE, the Syrians were defeated, the Maccabeans made their way to the Temple, cleansed it, reconsecrated it, and relit the menorah, the light of which signified God's presence.

Miraculously, the special oil that was found and which should have lasted for only one day was enough for eight days, giving the priests enough time to obtain a new consignment of oil. In commemoration of these events, candles or oil lamps are lit for eight days in Jewish homes.

Jewish children may attend school on these days.

# CHRISTIANITY

## AN INTRODUCTION TO CHRISTIANITY

Two thousand years ago, Jesus of Nazareth, a Palestinian Jew, was baptised in the Jewish tradition by John the Baptist and afterwards presented himself as 'the way, the truth and the life'. He attracted a core of 12 disciples and commenced a vigorous mission. To those who followed him, he promised salvation and chartered the route towards its achievement. The route contained both divine and human considerations.

Jesus was a charismatic and authoritative prophet preacher. He posed a threat to the religious leaders and the civil rulers at the time. The former persuaded the latter to take action against him. Pontius Pilate, the Roman governor, condemned Christ to death. He was crucified. After three days he rose from the tomb in which he had been interred. He appeared to his disciples and, a month or so later, he ascended into Heaven.

The immediate disciples commenced a Jesus movement. Initially the movement engaged Jewish followers and continued Jewish practices such as baptism and circumcision. Within a short while, it attracted Gentiles (non-Jews), Greeks and other outsiders. The members of the new movement were essentially followers of Jesus, the Messiah of the Old Testament, or the Christos as the Greek converts translated his messianic title. By the second half of the first century, the followers of Jesus were known as Christians.

### The Last Supper

On the night before he was killed, Jesus celebrated a meal with his 12 disciples. Having warned them of his imminent betrayal and death, he broke bread and drank wine with them. He described the bread and wine as his body and blood and asked them to continue sharing bread and wine together in memory of him. The continued celebration of the last supper became known as the Eucharist or Communion. It is also called the Mass.

There are many strands of Christianity. However, all Christians are followers of Jesus and almost all celebrate the Eucharist.

## THE BIBLE

All Christian knowledge about the messianic predictions and about the birth, life, teachings, death and Resurrection of Jesus is acquired from the scriptures or Bible. The Bible in Christian terms is comprised of the Old Testament (pre-Jesus writings) and the New Testament. Christianity shares the Old Testament with Judaism. The scriptures, representing the revealed word of God, are treated with respect. In public ceremonies the Bible is the object of ritualised honour.

The concept of revelation in the Bible is complex. The Bible is not a verbatim record. Although the authors are the messengers of the word of God, they are not word-for-word scribes hastening from vision to parchment. The human instrument is significant. Jesus, sometimes referred to as the 'word of God', left nothing in writing. Shortly after his death, and after considerable reflection under the guidance of the Spirit of God, the various authors wrote all that is known about the life and teachings of Jesus.

The revealed word of God unites all Christians. The complexity of revelation positions Christians on a diversity of pilgrimage routes in a common and occasionally conflicting search for fulfilment in truth.

## The Trouble with Revelation

The Bible, in common with revealed sacred writings in all religions, has a certain vulnerability. Isolated texts have been and continue to be to be misused to justify hatred, oppression of women, ethnic cleansing, castigation of the poor and the unemployed, car bombings, cruelty to animals, exploitation of children and even wars of religion.

Extracts from the letters of St Paul can illustrate the dangers of quotations out of context. In places his harshness of expression seems to mirror well the social climate of his time and to relegate women to a subordinate status. A balance can only be struck by reviewing the Christian message as a whole and by understanding the role of the human instrument in the delivery of divine revelation. The slick one-verse approach to truth is the antithesis of biblical revelation.

# CHRISTIAN BELIEFS

Christians acknowledge the manifestation of God through the Bible. The manifestation of the divine being reveals to them a single God in whom are three persons, namely Father, Son and Spirit, sharing a single 'substance'. This aspect of the godhead is called the Trinity.

All Christians have faith in the existence of Jesus Christ, the Son of God, born of the virgin Mary, and in the need for personal commitment to him.

Christians believe that whereas they understand and relate to God in a somewhat clouded manner in the here and now, they have the promise and hope of seeing God 'face to face' in a life of permanent happiness after death.

They understand God to be the creator of the entire universe. In the main they have no problem with the theory of evolution; Christian cosmologists are as much theologically intrigued by what happened before the 'big bang' as by what developed after it. For them God is the first cause.

On formal liturgical occasions the Christian congregation frequently recites a creed, or summary of beliefs, called the Nicene Creed, originating in the fifth-century Council of Nicea. The following are extracts from the creed:

*We believe in one God, the father, the Almighty, maker of heaven and earth. We believe in one Lord, Jesus Christ the only Son of God … of one being with the father. For us and for our salvation he came down from heaven, was incarnate of the Holy spirit and the virgin Mary and was made man … he suffered death and was buried. On the third day he rose again and ascended into heaven. … We look for the resurrection of the dead and the life of the world to come.*

For Christians the moral code is imbedded in the precept of charity, which Jesus expounded:

*You must love others as yourself. By this will everyone know that you are my disciples if you have love one for another.*

The implications of the Christian imperative to love 'without keeping a record of wrongs' are still being worked out. The guidelines for the ideal of Christian morality are expressed in the Ten Commandments.

## The Ten Commandments

1  You shall have no other gods before Me.
2  You shall not make for yourself an idol in the form of anything in heaven above or on the earth beneath or in the waters below. You shall not bow down to them or worship them; for I, the Lord your God, am a jealous God, punishing the children for the sin of the fathers to the third and fourth generations of those who love me and keep My commandments.
3  You shall not misuse the name of the Lord your god, for the Lord will not hold anyone guiltless who misuses His name.
4  Remember the Sabbath day by keeping it holy.
5  Honour your father and your mother.
6  You shall not murder.
7  You shall not commit adultery.
8  You shall not steal.
9  You shall not give false testimony against your neighbour.
10 You shall not covet your neighbour's house. You shall not covet your neighbour's wife, or his manservant or maidservant, his ox or donkey, or anything that belongs to your neighbour.

# CHRISTIAN PRACTICES

## The Sabbath

The concept of sabbath was inherited from Judaism. It was progressively applied to Sunday rather than the Jewish Saturday, because the Resurrection of Christ occurred on the first day of the week.

As Christianity spread and in many places became the established religion, three aspects of the Sabbath evolved, namely, religious observance, remission of secular duties and recreational activity.

Religious observance acquired a public dimension and required attending a common place of worship, where the Eucharist, scriptural readings and prayers were offered.

## The Eucharist

The celebration of the Eucharist is also called Holy Communion and the Mass. It is a re-enactment of the Last Supper. The service is normally led by an ordained minister. The congregation makes an expression of humility, asks forgiveness for failings, listens to appropriate scriptural readings and, after the minister has recited the words of the Last Supper over the bread and wine, they receive what has been blessed as the body and blood of Christ.

On some occasions the Mass is celebrated with extensive ritual. This is particularly common in the Eastern Orthodox Church.

## Bible Readings

Scriptural readings are often part of wider spiritual activities, such as funerals, weddings, ordinations of ministers, or simply services in their own right. In general there is a balance of readings between the Old and New Testament.

New Testament readings will also often have a balance between the Gospels and the other books. The Gospels according to Matthew, Mark, Luke and John deal with the life of Christ; the other books, including the Epistles and the Acts of the Apostles, deal with the life and activities of the early church.

## Prayer

Prayers are said both in private and in public. Where prayer is formalised it normally contains recognition and worship of God, an element of thanks and a hope or a request for the future.

The best known of all Christian prayers is the prayer that Jesus taught his disciples when they asked him how they should pray. It is now called the Lord's Prayer:

*Our Father in Heaven*
*Hallowed be your name.*
*Your kingdom come,*
*Your will be done,*
*On earth as it is in Heaven.*
*Give us today our daily bread.*
*Forgive us our sins,*
*As we forgive those who sin against us.*
*Lead us not into temptation,*
*But deliver us from evil.*
*For the kingdom the power and the glory are yours,*
*Now and forever. Amen.*

## Sacraments

These are solemn religious acts which, through external signs, confer internal grace on recipients who are properly disposed.

In the pre-Reformation tradition, in the Roman Catholic and Byzantine traditions there are seven sacraments: baptism, confirmation, the Eucharist, penance, extreme unction, orders (ordination) and marriage.

For some reformed churches, sacraments are limited to

baptism and the Eucharist, the two sacraments clearly identified in the Bible.

Quakers and the Salvation Army do not accept the concept of sacramental ritual.

## Celibacy

Catholic clergy may not marry and, with very few exceptions, married persons may not be ordained. Anglican and Protestant clergy may marry. Eastern Orthodox priests may marry; their bishops may not, and for that reason are usually chosen from the Orthodox monasteries where celibacy is the rule.

## DISAGREEMENTS AND DIVISIONS

Within 30 years of the Ascension of Christ to Heaven and his promise that he would come again in glory at the end of the world, Christians experienced disagreements about the second coming of Christ, about the metaphysics of the human and divine natures of Christ, and about adherence to religious practices.

Major theological issues were debated and defined in ecumenical (worldwide) councils. The four major councils were the Council of Nicea in 325, Council of Constantine in 381, Council of Ephesus in 431 and the Council of Calcedon in 451.

The frequency, the dating and the conclusions or definitions of the ecumenical councils reveal the high-risk strategy of a Christian God who gave so much scope to the human instrument in taking his message of salvation to humankind.

After each council there was a certain shedding of members. The Oriental Orthodox Church, for example, which has most of its members in Ethiopia, Armenia, Egypt and Syria, rejected the definition of the two natures of Christ as defined at the Council of Calcedon (451) and went its own Christian way.

At various stages in the Church's history the imperfections of the human instruments became too intrusive and had to be reformed. In the eleventh century the Latin or Roman tradition in the Church and the Eastern Churches finally split. The Protestant Reformation of the sixteenth century took reformation on to a new plane.

### The Eastern Orthodox Church

The first formal schism between east and west occurred in 863. The divide was temporary. A permanent schism occurred in 1054 and was consolidated when the western crusaders, while trying to regain the Holy Land, attacked Constantinople and looted the eastern churches in 1204.

The schism crystallised around points of doctrine and authority. In practice it was long in the making, being influenced by cultural and political factors.

The Eastern Orthodox Church reject the authority of the pope and see themselves as a fellowship of autonomous churches governed by their bishops, with the Patriarch of Constantinople holding the position of first among equals. The Eastern Orthodox Church claims a direct link to the original apostolic church.

The largest Orthodox community is in Russia. There are also substantial population proportions in Greece, Serbia, Romania, Bulgaria and Cyprus.

The most distinctive characteristic of the Eastern Church is the prevalence of icons. The veneration of the icon is an aid towards entering into a state of Christ-mindedness.

### Sixteenth-century European Reformation

### Lutheranism: Martin Luther (1483–1546)

A German priest and professor of biblical studies, Martin Luther, reacted to the Church's perception of itself as the reservoir of grace, promising eternal happiness after death and mediating in the process of judgement through the use of what were called indulgences.

Luther preached justification by faith alone. He asserted that scripture was the sole rule of faith. Each individual should find Christ in the Bible and have faith in Him.

The immediacy of Luther's theology, in which Christ rather than the Church is the central point, reduced the importance of the Church and the sacraments, questioned the superiority of the clergy, and opposed the supremacy of the pope.

The invention of printing greatly assisted Luther. Translations of the Bible were becoming accessible to believers who previously depended upon their clergy for an explanation of the Latin text. And the 95 theses in which Luther criticised malpractices in the Church were widely disseminated.

Lutheranism, although initially opposed in England, was influential in the English Reformation. His reforms rapidly gained prominence in northern Europe, in Scandinavia, Iceland, Prussia and the Baltic countries.

## Calvinism: John Calvin (1509–64)

The French theologian John Calvin is the outstanding author of the Reformation. He taught that at the heart of the Christian life lies union with Christ and that such a union is an utterly unmerited relationship, brought about by the Holy Spirit. The unmerited nature of the gift led Calvin's followers to preach a theology of 'predestination'.

Calvinism influenced the Puritans in England, the Presbyterians in Scotland and the Calvinistic Methodists in Wales.

## Anabaptists (Origins in Switzerland in 1525)

The Anabaptists were the most radical of the sixteenth-century reformers. They had a left-wing, maverick reputation and a scattered membership that makes it difficult to represent them fairly in a brief entry. They were equally disliked by both other Protestant reformers and by the State.

The organised believers' groups were made up of families of believers who had submitted themselves to adult baptism, which was more a symbol of faith rather than a sacrament that conferred grace. They found much of the existing Church structure to be irrelevant. They opposed military service, involvement in politics, the taking of the oath in civil matters, and participation in public office.

They suffered considerable persecution from their earliest days and were actually driven out of Munster, in Germany, for preaching polygamy.

Baptists, Congregationalists, Mennonites, and Quakers inherited theological principles and practices from the Anabaptists.

### The English Reformation

The English or Anglican Church is variously described as Catholic, Anglo-Catholic or Protestant.

Henry VIII (1509–47) had personal reasons to rule both Church and State. Personal need and commitment to tradition led him to seek a middle-way reformation. He rejected papal authority, set about reforms and fathered the English Reformation.

There are now 37 autonomous Anglican Churches throughout the world. They are bonded by the Book of Common Prayer, which dates to the sixteenth century. It states the doctrines of the Church, which are biblically based. Major changes in doctrine, liturgy and canonical matters are subject to a consensus of the bishops, the clerics and the laity in synod.

The Church of England is the only State-established Anglican Church.

# THE CONTINUING PROCESS OF REFORM

In keeping with the spirit of the Continental and the English Reformations, various groups have followed the sixteenth-century desire for a purer Church, a more biblically based Church, a less-governed Church, an Anabaptist-type of affiliation of believers displacing the Church, or a more caring Christian community. Below are listed some of these reform groups.

### Baptists

The Baptists founded a separate Church in England in 1612. Their most characteristic beliefs and practices are clearly implied in their name: they believe that only adults can be baptised, as each individual should be old enough to make that decision for himself or herself. They further believe that baptism must be by total immersion and not by mere sprinkling with water. Baptists do not have bishops and are less hierarchical in their orders of ministry than Roman Catholics or Anglicans.

## Methodists

The same is true of Methodists, so called because of the methodical way in which their founders John and Charles Wesley organised study of the Bible and meetings for prayer when they were students at Oxford in the eighteenth century. Later on they travelled the country, preaching in the open fields to large congregations and placing great emphasis on the need for each individual believer to undergo a personal experience of conversion, of having their lives or sense of direction dramatically changed. Initially, the Wesley brothers were not intending to set up another Church but to 'revive' the Church of England from within. However, in 1784, the Methodist Church was founded and has become one of the strongest of Protestant Churches in Britain, Australia and the USA.

## Quakers

The Society of Friends, or Quakers, was founded by George Fox in the 1660s. They have no clergy and no set form of service. When they meet in their meeting houses, they wait for God's spirit to guide one of them to speak: sometimes it means that a number of worshippers will stand up to speak but at other times they will sit in complete silence.

## Unitarianism

Unitarians affirm the unipersonality of God, as opposed to the doctrine of the Trinity, three persons in one God. They see Jesus as the great 'humanitarian' exemplar.

As with the Quakers, they have a non-creedal basis for membership. Principles of freedom, reason and tolerance bind the seekers together. In their weekly assemblies there are readings from the Bible, from other religions and from secular sources. Major Christian festivals are celebrated with a liberal and modernist interpretation, as are some festivals of other faiths and humanitarian causes.

Although actively and internationally associated with inter-faith movements, Unitarians have recently been excluded from the British Council of Churches.

## The Salvation Army

The Salvation Army was founded by William Booth in 1865. It is an evangelical movement, respected worldwide for its social work and help to the impoverished. Salvation Army meetings are joyful, led by their famous bands, and often take place on street corners as a witness to their faith. Instead of clergy, they organise themselves on military lines with captains, majors, etc., and they do not observe sacraments such as baptism or Holy Communion.

## Pentecostal Churches

The Pentecostal Churches include the Elim Church (1915) and the Assemblies of God (1924). As the name 'pentecostal' suggests, they place emphasis on the gifts of the Holy Spirit which, it is believed, were first conveyed to Christian believers shortly after the Ascension of Jesus. Most characteristic of these gifts is to be able to speak in an ecstatic, unlearned language other than one's own, which can then be interpreted by another worshipper.

## Open or Christian Brethren (Plymouth Brethren)

This movement began with a group of Anglicans living in Dublin in 1829. The group members, in wishing to model their lives more closely on the intentions of the original founder, Christ, rejected what they later called 'churchianity'. Although not co-ordinated by a central administration, the Brethren coalesce into two main bodies namely 'Open' and 'Exclusive' Brethren, descriptions which in part reflect their orientation towards other Christians. Believing that the second coming is imminent, the Brethren are committed to an urgent evangelism.

## Jehovah's Witnesses

Although Jehovah's Witnesses are few in number, they are well known because of their emphasis on home-visiting to convert new members, their strict application of religious principles to certain medical interventions, and their frequently expressed desire to withdraw their children from religious education in schools.

## The Church in Scotland, Ireland and Wales

The Established Church in Scotland is the Church of Scotland, which is organised on Presbyterian lines. Presbyter is the Greek word for elders. Direction by the elders, senior or respected lay people, appears to have been one of the systems of church government in the early Church. Presbyterians lay great emphasis on orderly, dignified worship and strong preaching. Scotland also has the Episcopal Church (Anglican) as well as Roman Catholic and the smaller Protestant Churches.

Presbyterianism is found in Northern Ireland, though Roman Catholicism is dominant in the rest of Ireland.

The Church in Wales, though Anglican, is separate from the Church of England and disestablished since 1920. The Presbyterian Church is the strongest among other Protestant Churches in Wales.

## RITES OF PASSAGE

The rituals that mark the major transitions in the lifecycle of a Christian are baptism, confirmation, matrimony, extreme unction and the funeral service.

### Baptism

Baptism is a right by which a person becomes a member of the Church. Originally baptism was requested by and granted to adults and involved immersion in a river, sea or pool. Now infant baptism is more or less universal and entails the pouring or sprinkling of water on the head of a child on whose behalf a sponsor speaks.

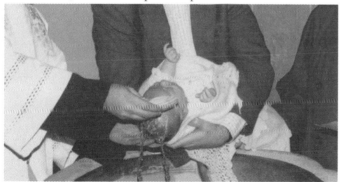

The Anglican baptismal rite has six elements:

1   An introduction of prayers, an address and gospel reading.
2   Baptismal vows made by the candidate or the sponsor who:
    • promises to renounce evil
    • promises to adhere to the Christian faith as stated in the Creed
    • promises to follow the Christian way of life.
3   Blessing of baptismal water to show this is more than a physical cleansing.
4   Pouring of the water on the head on the person being baptised using the Trinitarian formula (that is, in the name of Father, Son and Holy Spirit).
5   Newly baptised is signed with cross and declared received into the Church.
6   Thanksgiving and address to sponsors who undertake to help the newly baptised person lead a Christian life.

An infant may be baptised at any age. Baptism is normally administered by a cleric, but in certain circumstances any Christian may baptise another.

### Confirmation

Confirmation is a ritual performed by a bishop in which the Holy Spirit comes upon an already baptised person in a renewed and fuller way.

In the Byzantine Orthodox Church, confirmation is conferred with baptism and is followed immediately by the Eucharist. In the West there is a considerable gap between each ritual.

Young persons are confirmed after the age of seven in the Roman Catholic Church and a little later in the Anglican Church. Before receiving confirmation, a candidate must be instructed in the faith and be able to show sufficient understanding of Christianity. Once confirmed, the young person may receive communion.

The ritual is in three parts:

1  The renewal of the baptismal vows.
2  The bishop extends his hands over them and prays that they may receive the Holy Spirit.
3  The bishop lays his hand on the head of each candidate.

In the Roman Catholic Church the bishop then anoints with oil the foreheads of those being confirmed. The anointing is optional in the Church of England.

# MARRIAGE IN THE CHRISTIAN CHURCH

Christian marriage is a monogamous life-long union of a man and woman who are not close relatives. It is seen as a symbol of the union of Christ with his Church, and the marriage service is one of considerable solemnity.

Before marriage the couple are offered an opportunity to discuss the implications of marriage and to prepare themselves for the ceremony.

The banns are the announcement of the planned wedding and an open invitation for anyone in the community to object to the marriage if they have just cause for doing so. The banns are published in the church on three Sundays prior to the marriage and request anyone who knows any reason in law why the persons should not marry each other to 'declare it now'.

## The Marriage Service

A valid Christian marriage requires the full knowledge and full consent of both parties.

When the bride and groom have arrived in church, the minister states the purpose and nature of marriage. Then the congregation is asked to consider if they know of any reason why the couple should not be married. The bride and groom are then asked if they know of any reason why they may not lawfully be married.

Marriage is exclusive and permanent.

The minister asks the groom:

*Will you take this woman (by name) to be your wife? Will you love her, comfort her, honour and protect her, and, forsaking all others, be faithful to her as long as you both shall live?*

The same questions are asked of the bride. The weddings vows are then exchanged. The couple solemnly promise to be husband and wife in sickness or in health, in poverty or in wealth until parted by death. In the traditional service, the bride promised to 'love, honour and obey' her husband, although she may now omit the word 'obey' from the promise if she so wishes.

The bride and groom then place wedding rings on each other's third finger.

Prayers are then recited for the happiness and success of the wedding, and the ceremony may be followed by the Eucharist.

## Registration of the Marriage

The law requires that the civil registers are completed immediately after the solemnisation of a marriage. If the priest is not also a recognised registrar, an external registrar must be brought in. Two persons, normally the best man and the bridesmaid, witness and sign the register.

## Divorce

The Christian ideal for marriage is exclusivity and permanence. The ideal is sometimes not achieved.

The Roman Catholic Church does not accept divorce and remarriage. The Church of England regrets the break-up of a marriage but accepts divorce and, at the discretion of the vicar, allows remarriage in church.

# FUNERAL RITES

## Anointing of the Sick (Extreme Unction)

In the Middle Ages, the anointing of the sick came to be numbered among the seven sacraments. It was originally connected with the healing of the sick. In the Graeco-Roman world of the early Christians, physical illness was associated with sin and evil and required a remedy, at once visible and spiritual, administered by a priest.

The rite became so closely connected with repentance and the whole penitential system that it was commonly postponed until death was approaching – hence the term 'extreme unction'. It is now most commonly called the 'anointing of the sick' and assumes a rather special significance when it is applied to a believer preparing to depart this world.

The sick person is anointed on the forehead and hands while the minister prays:

*As you are outwardly anointed with this holy oil, so may our heavenly Father grant you an inward anointing of the Holy Spirit.*

The Eucharist is then offered to the sick person and to any others who may be present. The rite may be received any number of times.

## Funeral Rites

Rites are the immediate extension of beliefs. Christian belief in the risen Christ is expressed with immense power and security throughout the entire funeral service.

If the coffin is being taken to the church for the funeral it may be received immediately before the service or on the day before. There is a short reception service. As the coffin is taken into the church, the minister reads from the gospel of St John:

*'I am the Resurrection and the life,' says the Lord. 'Those who believe in me, even though they die, will live, and everyone who lives and believes in me will never die.'*

The theme of hope is repeated in many readings and prayers until the body has been placed in the grave or the crematorium.

On the day of the funeral, the church service may include the Eucharist.

The prayers, readings and sermon, while showing that death is merely the end of the beginning, also confront the pain, loss and destruction of death. Support is given to the bereaved, and all present are encouraged to focus on the event as a spur to better Christian living.

After the church service, the coffin is taken to the cemetery or crematorium, for a service of committal.

It is customary for those who have attended a Christian funeral to share a meal or refreshments together immediately afterwards.

There are no specified mourning patterns, but it is quite common to have memorial services at set times commemorating the life and death of the deceased. Immediate male relatives often wear black ties to the funeral, whereas the women wear dark clothes to signify mourning. Flowers are usually placed on the coffin and on the grave.

# CHRISTIAN FESTIVALS AND HOLY DAYS

## New Year's Day

Celebrated both as a popular festival and holiday, and by the Church. 1 January is traditionally seen as a time for fresh starts and opportunities. 'A happy New Year' is a greeting understood by everyone.

The feast of the Circumcision is also on this date, remembering the circumcision of Christ, as is the Jewish custom, eight days after birth.

## Epiphany

This festival, twelve days after Christmas, was originally associated with the baptism of Christ, and was one of the main festivals of the early Christians.

In the West, it celebrates the manifestation of Christ to the Gentiles in the story of the wise men or Magi. They brought presents of gold for a king, frankincense for a priest and myrrh for the suffering he would endure. These gifts are presented at the altar in St James's Palace, Chapel Royal by the British royal family. This has been done for the last 700 years.

In Orthodox churches, both on the vigil (the day before) and on the feast itself, services of blessing of water take place. The first of these is for the blessing of water in a font or tank for use in church blessings and for the devotional use of the people. The second often takes place outdoors, for the blessing of a local river or spring or even the seaside. The high point of each of these services comes when the priest plunges a cross three times into the water in commemoration of the baptism of Jesus in the Jordan.

In some places where the climate is warm, the priest flings the cross into the sea, and boys are ready to dive in to retrieve it.

## Week of Prayer for Christian Unity

Special services are held in which members of different denominations visit one another's churches, and pulpits are shared by visiting preachers.

## St Brigid's Day

This in Celtic tradition is the first day of spring. Rebirth was associated with Brigantia, the fertility goddess.

In Christian tradition, St Brigid (or Bridget), a secondary patron saint of Ireland, is said to have been inspired by the teaching of St Patrick and to have established the first community of nuns in Kildare, an area which is now well known for its racehorses.

## Candlemas – Feast of the Purification

This festival celebrates the presentation of Christ in the Temple in Jerusalem a few days after his birth, as the Jewish custom, and the purification ceremony of the Virgin Mary at the same time.

The English name Candlemas refers to the custom of blessing and distributing candles and carrying them in procession before the Mass. The light of the candles is symbolic of Christ as the light of the world.

## Shrove Tuesday

Shrove is a term that is associated with confessing sins. A person is said to be shrove or shriven when they have confessed. It is thought necessary to confess sins before the solemnity of Lent which, historically, is a special period of penance for repentant sinners received back into the community or indeed for those who wish to enter the believing and repentant community for the first time.

The day is just before Ash Wednesday, which marks the beginning of Lent. The seriousness of Lent was preceded by merrymaking, and people used up all the rich food in the house in preparation for a fast. Pancakes were a good way to use up food, and pancake races are a traditional sport.

The Mardi Gras carnival is now celebrated on an extravagant scale on this day.

The Orthodox equivalent to Shrove Tuesday is Cheese-Fare Week. During the week before Lent begins, meat is not eaten. But egg and milk foods, which will not be allowed during Lent itself, are taken. The last day on which meat may be eaten before Easter is the Sunday called Sexagesima in the Western churches.

## Ash Wednesday

This marks the first day of Lent. In Roman Catholic churches, the previous year's palm crosses are burnt and the ashes sprinkled with holy water and then an ash cross marked on the participants as a sign of their penance. This is a reminder that sackcloth and ashes were a sign of penance in the Old Testament. Ash Wednesday is a day of fasting in the Catholic Church. As the minister signs each penitent he says, 'Remember man thou art but dust, and into dust you shall return.' This reminder of the mortality of man starts the preparation of prayer, penance and meditation for the great Easter festival.

Ash Wednesday commences the great liturgical cycle that culminated in the death and Resurrection of Christ on Easter Sunday.

## Lent

Ash Wednesday to Holy Saturday – 40 weekdays; Sundays are always festive. This period remembers the 40 days in the wilderness when Christ was tempted. Various degrees of fasting used to be practised, but now people usually give up luxuries, give to others and spiritually prepare for Easter.

In the Orthodox (Eastern) Churches, Lent begins two days earlier, on the Monday after the seventh Sunday before Easter. The fasting is strict: not only meat, but eggs and milk products are forbidden. On Sundays, olive oil and wine are allowed, and on Palm Sunday and Annunciation Day, fish may be eaten as well.

## St David's Day

St David is the patron saint of Wales, and his feast day has been observed since the fourteenth century. Welsh people wear leeks or daffodils on this day. Very little is known about St David except that he lived in the far south-west of Wales, became an Archbishop and Primate of Wales, and advised kings in Ireland.

## St Patrick's Day

The patron saint of Ireland is remembered and honoured for his work as a missionary and evangelist. Legend says that as a teenager he was carried off to Ireland from England and later escaped and returned home as a priest to introduce the Christian faith. He built a monastery at Armagh. The Irish celebrate this day as a public holiday and wear the shamrock, which is also a reminder of the Holy Trinity. The deep historic links of Catholicism and nationalism in Ireland are reflected in the St Patrick's Day processions, speech-making, drama and musical activities. In North America, and in the countries where Irish missionaries have been active, celebrations are enthusiastically pursued.

## Mothering Sunday

This is held on the fourth Sunday in Lent. It was considered to be a break in the solemnities of Lent, being a cheerful day when girls in service visited their mothers, taking simnel cake (fruit cakes with almond paste) as presents. These cakes were generally kept until Easter.

People in villages also went to the Mother Church to give gifts. Today it is celebrated by people buying cards and flowers for their mother and giving her a day of rest. Churches often provide flowers and cards for children to give to their mothers.

## Palm Sunday

This marks the beginning of Holy Week, the last week of Jesus's life on earth, and celebrates the story of Jesus entering Jerusalem on a donkey, when he was welcomed by crowds waving palm branches (Matthew 21, 1–9).

Processions are made around churches and between churches, carrying and distributing branches or fronds of palms. Churches are usually decorated with palms or willow. Crosses shaped from palms are often distributed to the congregation on Palm Sunday.

## Maundy Thursday

This day begins a special commemoration of the last acts of Jesus's life and remembers the Last Supper, which Jesus shared with his disciples where he instructed them to 'Love one another', washed their feet, and instituted the Eucharist. (Maundy comes from the Latin word *mandatum* meaning command.)

In England, up until the time of Queen Anne, the monarch or his/her representative washed and kissed the feet of the poor and gave them money. The Georges discontinued the washing – or, rather, commuted it to a further gift of coin. The Royal Almoner still wears a folded towel at the Maundy ceremony, in case the monarch were to revive the custom!

## Good Friday

This Friday before Easter Day is the day on which the anniversary of the crucifixion of Christ is kept. It is a day of fast, abstinence and penance in some Churches, but in others – notably the Free Churches – it has become a feast day.

It is called Good Friday because Christians believe that, as Jesus died for mankind, everything will be right between them and God. His love and his sacrifice are remembered.

Services are usually held in churches some time between noon and 3.00 p.m. when, as Mark (15, 33–34) says, Jesus died on the cross. There are often united services and processions and passion plays portraying the Easter events.

Hot cross buns are eaten. They used to be kept just for Good Friday, in keeping with the symbolism of the cross, although it is thought that they originated in pagan times with the bun representing the moon and its four quarters.

## Holy Saturday

This is the last day of Holy Week, once known as the 'Great Sabbath' and now also known as Easter Eve. It commemorates the period during which Jesus lay in the tomb after he had been taken down from the cross.

The day is traditionally honoured as a focus upon the forgiveness of sins.

## Easter Sunday

This is the most important festival in the Christian Church, celebrating the Resurrection of Jesus. Traditionally it is the day when new members are baptised into the Christian community and comes at the end of Lent, which is a period of preparation for the great event.

Easter is often celebrated with a midnight mass, where the priest lights one large candle from which the many smaller candles of the congregation take light and pass on the flame, while the people say or sing 'Christ is risen'. Dawn services and outdoor services are quite common on Easter Day.

The word 'Easter' is connected with the Anglo-Saxon spring goddess Eostre, and it seems that Christian celebrations displaced the pagan festival. The custom of giving eggs is an ancient one celebrating new life. People often spring-clean or decorate and make a fresh start at Easter. New clothes are worn and there are Easter parades.

The date of Easter is determined by the paschal full moon, the first full moon after 21 March, and can be anywhere between 21 March and 25 April. There was early controversy whether Easter should follow the fixed lunar month and be celebrated at the time of the Jewish Passover, and various Churches celebrated it at different times. The Alexandrian calculation was accepted in the year 325, but in the fourth and fifth centuries the Roman Church disagreed. In Britain, the Celtic churches had their own system of calculations, but the Roman method was adopted by the Synod of Whitby in the year 664.

## St George's Day

St George became patron saint of England during the reign of Edward III, when the Order of the Garter was founded under the saint's patronage. Although once a very prominent holy day in the Christian calendar, St George's Day is today celebrated mainly by special parades and rallies. Many legends have been built up around the figure of St George, but all that is known with a degree of certainty is that he suffered martyrdom in Palestine, before the reign of the Roman Emperor Constantine, where he may have been a soldier in the Roman army.

## Ascension Day

This is kept on Thursday, the 40th day after Easter. It commemorates Christ's last earthly appearance to his disciples after the Resurrection and his ascension into Heaven into divine glory, which traditionally happened on the Mount of Olives. (See Mark 16, 19, Luke 24–51 and Acts 1, 1–11.)

The purpose of the commemoration is to remember that Christ's spirit lives on. In the Western Church, the paschal candle lit during Easter is extinguished on Ascension Day in commemoration of Christ's departure from the apostles.

## Christian Aid Week

This is a week in which Christians focus on the need to care both spiritually and materially for people everywhere. Third World countries are especially remembered – in special prayers and the raising of funds. The organisation of

Christian Aid usually has a theme for raising money, such as the provision of wells for villages.

## Whit Sunday or Pentecost

This is held on the 50th day after Easter and commemorates the gift of the Holy Spirit to the followers of Christ. It is often called Pentecost because, when the disciples received the Holy Spirit and began to go out and preach about Jesus, it was the Jewish festival of Pentecost.

Because it marked the first preaching about Jesus, it is called the birthday of the Christian Church. It is a favourite day for baptism. As converts are often dressed in white for baptism, it was probably originally 'White Sunday'. It is marked by miracle or mystery plays and processions, particularly in the north of England where the 'Whit Walk' is common and new clothes are worn. It is a major Christian festival and celebrated as a Holy Day of Obligation in the Catholic Church.

## Corpus Christi

Corpus Christi, literally the Body of Christ, is celebrated on the Thursday after Whit Week. In the Catholic Church it is a Holy Day of Obligation on which people are expected to attend church.

It celebrates the institution of the Eucharist at the Last Supper. The Eucharist is celebrated on the Thursday of Holy Week but, being placed then between the austerity of Ash Wednesday and the dramatic tragedy of Good Friday, a joyous commemoration is difficult.

## Feast of St Peter and St Paul

Saints Peter and Paul are seen as two powerful pillars of the Christian Church. Peter became the first Bishop of Rome, and Paul took the Christian message with vigour and eloquence to a new Gentile audience.

This is a Holy Day of Obligation in the Catholic Church.

In the Orthodox Church, this feast is preceded by a fast, which begins on the Monday eight days after Whit Sunday. The earlier Easter comes, the longer the Saints Peter and Paul fast!

## Assumption of the Blessed Virgin

This feast is celebrated in the Roman Catholic and Orthodox Churches to commemorate the Resurrection of the Virgin Mary, believed taken body and soul into heaven immediately after death. The Feast of the Assumption dates from the sixth century, and in many Western European countries the day is observed both for its religious significance and as a public holiday.

In the Orthodox Church this festival is observed as the Falling Asleep of the Blessed Virgin Mary. Pope Pius XII declared the Corporal Assumption of the Blessed Virgin as an official dogma of the Catholic Church. Protestants reject this doctrine.

## Harvest Festival

This is one of the oldest festivals known to man. After prayers for a good harvest, it seemed natural to give offerings or sacrifice part of the crops. The Jews celebrate three harvest festivals dating from their wanderings in the wilderness with Moses. In Christian Britain, harvest is an unofficial religious festival of thanksgiving, usually observed on a Sunday in September or October to give thanks for the harvest being gathered in.

It is customary to display fruits, vegetables and flowers in the Church of England and the Free Churches, and these are later given to charitable causes.

In medieval times, Lammas Day, 1 August, was a celebration of the offering of the first fruits (Deuteronomy 26, 1–11). A loaf made from the first grain was baked and used in the Eucharist. The service was called Loaf Mass, in Saxon 'Half Masse', which gradually became Lammas. The arrival of Lammas Day also meant that the Lammas Land in some villages could be used for general grazing of stock by all villagers as the hay would have already been reaped. Country fairs were also held around Lammas Day.

When all the harvest had been gathered in, Harvest Home would be celebrated at the farmer's house, with a supper. The last of the corn would be twisted into a person or cross corn dolly. It was believed that the corn spirit was contained in the dolly and had to be kept alive during the winter and sown with the new corn to ensure a good harvest. It was often taken to the church for the harvest service before being hung in the barn. Some churches still have harvest suppers.

In seaside towns, churches may celebrate a harvest of the sea and, in some manufacturing towns, tools or machinery may now replace the traditional displays. Special hymns are sung and the Church of England has a special service.

## All Saints' Day (Allhallows)

This festival celebrates Christian saints known and unknown. Although it was originally held in May, its date is now 1 November and probably stems from Gregory III (died 741) who dedicated a chapel to 'All Saints' at St Peter's Basilica on that day, and Gregory IV (died 844) ordered its universal observation. In the Eastern Church it is still kept on the first Sunday after Whitsun. It is a Roman Catholic Holy Day of Obligation; Roman Catholics are expected to attend church.

## All Souls' Day

This festival has been kept for nearly one thousand years. A shipwrecked pilgrim was told by a hermit that the souls of the dead who had not yet gone to Heaven were crying out because people were not praying enough for them. The pilgrim told Odila, Abbot of Cluny, who set aside the day after All Saints' Day as All Souls' Day. Christians pray for the souls of the dead and often take flowers to the family grave.

As the Orthodox Churches do not observe All Saints' in November, neither do they observe this All Souls' Day. But they have several similar days in their calendar on which the dead are especially prayed for: most notably the Saturday before Lent and the Tuesday after Low Sunday (the first Sunday after Easter).

## Advent

The four Sundays preceding Christmas Day, 25 December, are called the four Sundays of Advent.

Advent is the season when Christians celebrate their condition between the two comings, the coming of Christ on the first Christmas and the second and final coming of Christ to deliver the world from darkness.

The scriptural readings during this season manifest a Christian sense of history together with a joyful expectancy. John the Baptist, the precursor of Jesus, is given a prominence, as are the thoughts of certainty, preparedness and joy in the future.

*John the Baptist appeared; he preached in the wilderness of Judea and this was his message, 'Repent, for the kingdom of Heaven is close at hand.'*
(Matthew, 1.12)
*Wake up, our salvation is even nearer now than it was when we were converted.*
(Romans 13, 11–14)

## St Andrew's Day

St Andrew is the patron saint of Scotland, of Greece, and of Russia. Andrew was a disciple of Jesus and the brother of Peter. Not much is known about him, except that, according to tradition, he was crucified on an X-shaped cross and that in the thirteenth century some monks brought his relics to Scotland to secure their own protection.

In the Anglican Church the day is used to make intercessions for foreign missions.

## Feast of the Immaculate Conception

Popular early Christian devotion to the Virgin Mary was confirmed at the Council of Ephesus in 431 when she was proclaimed to be the Mother of God. In subsequent centuries Christians, both Eastern and Western, advanced and extended devotion to the Virgin Mary. In honour of her special position in the history of mankind's redemption, the redemptive effects of her life, death and Resurrection of Jesus were anticipated at her birth. Thus in 1854, Pope Pius IX declared that Mary was conceived free from original sin (the Immaculate Conception).

Four years after the declaration of Pius IX, a young French girl, Bernadette Soubirous, had a vision of Mary at Lourdes. In the apparition, Mary introduced herself as the 'Immaculate Conception'. Since then Catholics from all over the world have flocked to Lourdes in pilgrimage. Pilgrims find that the great chorus of hymns, the torchlight processions and the rows of hopeful sick create a deep sense of pilgrimage.

The Orthodox Churches observe a feast on the Conception of the Theotokos, but they reject the papal doctrine of the Immaculate Conception because they say it is based on a faulty quasi-Calvinistic doctrine of original sin.

This is a fixed feast day and is celebrated on 8 December.

## Christmas Eve

On Christmas Eve, carol services and midnight masses are held at churches and cathedrals throughout the world to celebrate the birth of Christ.

## Christmas Day

This festival celebrates the birth of Christ. Although it is likely that Jesus was born at a different time of the year, 25 December was used, probably to coincide with and to change the Roman festival of the birthday of the unconquered sun. (21–22 December is now the shortest day of the year due to a calendar correction in 1752.)

The first Christians did not keep Christmas, but by the fourth century it was celebrated. 6 January was used a lot in the East, originally for a commemoration of a heresy that 'divine Christ' appeared only at his baptism by John. The Eastern Church still uses Epiphany (from the Greek for 'appearing'), whereas the Western Church adopted 25 December because Rome did so between 336 and 353.

Although the Western calendar dates from Christ's birth, there have been miscalculations. Jesus was born when Herod was king and the Romans were ruling, and Herod died in what is referred to as 4 BCE. The Roman calendar was used when Jesus was born and continued to be used until the sixth century. In AD 533, a Russian monk named Dionysius made the Christian calendar but miscalculated. It is reckoned Jesus was born some time between 7 BC and 4 BC.

Christmas is celebrated with joy and merrymaking. Friends and families get together and give presents, remembering the gift of Christ and the gifts given to Jesus. Peace and goodwill to all men is proclaimed in the singing of Christmas carols. Often candlelit services are held.

It was a belief of the church fathers that Christ, in the perfection of his life, lived a perfect (complete) number of years. Therefore, the date of his death ought to be the date of his conception. Early astronomers reckoned that Good Friday AD 34 was 25 March. Therefore, the feast of the Annunciation of the Angel to Mary was 25 March, and the Nativity of Christ, 25 December. The suggestion that Christmas was deliberately invented to replace Sol Invicta (the festival of the unconquered sun) was first mooted by the Puritans, who hated the joy of Christmas, and it was revived by the Deists and their successors, who hated the religion of Christmas.

## Christmas Customs

Many of the modern Christmas customs are directly derived from ceremonies associated with ancient mid-winter feasts. One of the oldest is probably the decoration of houses and churches with greenery. Evergreens – the symbol of everlasting life – were commonly used to decorate dwellings and sacred buildings in ancient times at the time of the winter solstice, and the custom has endured and been absorbed into Christmas customs, despite the efforts of the early Christian Church to put an end to the practice.

Holly and ivy were the favourite plants, although laurel was also used. Mistletoe, sacred to the Druids, was used in houses but it was, and still is, banned from some churches. The custom of kissing under the mistletoe is entirely English in origin.

The Christmas tree is a relative newcomer to England. It came originally from Germany, and went to America with the German settlers before it reached the British Isles sometime in the early nineteenth century. The first English Christmas tree of which there is any clear record was one set up at a children's party by a member of Queen Caroline's Court in 1821. The custom of having a Christmas tree as an important symbol of the festival, however, became widespread only after Prince Albert, the Consort of Queen Victoria, set up one at Windsor Castle in 1841.

Since 1947, the Norwegian capital, Oslo, has made an annual gift of an immense Christmas tree to the people of London. This stands brightly lit, in Trafalgar Square, close to Nelson's Monument.

Many churches now have a Christmas crib, although not so long ago these were rarely seen except in Roman Catholic churches and homes. Tradition says it was St Francis of Assisi who made the first crib in 1224.

Exchanging presents and Christmas cards are essential features of the Christmas festival, though the custom has its roots in pre-Christian times. Presents were given to the poor and relatives at the feast of the Saturnalia in ancient Rome. The Christmas card began its existence as the 'Christmas piece' – a decorated sheet of paper on which schoolchildren wrote polite greetings for the season in their best handwriting and presented these to their parents.

Father Christmas is the traditional bearer of gifts in Britain. Originally he was more the personification of the joys of Christmas than a gift-giver. He is mentioned in a fifteenth-century carol, which began, 'Hail, Father Christmas, hail to thee!' and has been a familiar figure for centuries. Parliament abolished him in 1644 but he came back after the Restoration. In the nineteenth century he acquired some of the attributes of the Teutonic Santa Klaus and now children think of him as the bearer of gifts, coming at night from the North Pole in his reindeer-drawn sleigh and entering homes through the chimneys.

The Yule log was one of the main features of Christmas festivities in England and other European countries. The traditional log was usually of oak or ash and as large as the widest fireplace in the house would allow. It was brought in on Christmas Eve with great ceremony and rejoicing and lit with a fragment of its predecessor of the year before. It had to burn steadily throughout the twelve days of Christmas and at the end was put out, and a portion saved to use in kindling the next year's log so that there would be a continuity of good fortune and blessing. It was never allowed to burn away completely.

Christmas food has been largely a matter of tradition. Turkey, the most usual dish on Christmas day, did not appear in Britain until about 1542 and was not very popular until much later. Its predecessors were goose and pork, or a huge Christmas pie made from a variety of birds. In richer houses, venison, swans or peacocks were eaten. However, the boar's head was always considered to be the most succulent dish of all. It was usually brought to the table on a gold or silver platter and with great ceremony.

The ancestor of the modern Christmas pudding was plum porridge, a mixture of meat broth, raisins, spices, fruit and wine. When puddings are made at home, every member of the family is expected to make a wish while waiting their turn to stir it. A few small charms such as a silver coin (promising wealth), a ring (promising speedy marriage) and a thimble (prophesying a single life) are often included in the mixture.

The tradition of eating mince pies is older than plum pudding as they were already well known by the end of the sixteenth century. They were originally more varied in content, including items such as chopped chicken, eggs, spices and raisins, all contained in little pastry cases known as 'coffins'. According to tradition, one should be eaten on each of the twelve days of Christmas to ensure twelve happy months in the coming year.

In England, the traditional Christmas drink was the wassail, which was always served in a large brown vessel made of apple wood. It consisted of ale, roast apples, eggs, sugar, nutmegs, cloves and ginger and was drunk while hot.

Wassail comes from two old Saxon words (was haile)

meaning 'your health'. In Victorian times, the wassail bowl was carried from door to door in rural areas. Neighbours would fill the bowl with ale or cider to ensure a good apple harvest the next autumn.

Carols were never considered to be religious hymns. Rather, they were the popular songs of the Christian religion that came into being after the religious revival of the thirteenth century. Puritanism swept away the English carols and they did not come back into general favour for nearly 200 years. Now, nearly all churches have a carol service, and groups of adults and children go from home to home, singing carols and being rewarded with mince pies and money.

The feast of St Stephen, the first Christian martyr, is on 26 December. In England, this anniversary is popularly known as Boxing Day. The name is thought to be derived from the alms boxes in churches that were opened on this day and their contents distributed among the poor, or else from the earthenware boxes that apprentices carried when they were collecting gifts of money from their master's customers. Until recently it was usual for the postman, dustman and other public employees to call at the houses they served to receive small gifts.

For over 800 years, one of the regular Christmas entertainments was mumming, when young men and women dressed up, sometimes in each other's clothes, wore masks and gave a display of dancing or enacted a play at the homes of the rich people. They were usually rewarded with a gift of money or food.

In the course of time, the dialogue and action underwent several changes, although the central theme continued to be the victory of good over evil. At the end of the play, there was usually some clowning and gaiety in which all the characters would join.

Plays about the Nativity were part of miracle plays, which became popular between the thirteenth century and sixteenth century. They were based on Bible stories and were originally performed as part of a church service.

The Reformation checked the popularity of miracle plays and gave rise to the morality play, which was mainly concerned with the behaviour of men and women.

Pantomime is an entirely British form of entertainment. It is believed to have originated in the eighteenth century and continues to be a popular feature of Christmas festivities and celebrations.

## Orthodox Christian Christmas Customs

Christmas in the Orthodox Christian tradition is marked by various distinctive customs. To symbolise Christ's entry into the world, a young oak tree is brought home, placed on the fire and burned on Christmas Eve. At the same time, straw is spread on the floor. A prayer service is conducted, after which a festive supper is served.

The first visitor to the home on Christmas morning has special significance in many East European countries. He/she represents the shepherds who had the honour to see and announce the birth of Christ.

Chesnica, a simple bread and nut pastry, is prepared on Christmas Day, with a silver or gold coin baked into it. It is cut open during the Christmas meal and the person served the piece with the coin is supposed to have good luck in the coming year.

Christmas customs are crowned with going to church for the Divine Liturgy.

## St Stephen's Day

St Stephen is celebrated as the first Christian martyr and his life is commemorated on 26 December. His story is beautifully told in the Bible, in the book called the Acts, chapters 6 and 7. He was chosen by popular choice to take up some of the excessive workload of the original 12 apostles. A wise, impartial and eloquent man and one with terrific drive, he was just too good at his job. He alienated the old guard in Jerusalem and was put on trial for sedition.

Having given a marvellous trial speech, he was taken out and stoned to death. His death was supervised by a man called Saul. Saul enthusiastically followed up the death of Stephen with a general persecution of the Christians in Jerusalem.

Saul was later converted to Christianity, changed his name to Paul and in time became another Stephen.

# Islam

## An Introduction to Islam

In the seventh century CE, a religious movement, which was called Islam by the Prophet Mohammed, emerged in the Arabian Peninsula. It took root quickly and within a century after the Prophet's death (CE 632), a large part of the world, from Spain across Central Asia to the Indian subcontinent, was brought under the influence of an Arab Islamic Empire. Today, approximately one-sixth of the world's population profess the Islamic faith.

The word Islam is derived from the Arabic verb aslam, which means 'to submit', and it epitomises the characteristic attitude of the true believer in relation to God. The followers of Islam are called Muslims. A true Muslim, by definition, is one who has submitted to the will of God.

Islamic beliefs and practices are based upon the Qur'an. Muslims regard it as the infallible, incontrovertible message of God (Allah) to mankind, as revealed to His Prophet, Mohammed.

## The Prophet Mohammed

The Prophet Mohammed is believed to have been born in Mecca around CE 570. His father, who belonged to the influential Quraysh tribe, died a few days before his birth. At the age of six, he lost his mother and was brought up by his grandfather. Two years later when his grandfather died, he was entrusted to the care of his paternal uncle, Abu Talib, who was the head of the tribe.

As a young man, Mohammed accompanied his uncle on various trading expeditions. At the age of 25, he managed the caravan trade of a wealthy widow named Khadijah, whom he subsequently married. They had two sons who died young and four daughters, of whom the best known is Fatima.

Marriage gave Mohammed high status within the Meccan community and considerable financial independence. He also had greater freedom to pursue his spiritual inclinations. He would retire periodically to the hill caves outside Mecca and spend time in meditation and contemplation. According to tradition, it was on one such occasion in the year CE 610, soon after his fortieth birthday, that Mohammed received his call to be a prophet through the archangel Jibril.

Until his death in CE 632, he received several verbal communications which he believed came directly from Allah. These messages, initially preserved in an oral tradition, were finally collected and committed to writing around CE 650. This compilation is known as the Qur'an.

The Prophet Mohammed condemned the polytheistic beliefs of the pre-Islamic Arab tribesmen as well as the prevailing practice of idol worship. Instead, he preached a strictly monotheistic creed and emphasised man's obligation to fulfil the purpose of his majestic creator. He also warned his followers of the final judgement awaiting humanity.

The Prophet soon attracted a large following. However, he also incurred the hostility of the wealthy merchants of Mecca who refused to give up idol worship and its associated beliefs. The deaths of his uncle Abu Talib and his wife Khadijah left him particularly vulnerable to attacks from the opposition.

The Prophet eventually decided to migrate to Yathrib (Medina) after receiving promises of protection from two of the leading tribes who had converted to Islam. Evading an attempt on his life by the Meccans, the Prophet, using various unfrequented routes, finally reached the safety of Yathrib on 24 September 622. This event known as Hijrah (severance of kin ties) marks a turning point in the history of Islam. The Muslim calendar dates from the year of the migration which began on 16 June 622.

From Yathrib, the Prophet led a number of raids on Mecca. Through skilful diplomacy and armed might he finally gained possession of Mecca in CE 630, the eighth year of the Hijrah. All the idols in the Kaaba and neighbouring shrines were destroyed and many Meccans embraced Islam, although no such condition was imposed by the Prophet. With the support of the people of Mecca, Mohammed soon became the most powerful leader in Arabia. He created a federation of Arab tribes and made Islam the basis of Arab unity.

The Prophet is believed to have gone on pilgrimage to Mecca for the last time in CE 632. Preparations were made for a military expedition to Syria, but his health failed and on 8 June 632 he died at Yathrib (later re-named al-Madinah) without designating a successor. Political leadership of the expanding Islamic community passed into the hands of the Caliphate at Baghdad. However, the controversy over the spiritual successor to the Prophet provoked the most important schism in the history of Islam.

Muslims consider the Prophet Mohammed to be the epitome of human perfection. There are numerous legends referring to various signs and wondrous events at the time of his birth and testifying to his great spiritual powers. In eschatological writings he is recognised as the intercessor for his people on the final Day of Judgement. Veneration of the Prophet reaches its greatest height in the devotion of the Sufi mystics.

# THE FUNDAMENTAL BELIEFS OF ISLAM

Islamic theology (kalam) addresses a number of issues. The most fundamental of these is the nature of God (Allah). The Prophet Mohammed's rigorously monotheistic stance is stated most simply in the first article of the Muslim creed:

*'La ilaha illa 'lla hu' (There is no God save Allah).*

Muslims believe that God is one and unique. He has no partner and no equal. God is the sole creator and sustainer of the Universe and He is eternal. The God of the Qur'an is majestic and sovereign. He is also described as just and merciful and His justice ensures order in His creation.

Islam rejects anthropomorphism: God's existence cannot be perceived by the senses. Attributing God's unique sovereignty to any one or anything (*shirk*) is regarded as the gravest sin. Muslims therefore believe that the Qur'an was created by God, rather than being eternal, for to grant the Book co-eternity would necessarily compromise divine uniqueness.

The Qur'an describes God as 'closer to man than his jugular vein'. Yet, it is believed that human beings can never fully comprehend His divine nature. God's indefinability does not, however, prevent man from addressing Him in terms of His several attributes. Islamic theology provides one of the most comprehensive lists of God's attributes. These are the 99 most beautiful names of God (*asma 'al-husna*). When making a petition to God, it is customary to choose a name from the list that is most appropriate to the request being made.

## The Nature of Man

According to the Qur'an, God created two apparently similar species – man and *jinn*; the former from clay, the latter from fire. Man is considered to be the noblest of all creation. His sole purpose is to serve and submit to God's will.

According to Islamic theology, every created thing is endowed with a defined and limited nature. Human beings, however, are full of pride and tend to ignore their limitations. They are frequently guilty of ascribing to themselves some of the attributes of God and of considering themselves to be in partnership with God, thereby denying the sovereignty and uniqueness of the divine presence.

## The Islamic Concept of Sin

Muslims regard sin more as disobedience to God's command than as a transgression of some moral or ethical standard. God's will pervades all aspects of life.

Consequently, Islam does not recognise any distinction between sacred and secular.

Islam, like Judaism, rejects the Christian doctrine of original sin. Human beings, according to Islamic theology, are imperfect and therefore bound to commit acts of disobedience. They do not, however, carry the burden of Adam's original sin and subsequent fall from Paradise.

According to the Prophet Mohammed, every human being is born pure and is personally responsible for subsequent acts of disobedience. Individuals are rewarded or punished by God according to their actions.

## Angels

Angels are frequently mentioned in the Qur'an as immortal beings who act as God's messengers and exercise great influence on man and the universe. They also act as intermediaries asking God to forgive the sins of true believers. At the time of death, the souls of human beings are received by angels who have kept a record of their deeds and will witness for or against them on the Day of Judgement.

## Prophets

Muslims believe that God sent prophets or messengers to all peoples in all ages to proclaim the oneness of God and to warn humanity of the impending Day of Judgement. Islamic theology recognises 28 prophets from Adam to Mohammed who are specially chosen Messengers of God (*rasul*). Each of these prophets has been identified by name in the Qur'an.

The Holy Book states very clearly that these special messengers are human and not part of divinity. They are simply the recipients of revelations from God. Mohammed is regarded by Muslims as the Seal of the Prophets through whom God revealed His message in its definitive form. The prophetic mission, it is believed, has been fulfilled for all time by Mohammed.

## The Prophetic Tradition

| | | | |
|---|---|---|---|
| 1 | Adam | 15 | Solomon |
| 2 | Idris (Enoch) | 16 | Job |
| 3 | Noah | 17 | Jonah |
| 4 | Lot | 18 | Zachariah |
| 5 | Abraham | 19 | Ezrah |
| 6 | Ishmael | 20 | Lugman |
| 7 | Isaac | 21 | Dhu'l-Qarnain |
| 8 | Jacob | 22 | Hud |
| 9 | Joseph | 23 | Salih |
| 10 | Moses | 24 | Shu'aib |
| 11 | Aaron | 25 | Dhu'l-kifl |
| 12 | Elijah | 26 | John |
| 13 | Elisha | 27 | Jesus |
| 14 | David | 28 | Mohammed |

# THE HOLY SCRIPTURES

Muslims accept five books as Divine revelations. These are:

- The Scrolls (*Suhuf*) – 10 scriptures revealed to the Prophet Abraham
- The Torah (*Taurat*) revealed to Moses at Mount Sinai
- The Psalms (*Zabur*) revealed to the Prophet David
- The Gospels (*Injil*) revealed to Jesus
- The Qur'an revealed to the Prophet Mohammed
- The Qur'an.

Muslims believe that the Qur'an is God's final revelation and as such is the noblest of the Holy Books. The contents of the Qur'an are considered to be infallible since they are an exact reproduction of an original protected by Allah.

The Qur'an is believed to have been dictated in Arabic to the Prophet Mohammed by the messenger of God, the Archangel Jibril (Gabriel) over a period of 23 years. His followers memorised these messages, which appeared on materials as diverse as palm leaves, fragments of pottery and the shoulder blades of camels.

After the Prophet's death, the revelations were collated. These were committed to writing nearly 25 years later during the reign of Caliph Uthman.

The Holy Book of Islam is divided into 114 chapters or *sura*, which means a degree or step by which the devout mount up. Each verse of the sura is called an *ayat*, which also means a sign. The sura are of differing lengths and each is named after a particularly important or recurring word in the text. All except the ninth sura (which is believed to be a continuation of the eighth) start with the words 'In

the name of God, the Merciful, the Compassionate'. The first sura, the *Fatiha*, consisting of seven verses, encapsulates the essence of the Islamic faith and is recited in every prayer of devout Muslims, at least 17 times a day.

Sura Al-Fatiha 1
*In the name of Allah, Most Gracious, Most Merciful.*
*Praise be to Allah the Cherisher and Sustainer of the Worlds:*
*Most Gracious, Most Merciful;*
*Master of the Day of Judgement.*
*Thee do we worship,*
*And Thine aid we seek.*
*Show us the straight way,*
*The way of those on whom*
*Thou has bestowed Thy Grace,*
*Those whose (Portion)*
*Is not wrath.*
*And who go not astray.*

The Qur'an is treated with great respect. When not being read, it is carefully wrapped in silk cloth and stored in a place where it is unlikely to be defiled. The Book is only touched or read by people after cleansing themselves.

Muslims consider Arabic to be a sacred language since it is the medium through which the Qur'an was revealed to the Prophet Mohammed. Although the Holy Book has been translated into various languages, pious Muslims believe that such works can only convey the meaning of the message and are not in any sense, the Word of God itself.

The Qur'an literally means recitation. A standardised mode of melodic intonation exists throughout the Muslim world, despite minor regional variations in reading and pronunciation. The correct art of Qur'anic recitation is taught in the seminaries (*madrasa*).

The Qur'an encapsulates the uncompromising monotheistic creed of Islam. It proclaims the existence of the one and only God who is the creator of the Universe and who is All-wise, All-just, All-compassionate, Omnipotent, Omniscient and Omnipresent. References to theology, jurisprudence, science and history are also scattered throughout the Qur'an. However, the dominant themes are the dignity of human existence, the folly of human perversity, the impending Day of Judgement, the eternal condition of bliss and doom and the reality of Allah's mercy.

The contents of the Qur'an provide the foundations for an entire way of life. They also provide the basis for Islamic Law (*Shari'a*).

## The Hadith

Next to the Qur'an, the most important sacred work for Muslims is the *Hadith*, the body of tradition (*Sunna*) and sayings attributed to the Prophet Mohammed. These were, at first, transmitted orally. However, within two or three generations after the Prophet's death, a large number of Hadith are believed to have come into circulation.

Muslim scholars recognised the need to establish the authenticity of the material and a science of Hadith criticism gradually developed from about the ninth and tenth centuries. Its primary objective was to gather reliable bibliographic evidence about the narrators of the Traditions.

It was agreed that to be considered authentic, an item from the Hadith must include the name of each human link in the chain between the Prophet (or one of his companions) and the individual who finally transcribed or transmitted it. A sound (*sahih*) tradition has strong links and is corroborated by other versions. The category of *daif* or weak traditions includes items that are demonstrably false or forged.

The Hadith literature is both a commentary on the Qur'an and a complement to its teachings. Collections in the Hadith deal with social, political and economic issues as well as more esoteric subjects as cosmology, metaphysics and eschatology. The Hadith is also considered to be a useful source of early Islamic history and is recognised as having played a vital role in the development of Islamic law and doctrine.

One of the most popular themes in the Hadith is the story of the Prophet's night journey to Jerusalem and his ascent to heaven. This event has been described in the Qur'an and is celebrated as the festival Lailat-al-Miraj.

## Islamic Eschatology

The final Day of Judgement is vividly described in the Qur'an and the Traditions (Hadith), as a cataclysmic event when 'the trumpet sounds, the sun shall darken, the stars shall fall, all the mountains shall turn to dust, the earth shall be crushed, the beasts shall be scattered all over, the sea shall boil, angels shall appear and terror shall strike everywhere'.

Muslims believe that on the Last Day, when the world comes to an end, the dead will be resurrected and a judgement pronounced on every person in accordance with their deeds. The pious, humble and charitable will enjoy all the pleasures of Paradise, whereas sinners will burn in Hell.

Islamic doctrines conceive of Heaven and Hell as spiritual concepts as well as physical entities. Thus, the blessed will experience spiritual happiness in addition to physical pleasures; whereas the damned, while suffering in Hell, will also experience 'fire in their hearts'. There is no doctrine of intercession in Islam, but it is told in the Qur'an that God in His mercy may forgive certain sinners.

According to Islamic theology, the end of the world will be preceded by the appearance of a messianic figure, the *Mahdi* or The Guided One. The identity of this Messiah is a major point of difference between the different Islamic sects.

# MUSLIM SECTS

Sectarian divisions within the Muslim community have arisen as a result of historical and political developments as well as doctrinal differences and varying interpretations of the Shari'a.

The main Muslim sects are the Sunnis, the Shi'ites and the Kharijites.

## The Sunnis

The majority of Muslims are followers of the *sunna*, or the orthodox articles of faith as laid down by the Prophet Mohammed and recorded in the Hadith or Traditions. After the death of the Prophet, the Sunnis recognised the legitimacy of the caliphate as the political leaders of the Muslim community. It was strongly believed, however, that guidance on doctrine and practice must come from the Qur'an, the Hadith and the Shari'a as interpreted by the scholar-jurists (*ulema*) and the consensus of the community of scholars (*ijma*).

## The Shi'ites

In the seventh century CE, a minority group broke off from the Sunnis over the question of legitimate leadership of the nascent Islamic community. The Shi'ites claimed that the caliphate should remain within the family of Ali, the son-in-law of the Prophet Mohammed, and that after Ali's death the rightful successor was Hussain (the grandson of the Prophet) who was murdered in CE 680 at the battle of Karbala. The Shi'ites believe that spiritual authority rests with the imam. According to the majority of Shi'ites, there have been 12 true and infallible imams, starting with Ali and a direct line of his descendants. The imamate is believed to have come to an end with the disappearance of the twelfth imam in CE 878. The responsibility for providing guidance on doctrine and practice was transferred to the ayatollahs, or religious scholars, although it is believed that the twelfth imam will return as the Mahdi just before the end of the world.

The Shi'ites have their own legal system and commentaries of the Qur'an. The tenth day of Muharram, the first month of the Muslim calendar, is observed by the Shi'ites as a day of mourning for the murdered Imam Hussain, the youngest son of Ali.

The Ismailis are a minority Shi'ite sect who believe that the Prophet Mohammed will be followed by seven imams who will be the source of religious instruction and guidance. The Nizaris, one of the two branches of Ismailis, consider the Aga Khan as their spiritual leader.

## The Kharijites

The Kharijites were strict conformists who believed that the Caliph or leader of the Muslim community could belong to any race or tribe provided he was a true follower of the Islamic faith. They also believed that the profession of faith alone was not sufficient to qualify as a Muslim, unless it was accompanied by good deeds.

# SUFISM

A deep vein of mysticism has run through Islam for centuries in the form of Sufism. The term is derived from the rough woollen garments (suf) worn by the early mystics to signify their search for an alternative approach to the divine, and their detachment from the world.

The mystical tradition is well rooted in the Qur'an and the Hadith. However, in addition to the orthodox rules for religious life, the Sufis also believe that there is a deeper level of spiritual knowledge which has been transmitted from the Prophet through an unbroken chain (silsillah) of saints (walis). Whereas mainstream Islam does not recognise the need for an intermediary between man and Allah, the Sufis believe that a lay-person cannot access this secret knowledge without the help of a spiritual guide and submitting to a strict discipline of meditation and asceticism.

From CE 900 onwards, a strong cult of mysticism developed which centred on Mohammed and conferred on the Prophet many supernatural qualities which orthodox belief took care to avoid.

Sufism is oriented towards discovering the truth of divine love and the extinction of individuality in the divine reality. The path (tariquah) to this goal begins with repentance. A mystical teacher (shaykh) accepts the seeker as a disciple and leads him into a disciplined ascetic life. Various rituals are also prescribed, including the chanting of the 99 'most beautiful names of Allah' and the profession of the faith 'There is no God but Allah and Mohammed is His Prophet'. Sufi devotion has also been expressed through music and poetry of great emotional intensity. The dervish, a semi-monastic Sufi order in Turkey intensify the ecstatic experience of union with God through vigorous dance movements and the repetitive chanting of Allah's names.

Sufism has drawn its following from both the Sunni and Shia sects and at various periods in history, certain mystical orders exerted considerable political and spiritual influence in the Islamic world. It is customary for devout believers to visit the tombs of the great Sufi saints (especially on the occasion of their death anniversary) to take offerings and to petition their help in a crisis.

# ISLAMIC LAW

The sacred law of Islam (Shari'a) is described as the 'pathway in which the true believer should walk in order to please God'. The law governs all aspects of a Muslim's life and applies equally to all followers of the faith. It is firmly believed to be the eternal, unchanging embodiment of divine will and is derived from four main sources: the Qur'an; the Hadith; the *ijma*, or consensus of the community of leading Muslim scholar-jurists and religious leaders; and *qiyas*, or analogical deductions from the first three sources. The Shari'a governs man's obligations to God as well as his obligations to fellow humans. The gravest sins are those against God and the faith, followed by those against fellow humans. According to the Qur'an, God forgives all sins except that of not believing. A high value is placed on human life and morality, and acts such as stealing, promiscuity and adultery should therefore incur severe punishment. Diet, dress and modes of social interaction also fall within the scope of the law.

According to the Shari'a, all actions fall into one of five categories:

- What God has commanded
- What God has recommended but not made strictly obligatory
- What God has left legally indifferent, such as actions that will not be rewarded by God and their omission will not be punished
- What God disapproves of but has not actually prohibited
- What God has expressly forbidden.

Islamic law is noteworthy for its comprehensiveness. Consequently, Muslims believe that the Shari'a does not require to be supplemented, but may be clarified and interpreted according to the needs of the time and place.

The Sunnis recognise four schools of interpretations of Islamic law.

The Hanafi school was the first to be developed and is the most widespread. It is also the most liberal and allows greater room for rationality and individual opinion than the other schools. This school is dominant in the Indian subcontinent, Central Asia, Turkey, Afghanistan and in parts of Egypt.

The Maliki school is more conservative, and its legal interpretations tend to be rather rigorous. This school is particularly influential in North and West Africa, the Sudan and Kuwait.

The Shafi'i school is the most systematic and upholds a position which is neither too conservative nor too liberal. It is dominant throughout South East Asia and parts of the Middle East.

The Hanbali school is the most rigid of the four law schools. It is predominant in Saudi Arabia and has some support in countries such as Syria and Iraq.

The Shi'ites stress the importance of rational reflection and the individual's own attempts to solve problems (*ijtihad*). The legal experts (*mullahs* or *mujtahid*) have an important role to play in interpreting the law and issuing opinions (*fatwa*).

## ISLAM IN PRACTICE

Muslims do not recognise the concept of a 'church', and Islamic theologians and religious scholars do not enjoy the status and privileges of priesthood. Each individual is expected to create a direct link to God, without the help of intermediaries. Conformity to the dictates of the Shari'a and observance of 'the five pillars of the faith' are the basic obligations of each individual towards Allah.

### The First Pillar: The Confession of Faith (al-Shahada)

The Islamic way of life is rooted in the al-Shahada, the declaration of faith: 'There is no God but Allah; I bear witness that Mohammed is the Apostle of Allah.'

This declaration is made many times a day, especially in the daily prayers. They are the first words whispered into new-born infant's ear and the last to be uttered by a dying person. They are a confirmation of Islam's monotheistic beliefs and a recognition of Mohammed as the last in the line of Prophets to whom God's final and authoritative word, the Qur'an, was revealed.

### The Second Pillar: Ritual Prayer or Divine Service (Salat)

Every Muslim is obliged to perform the ritual of prayer (*salat*) at the five prescribed times of dawn (*fajr*), midday (*zuhr*), afternoon (*'asr*), sunset (*maghrib*) and night (*'isha*). The daily salat may be performed in the company of other believers in a mosque under the leadership of an *imam*. It may also be performed by individuals on their own on any clean ground or prayer mat, facing the direction of the sacred Kaaba in Mecca.

The noon prayer on Friday is the principal congregational service of the week. It is distinguished by a formal address (*khutbah*) which is partly a sermon delivered in the local language and partly a recitation from the Qur'an in Arabic. Attending the Friday prayer is obligatory for all except women during their menstrual periods.

Congregational services are also held on two major festival days. These are the day of the Breaking of the Fast, the day after the month of Ramadhan (Eid-ul-Fitr) and the Feast of Sacrifice at the Pilgrimage (Eid-ul-Adha). Muslims believe that congregational prayers are far more meritorious, because they heighten the feeling of solidarity and equality of the worshipping community.

The call to prayer is announced in Arabic by the *muezzin* from the minaret of a mosque. Before commencing the ritual of salat, the worshipper is required to cleanse the face, head, arms, feet and ankles (*wudu*). The salat consists of one or more ritual cycles (*rak'a*), which include several bodily movements accompanied by expressions of adoration and praise. Each rak'a begins with the *qira'a* or recitation of the al-Fatiha, the first sura of the Qur'an and another short passage. Then comes the *ruku'* or bowing from the waist, hands on knees, accompanied by the words 'Praise be to God'. After briefly returning to the upright position, the worshipper then prostrates himself, touching the ground with his forehead, palms, knees and toes (*sujud*), while saying the *takbir*, 'Allahu Akbar' (God is great). From this he changes to a position of sitting on his heels and says another

*takbir* before making a second prostration in which he asks for God's mercy. This action concludes the first rak'a.

The dawn worship consists of two ritual cycles; the sunset worship, three; and the others, four. After the second prostration of the last rak'a, the worshipper assumes an upright sitting position (*qu'ud*), hands on knees, while professing the faith (al-Shahada) and praising God and the Prophet. The concluding act is the *sluam* or *taslimat al-tahil* which consists of repeating the Arabic words of peace, 'as-salaam 'alaikum wah rahmatu 'llahi'. Private prayers may be offered after the communal service.

When there are many people, as at the Friday noon prayers, the worshippers stand in rows, facing the direction of Mecca. The imam, or prayer leader, stands in front to give the cues for the various movements, which the entire congregation performs together.

According to Islamic doctrine, the five daily prayers are compulsory for all true believers, even for the sick who may pray in bed. However, under certain circumstances, such as when travelling, the noon and mid-afternoon prayers may be combined as one. Similarly, the sunset and night prayers may be offered together. Muslims who live and work in non-Islamic countries are often forced to make these adaptations. Women are exempt from daily prayers during their menstrual periods and for forty days after childbirth.

Worship in Islam is not necessarily confined to the five daily prayers. Whereas these help to focus the true believer's mind on God despite the hustle and bustle of everyday life, salat may also be performed at other times of the day or night as a non-obligatory devotion. Muslims also believe that every virtuous action which has been sincerely performed is in itself an act of worship.

### The Third Pillar: Almsgiving (Zakat)

The act of prayer is closely linked with the practice of alms-giving. From its very early beginnings, Islam emphasised the moral obligation of sharing one's wealth with the poorer and less fortunate sections of the community. Alms-giving was also regarded as a form of piety which cleansed the soul. Zakat paid out of wealth earned through unlawful means such as gambling, moneylending or stealing is, however, unacceptable.

The Shari'a has laid down the amount of alms that should be given against different categories of property. In modern Islamic countries, the base line rate has been fixed at 2 per cent of the accumulated wealth of a man or his family at the end of each year.

Zakat was traditionally levied by the State. Nowadays, however, the fulfilment of this obligation is largely left to the individual. Voluntary acts of charity (*sadaqah*) and simple acts of kindness and hospitality also earn special merit for the bestower.

> *To spend of your substance, Out of love for Him, For you kin,*
> *For orphans, For the needy,*
> *For the wayfarer,*
> *For those who ask …*
> *And give Zakat,*
> *To fulfil the contracts Which ye have made;*
> (Qur'an; Sura 2: Ayat 177-178)

## The Fourth Pillar: Fasting (Sawm)

The Qur'an makes it obligatory for all Muslims to fast during the hours of daylight throughout the holy month of Ramadhan (the ninth month in the Islamic calendar during which the Qur'an was revealed to the Prophet Mohammed). The fundamental intention of fasting is thanksgiving. Fasting commences officially when the new moon is sighted and it concludes when the new moon of the following month is seen. If due to bad weather, the moon cannot be sighted, then the duration of fasting is 30 days. Fasting begins at dawn and it continues until sunset. Following the practice of the Prophet, Muslims customarily break the fast each day by consuming a few dates.

> *Ramadhan is the (month) In which was sent down*
> *The Qur'an, as a guide*
> *To Mankind …*
> *So every one of you*
> *Who is present (at his home)*
> *During that month*
> *Should spend it in fasting …*
> *And eat and drink, Until the white thread of dawn appear to you*
> *Distinct from its black thread;*
> *Then complete your fast*

> *Till the night appears …*
> (Qur'an; Sura 2: Ayat 185-187)

Fasting involves total abstinence from food, drink, smoking, sex and the use of perfume. Unintentional eating or drinking does not necessarily render the obligatory fasting invalid; neither does medication such as eye or nose drops, even if these enter the throat. Intravenous, muscular and subcutaneous injections and enemas are also permitted on medical grounds. Fasting during the month of Ramadhan is obligatory for all adult Muslims except those who are ill or on a journey at the time. Women are exempt from fasting during their menstrual periods and for 40 days after childbirth. Pregnant women and nursing mothers are free to choose between breaking the fast or observing it.

In principle, all those who have missed some days of fasting for any one of the above-mentioned reasons, are required to compensate an equal number of days at any time during the year, preferably before the next Ramadhan. However, those who break the fast for even one day without a valid reason cannot make up for it at any other time.

The month of Ramadhan moves through all the seasons of the year in cycles of approximately 33 years. It is a period of heightened devotion, repentance as well as the reaffirmation of social relationships. Ideally, by the end of the month, the whole Qur'an would have been recited.

Muslims also perform other acts of devotion in addition to the obligatory fasting. Following the practice of the Prophet, all Muslims are supposed to go into retreat (*I'tikaf*) during the last ten days of Ramadhan. The night of Lailat-ul-Qadr (The Night of Power, which occurs on any odd day in the last ten days of Ramadhan), which commemorates the revelation of the Qur'an, and is considered to be particularly appropriate for an act of devotion.

The month-long period of fasting culminates in a grand celebration. The festival of Eid-ul-Fitr is observed by Muslims throughout the world as a joyful occasion when gifts are exchanged and friends and relatives are treated to grand feasts. Special congregational prayers are also held on this day, and it is an occasion for sharing food with people who are in need.

Voluntary fasting may be observed at any time during the year. Since the Prophet used to fast on Mondays and Thursdays, these days are especially recommended. Fasting during the months of Muharram and Sha'ban is also considered to be highly meritorious.

However, fasting is prohibited on the days of Eid-ul-Fitr and Eid-ul-Adha, as well as the three days following the latter festival. Women are not allowed to fast without their husband's permission except during the holy month of Ramadhan.

### The Fifth Pillar: The Pilgrimage (Hajj)

At least once in their lifetime, Muslims, if they have the means, are expected to undertake a pilgrimage to the sacred mosque at Mecca and its vicinity during the 12th month of the Islamic calendar (Dhu'l Hijja). The profoundly spiritual experience as well as the sense of community engendered by participation in rituals and congregational worship, give the pilgrimage considerable significance within Islam.

The Hajj consists of a series of ceremonies. After visiting the Great Mosque at Mecca and walking around the Kaaba seven times (tawaf) the devotee performs sa'y, which involves running seven times between the two small hills of Safa and Marwah. This ritual commemorates Hagar's (the wife of Ibrahim or Abraham) search for water for her thirsty infant, Ishmael (the forefather of the Arab people). The pilgrim then drinks water from the sacred spring of Zamzam, which sprang miraculously from beneath the feet of Ishmael in answer to his mother's prayer. On the seventh day of Dhu'l Hijja, the whole assembly of pilgrims listen to a sermon on the meaning of Hajj.

The next stage of the pilgrimage is an overnight stay at Mina before visiting the Plains of Arafat where the Prophet preached his last sermon. Here the pilgrims observe the rite of standing in meditation from midday to sunset. On the following day, the tenth day of Dhu'l Hijja, the pilgrims return to Mina to celebrate the Feast of Sacrifice, Eid ul-Adha, when Muslims all over the world remember the obedience of the Prophet Ibrahim to God's command to sacrifice his only son Ishmael. Eid ul-Adha lasts for four days. The pilgrims then return to Mecca for a farewell visit.

Other traditional rites connected with the Pilgrimage include the kissing of the Black Stone set in one of the four corners of the Kaaba and the casting of seven pebbles at the largest of the three pillars (the Jamarat) in the vicinity of Mina which is supposed to represent the devil (shaitan) who tempted Ibrahim to disobey God's command. Some pilgrims also visit the Prophet's mosque at al-Madina.

The ceremonies at Mecca alone constitute the Lesser Pilgrimage (umra). These may be undertaken at any time during the year.

Before embarking upon the umra or the Hajj, the pilgrim must be in a state of ritual purity. Men shave their heads and put on a simple garment of two seamless sheets of white cloth (ihram). Women may dress in ordinary clothes but do not wear the veil. The simple garments serve to symbolise equality and the irrelevance of material possessions and social distinctions in the sight of God. The completion of the pilgrimage is symbolised by the shaving of the head for men and the cutting off of a few locks of hair for women, putting off the ihram and the resumption of ordinary clothes.

## MUSLIM DIETARY LAWS

As with other aspects of life, eating and drinking are also governed by religious dictates. The Qur'an stipulates very clearly the categories of food items which are lawful and therefore can be consumed and those that are forbidden.

In general, all vegetables are permitted but pork and all pig products are prohibited. All carnivorous animals, rodents, reptiles and birds and beasts of prey are classed as 'unclean' and therefore forbidden. The consumption of blood products is also not permitted.

All other types of meat may be eaten provided they are *halal* or ritually slaughtered. The correct method of slaughter, Muslims believe, consists of slitting the animal's jugular vein with one clean stroke and then draining the blood out immediately. The invocation which precedes every *sura* in the Qur'an, 'In the name of God, the Merciful, the Compassionate', is pronounced over the act, to show that a life is being sacrificed only to satisfy a genuine human need for food.

In order to be fit for human consumption, food must be lawfully prepared as well as bought with money that is honestly earned. When in doubt, many Muslims may prefer to eat vegetarian food rather than risk contamination from meat prepared in ways declared 'unlawful' by the Qur'an. They may also be cautious about eating manufactured foods such as bread and biscuits in case they include lard as one of the ingredients.

Muslims always eat with the right hand and avoid, if possible, touching food with the left, which is considered to be unclean. A blessing is recited over the food before it is eaten. The rules of etiquette dictate that a person must sit properly to eat, must not eat quickly or in excess, and must eat what is served, although it is permissible to pick and choose fruit.

Traditionally, all Muslims ate from a common plate to symbolise brotherhood. The practice is kept up to this day by the Bedouin Arabs. It was customary for men and women to eat separately, but this is not always adhered to nowadays.

Intoxicants of any kind are forbidden, except when no other substitute may be found to alleviate a serious medical condition. According to the religious teachings, alcohol and other intoxicants should not be offered even to guests of other faiths, nor should Muslims sell them in their shops.

## THE PLACE OF WORSHIP

The Muslim place of worship is called a mosque. This word is derived from the Arabic word *masjid*, which means a place of prostration, or *sujud*, a place of congregation. The mosque is a place where Muslims can worship congregationally. It is also often used for educational purposes (*madrasa*).

The history of Islam reveals the gradual increase in the sanctity of the mosque. Originally a place of public assembly, the expression, *beit Allah*, or House of God, which was first used only of the Kaaba in Mecca, came to be applied to any mosque. A state of ritual sanctity (*tahara*) became necessary for all those entering, and the admission of women was restricted.

The construction of mosques came to be regarded as a social obligation of Muslim leaders and often the first act of Muslim generals was to establish a mosque in a newly conquered territory which would serve as a centre of administration as well as worship.

Mosques vary from simple roofless constructions of palm trunks to the architectural splendours of the great mosques of Cairo, Istanbul and Isfahan.

The distinctive features of a mosque include the provision of a fountain or cistern (*wudu*) for the performance of preparatory ablutions, or a niche in the middle of the front wall of the mosque which is oriented towards Mecca (*mihrab*), and next to it, the pulpit (*minbar*) from which the imam delivers the sermon (*khutbah*). Larger mosques are characterised by a dome, which represents the universe, and a minaret or tower, which the caller (*muezzin*) ascends to give the call to prayer (*adhan*). Most mosques also have special sections for female worshippers.

The floor of the mosque is often covered in carpets and the walls may be decorated with Qur'anic inscriptions in fine calligraphy or intricate geometric designs. Pictures and images are excluded from mosque, in keeping with the strict monotheistic beliefs of Islam and the Qur'anic injunctions against idolatory. One of the first acts of the Prophet on his triumphant entry into Mecca in CE 630 was to cleanse the Kaaba of its idols. Since then, there has been a strong prohibition against worshipping God in the form of any visible icons.

Certain regulations for decent conduct also prevail, the object of which is to preserve the dignity of the house of prayer. Public announcements may not be made, and talking and calling out aloud are frowned upon as they disturb the meditations of other worshippers. It is also customary to remove footwear before entering the mosque and many cover the head as a mark of respect. For the Friday service, it is mandatory to wear fine clothes and rub oneself with oil and perfume.

Memorial mosques associated with the Prophet and other saints are frequently the focus of pilgrimage. Of these, three are particularly significant for Muslims: the Holy Kaaba in Mecca, the Tomb Mosque of the Prophet Mohammed in Medina, and the Dome of the Rock in Jerusalem, built on the rock from which it is believed the Prophet Mohammed ascended to heaven one night to receive Allah's message which he then preached on his return to earth.

### The Holy Kaaba

According to Qur'anic references, the Holy Kaaba in Mecca is the first house on earth dedicated to the worship of Allah. The cube-shaped mosque, built by the Prophet Ibrahim and his son Ishmael, is draped each year in a new black velvet cloth (kiswah) on which passages from the Qur'an are embroidered in gold thread. During the period of Hajj, the black cloth is replaced with a white one.

One of the most important rites associated with the pilgrimage is the circumambulation (tawaf) of the Kaaba. Starting at the corner where the sacred Black Stone is embedded in one of the pillars, the pilgrims go around the shrine seven times, in an anti-clockwise direction, all the while reciting prayers to Allah. Legend has it that the sacred Black Stone, brought by the Archangel Gabriel, was originally white but has, in the course of time, become blackened by the sins of men.

### Admission of Women into Mosques

During the Prophet's time, women were free to participate in the religious services held at the mosque. According to one Hadith, even nursing mothers would attend prayers at the mosque and when the Prophet heard the cry of an infant he would shorten the service so that the mother could feed her child. It was around CE 256 that the segregation of the sexes was instituted in places of worship. Women were required to sit in special places inside the mosque and, as the adoption of purdah or seclusion became more widespread, women's attendance at the mosque became less frequent. Since women in an 'impure' state had necessarily to abstain from prayers, it gradually became more usual for women to worship in the privacy of their homes instead of participating in congregational prayers.

## LIFECYCLE RITUALS

### Birth and Naming Customs

The Prophet Mohammed taught that showing kindness and affection towards children was very much a part of being a good Muslim. The first words whispered into a new-born infant's ear is the Declaration of the Faith: 'There is no God but Allah and Mohammed is His Apostle.' Parents are recommended to be selective in their choice of names, to treat their sons and daughters equally and to ensure a sound religious and secular education for their children.

The Prophet recommended that the most beautiful names are those which offer servitude or praise to Allah. The names of Allah, however, are never used alone. They are usually preceded by Abdul or combined with another name in such a way that the final name is never a specific attribute of Allah.

Thus, in the case of male names, the following conventions may apply:

Names of Allah are preceded by Abdul. For example, Abdul Aziz, or Abdus if a name starts with the letter 'S' as in Abdus Saadiq.

Ahmad and Mohammed are often used before and after the names of Allah or Mohammed. For example, Mohammed Ali or Basheer Ahmad.

Biblical names in Arabic may be combined with the

names of Allah, Mohammed and others. For example, Mohammed Ali or Haroon Ghaffar.

Abu added to the name of a married man indicates that he is the father of the child of the same name. For example, Abu Haroon means father of Haroon.

Ibn or bin mean 'son of'. For example, Adam bin Kareem Hussain means Adam son of Kareem Hussain.

Female names also have a distinctive structure.

A single woman may use the name of her father after the chosen name. For example, Maryaam Ahmad.

The chosen name may be followed by Akhtar, Begum, Khanoom, among others – for example, Zainab Begum or Fatima Akhtar.

The prefix Umm means 'mother of'. For example, Umm Hanifa means 'mother of Hanifa'.

Bint after a female name indicates that she is the 'daughter of'. For example, Salma Bint Zubaida means Salma daughter of Zubaida.

The naming of a new-born infant is always an occasion for joy, feasting and celebration. Male children are circumcised in keeping with the Qur'anic emphasis on personal hygiene, which is reflective of moral convictions and inner purity.

The Prophet Mohammed recommended performing circumcision at an early age. This ritual is customarily performed on the seventh day after birth, but it can be carried out within 40 days after birth or thereafter until the age of seven, depending upon the health of the infant.

# ISLAMIC MARRIAGE AND WEDDING RITUALS

Marriage is regarded as a sacred duty by Muslims, and celibacy was frequently condemned by the Prophet. It is related in the Hadith that the Prophet Mohammed once said: 'When the servant of God marries, he perfects half of his religion.' Consequently, in Islam, even the ascetic orders tend to be married.

Marriage, according to the Shari'a, is a civil contract. Its validity depends upon the consent of the contracting parties, the presence of two male witnesses (or one male and two female witnesses) and the settlement of a dower upon the woman.

## The Rules of Marriage

The Qur'an does not stipulate the minimum age for a legal marriage. However, the Shari'a declares that among the conditions required for a valid marriage, the most important are understanding, puberty and freedom. The marriage contracted by a minor who has not arrived at the age of discretion, who does not possess understanding or who does not comprehend the consequences of the act, is regarded as null and void. In many Islamic countries, the minimum age of marriage has been laid down by secular law.

A contract of marriage is decreed to be invalid unless both the parties understand its nature and mutually consent to it. The various schools of Islamic law, however, tend to differ with regard to the necessity for obtaining the consent of the woman.

According to the Hanafi and Shia schools, a woman may consent to her own marriage with or without a guardian. Under the Maliki and Shafi'i law, however, the presence of a *wali* or guardian is essential to give validity to the contract, since it is presumed that women are incapable of understanding the complexities of the marriage contract and need to be protected from unscrupulous suitors. The guardian (who is usually a male relative) can only give the girl in marriage with her consent.

The validity of the marriage contract also depends upon the absence of any legal disability or bar to the union. The most important of the legal impediments are:

- Consanguinity or blood relationship. A man is forbidden to enter into a marriage with his sister, niece, aunt, and so on.
- Affinity or relationships through marriage. Marriage is forbidden to one's mother-in-law, daughter-in-law, step-daughter, and so on.
- Fosterage, which by tradition is treated almost the same as a blood relationship. Thus a man cannot marry his foster mother nor his foster sister, although he is permitted to marry the mother of his foster sister or the foster mother of his sister.
- Marriage with two sisters or with an aunt and niece at the same time is forbidden.
- It is considered unlawful for a man to marry the wife or widow of another until the expiration of the

woman's period of waiting between marriages (*iddah*). This is a stipulated period of three months to ensure that the woman is not pregnant. All the schools of Muslim law regard with extreme disapproval marriage with a woman who is already pregnant (by another).

A wide divergence of opinion exists between the Shia and Sunni schools of law regarding inter-marriage between a Muslim and a non-Muslim. The Sunnis recognise a marriage contract between a Muslim man and a woman believing in a revealed religion such as Judaism and Christianity (*kitabiya*) as legal and valid. Some Shia sects, however, place conditions on such marriages.

The Qur'an recognises polygamous marriages. The Shari'a, however, states quite clearly that a man can have a maximum of four wives at any one time provided he can treat all of them equally. Muslim law recognises that the validity of any marriage is determined by the laws prescribed in the place where the marriage is celebrated. Consequently, Muslims domiciled in Britain cannot have more than one wife at a time since bigamy is a criminal offence.

## Wedding Rituals

Muslim law stipulates no specific religious ceremony to validate the contract that has been entered into by two parties. All that is required for the performance of a valid marriage is a proposal made by, or on behalf of, one of the parties and acceptance of it by, or on behalf of, the other party at one and the same meeting. No specific words have been laid down in the Qur'an for either making a proposal or for its acceptance. However, since marriage in Islam is a legal contract, the Shari'a stipulates that the consent of both parties must be expressed unequivocally.

Muslim marriages are solemnised by a *quazi* or *mullah* who is conversant with Islamic law. The terms of marriage, such as the amount of dower, the mode of its payment, matters relating to custody of children and any other conditions that the parties concerned wish to stipulate, are embodied in a document called the *Kabin Namah*.

Weddings are rarely solemnised in a mosque; neither is it essential for the bride to be present at the ceremony. Two persons, formally appointed for this purpose, act on behalf of the contracting parties with the required number of witnesses. Once the amount of dower (*mahr*) has been settled, the religious ceremony (performed entirely at the discretion of the *quazi*) proceeds with the bridegroom repeating after the quazi the following:

*The Istighfar:* 'I desire forgiveness from God.'

*The Four Quls:* The four chapters of the Qur'an starting with the word 'Qul' (chapters CIX, CXII, CXIII and CXIV). These chapters are not particularly relevant to the subject of marriage and perhaps have been selected on account of their brevity.

*The Kalimah or Creed:* 'There is no God but Allah and Mohammed is His Prophet.'

*The Sifwatu'l-Iman:* A declaration of belief in God, the Angels, the Scriptures, the Prophets, the Resurrection and the Absolute Decree of good and evil.

The *quazi* then requests the bride's guardian to take the hand of the bridegroom and to say: 'Such as one's daughter, by the agency of her attorney and by the testimony of two witnesses has, in your marriage with her, had such a dower settled upon her. Do you consent to it?'

To which the bridegroom is expected to reply: 'With my whole heart and soul, to my marriage with this woman, as well as to the dower settled upon her, I consent, I consent, I consent.'

The religious ceremony concludes with the recitation of a short prayer and a benediction by the *quazi*.

*Nikkah* or the celebration of the marriage contract is preceded and followed by various festivities. Muslim law recommends simple ceremonies of marriage and the Prophet himself is believed to have declared that 'the best wedding is that upon which the least trouble and expense is bestowed'. However, right across the Islamic world, local customs (*adat*) have modified the Qur'anic ideal so that the Nikkah is usually a joyous and festive occasion.

Among Muslims in the Indian subcontinent, wedding celebrations traditionally went on for three days. The homes of both the bride and groom would be filled with guests, and the women of the family play a prominent part in the celebrations, although the bride herself would be kept in strict confinement.

Of the several long-established customs, the most important, in some parts of the Islamic world, is the gift of *mehndi* or *henna* sent by the bride's family to the bridegroom. Various presents in keeping with the means of the bride's family would also accompany the trays of mehndi. These gifts often include clothes for the bridegroom, toiletries, confectionery, dried fruits, sugar candy and *paan* (betel leaves filled with a sweet spice mixture and decorated with edible silver foil).

At the bridegroom's house, the female friends and relatives of the bride who accompany the trays of mehndi and other gifts are entertained in the women's quarters. The bridegroom is then summoned to the women's quarters (*zenana*) and the henna is applied to his hands and feet. The entire ritual takes place in a convivial atmosphere, throughout which the bridegroom is fed pieces of sugar candy and other confectionery.

On the third day, the bride's family prepare to receive the bridegroom's party (*barat*). The bridegroom traditionally arrives mounted on a horse, the legs, tail and mane of which are dyed with henna.

The marriage ceremony is performed in the presence of witnesses, although the bride is not seen by any of the males, not even by her husband-to-be, until they have been lawfully united. According to some local traditions, the bridegroom must first see his wife's face in a looking glass, which is placed in front of the young couple.

After the consummation of the marriage, the bridegroom's family traditionally host a reception (*walimah*) to publicise the lawful nature of the union.

## Divorce

Whereas the Shari'a recognises the woman as an equal partner in so far as the actual marriage ceremony is concerned, the right to a dissolution of a marriage by extra-judicial means is generally exercised by men alone. Divorce operates from the pronouncement of *talaq*, which literally means 'getting free (from a bond)'. A man can obtain a divorce in the presence of a *quazi*. The Shi'ites insist on the presence of two male witnesses as well, although this is not a legal requirement for Sunnis. The wife's presence on this occasion is not considered to be necessary by both the Sunnis and Shi'ites.

The talaq pronounced three times is held to be irrevocable and the husband is obliged to pay the entire dower (*mahr*) which had been decided at the time of marriage. A divorced couple can marry one another again only after the woman has consummated and dissolved a marriage with another man.

To be able to pronounce the talaq, the man must have attained his majority and must be of sound mind. The talaq is a personal right, which the husband must exercise himself or through a representative specially appointed by him. He may also entrust this mandate to his wife, who can then pronounce the talaq on herself.

Once the talaq has been pronounced, the woman has to wait for a period of three months before concluding a new marriage. During the waiting period (*iddah*), the woman has a claim on her husband for lodging, but has the right to maintenance only if she is pregnant. If the marriage has not been consummated, the woman is not required to observe the three-month waiting period, but can only claim half the dower.

Various attempts have been made to modernise the laws pertaining to marriage and family. In many Islamic countries, the right of wives to seek a judicial dissolution of their marriage has been recognised, and the arrangements for the payment of mahr at the time of marriage ensure that the wife can claim maintenance if there is a divorce.

The *khul* is a special form of divorce by which the woman can purchase her freedom by returning a portion of the mahr. The term comes originally from the symbolic act of 'taking off ' or throwing away an item of clothing. The khul was in existence in pre-Islamic times and continues to be practised in some parts of Muslim world, although there are differences of opinion as to whether it is a repudiation (talaq) or the annulment of a marriage.

# MUSLIM BURIAL CUSTOMS

The Islamic concept of death is quite simple, the idea being that 'from God we have emerged and to God we return'. The official mourning period tends to be of a relatively short duration (three days), the only exception being widows who observe strict mourning for a prescribed period of three months and ten days. When death is imminent, the person is asked to declare his faith by repeating the simple declaration of faith, 'There is no God but Allah and Mohammed is His prophet.' The imam at the mosque is informed as soon as possible after death occurs, and prayers from the Qur'an are recited over the body.

The body is then washed by family members of the same sex as the deceased and swathed in a simple white cotton sheet or shroud. All Muslims are dressed alike to symbolise the equality of all men before God. The body is then placed in an unlined coffin. If the body has been taken to a funeral director's premises, it is customary to conduct the ritualistic washing in a room which has been purified and from which all religious icons and imagery have been removed.

The prescribed mode of disposal of the dead, according to strict Islamic tradition, is by burial and, as far as possible, this should take place on the day of the death itself. The usual practice is for the deceased to be taken to the mosque, where special prayers are recited, before proceeding to the graveyard. A brief prayer service is also held at the cemetery, after which the body is buried in the grave with the head facing Mecca. Women rarely attend burial ceremonies.

Among some Muslims, on the third day following the burial, relatives and friends of the deceased gather together in the house of mourning and recite prayers for the dead. An offering in kind is made and, with this, the official mourning period comes to end.

Muslims from the Indian subcontinent, particularly in Western India, conduct a special ceremony on the 40th day following the death (chalismoh), when prayers are recited and food is distributed to all relatives of the deceased.

Besides the specific rituals, the dead are also commemorated in various ways. On Thursday evenings, prayers are offered to the dead after the prayers recited at sunset (Maghrib namaz). Similarly, after the Eid prayers at the mosque, cemeteries are visited and prayers are offered to the dead. It is customary to visit families who have been bereaved in the course of the year to offer condolences.

# MUSLIM FESTIVALS

For Muslims, all religious festivals have a special significance. At the end of different modes of worship, Islam has instituted a festival. Thus, for instance, the daily prayers of the week culminate in the festival of the Friday Prayer, called Juma Prayer. The festival following the month of fasting is called Eid-ul-Fitr, while that following the ceremony of Hajj is known as Eid-ul-Adha.

Festivals are not merely occasions of joy and happiness. They are also a form of worship in themselves, as Islam grafts the remembrance of God with every activity of a Muslim, even sitting, walking, sleeping, wearing shoes or garments, going in or out of the house, setting out on a journey or returning from one, selling or buying, eating, drinking, washing, bathing, entering or leaving a mosque, meeting a friend or facing an enemy, seeing the moon, starting any work or finishing it; even sneezing, yawning or taking medicine.

The day of a festival is spent in praising Allah, remembering his attributes and thanking Him for his countless bounties, as well as in merry-making. Islam, however, forbids its followers from indulging in extravagance at any time. The faithful are exhorted not to go to extremes so as to stand on the brink of insanity, either with excessive joy or with grief and sorrow. Followers of the religion are also instructed by the Qur'an to share their happiness with others, especially the poor and the needy.

*Children of Adam, put your minds and bodies in a state of tidiness at every time and place of worship and eat and drink but be not wasteful; surely, he does not love the wasteful.*
(The Qur'an 7:32)

Islamic festivals are based on lunar sightings rather than lunar reckonings.

## Hijrat – Muslim New Year

This is celebrated on the first of Muharram. Hijrat means leaving one place of residence for another. In the history of Islam, it occurred when the Holy Prophet of Islam migrated from Mecca, where he and his followers were persecuted, to Medina where they were welcomed by the populace in CE 622. The first mosque was built at Medina, and the Islamic social order and code of practice established.

## Muharram

Muharram is the name of the first month of the Muslim year. The first day of Muharram is declared a public holiday in Muslim countries. The Muslim calendar dates from the year the Prophet Mohammed – under pressure of persecution from the Mecca unbelievers – accepted the believers' invitation and emigrated to Medina in CE 622.

## Ashuraa – Tenth Day of Muharram

Shi'ites observe this festival with great respect, through prayers, talks and vigils, and singing dirges in memory of Imam Hussain, the grandson of Prophet Mohammed. It commemorates the great tragedy at Karbala, in Iraq, in which Imam Hussain was brutally speared to death in the 61st year of the Hijrah (AH), and when practically all of the Prophet's family including his son-in-law, Hazrat Ali, were annihilated.

Members of the Shia sect dress in black clothes as they spend the first ten days of the year in mourning. Assemblies are held every day for the first nine days, where Shia orators relate the incident of the death of Imam Hussain and his party in great detail. On the Tenth Day of Muharram, large processions are formed and the devoted followers parade the streets holding banners and carrying models of the mausoleum of Imam Hussain and his people who fell at Karbala. They show their grief and sorrow by inflicting wounds on their own bodies with sharp metal pieces tied to a chain with which they scourge themselves to depict the sufferings of the martyrs. It is a sad occasion and everyone in the procession chants 'Ya Hussain' with loud wails of lamentation. Usually, a white horse, beautifully decorated for the occasion, is also included in the procession, perhaps to symbolise the riderless mount of Imam Hussain after his martyrdom.

During these ten days, drinking posts are also set up temporarily by the Shia community where water and fruit juices are served to all, free of charge. It has also become customary to serve milk or *sharbat* (soft drinks) at these functions to remind Muslims of the way Imam Hussain and his followers were starved and tortured to death.

On this day, God saved Moses and his followers from the pursuing army of the self- appointed god, Pharoah. The Prophet asked his followers to honour this occasion by fasting.

## Eid Milad-un-Nabi

This festival commemorates the anniversary of the birth of the Holy Prophet Mohammed. It is celebrated on the twelfth day of Rabee-ul-Awwal. From the point of view of Muslims, this date marks the most important event in the history of the world. Mohammed is regarded as the last and the chief of the Prophets, the perfect man to whom the Qur'an was revealed, the best example, and the greatest benefactor of mankind. He is the person for whom God has proclaimed:

*Allah sends down his blessings on the Prophet, and his angels constantly invoke his blessings on him. Do you O believers also invoke Allah's blessings on him and offer him the salutation of peace.*
(The Qur'an 33:57)

The extent of festivities, on this occasion, is, however, restricted, because the same day also marks the anniversary of his death.

On this occasion, therefore, public meetings are held in the mosques, where religious leaders make speeches on different aspects of the life of this great man. The stories of the Prophet's birth, childhood, youth and manhood, character, teachings, sufferings and forgiveness of even his most bitter enemies, his fortitude in the face of general opposition, leadership in battles, bravery, wisdom, preachings and his final triumph through God's mercy over the hearts of the people, are narrated in detail.

Salutations and songs in his praise are sung. In some countries, streets, mosques and public buildings are decorated with colourful bunting and pennants and are well illuminated at night.

Devout Muslims give large sums of money to charity. Feasts are arranged and rice and meat dishes are served to the guests and also distributed among the poor. In some big cities, large processions are also formed, and people in jubilant mood chant verses in praise of the Holy Prophet Mohammed as they work.

Some Muslims, however, do not celebrate this occasion as his birthday or death anniversaries as they believe such celebrations are not part of Muslim society as such. Instead they hold Seer-un-Nabi meetings where speeches are made on different aspects of the life of the Prophet.

## Shab-e-Miraj

Shab-e-Miraj means the night of the ascent. It is a blessed night when the Holy Prophet of Islam was spiritually transported to heaven and reached such a high stage of nearness to God Almighty as was beyond human mind to conceive. The ascent took place in the fifth year of the call, about seven years before Hijrat. On the way to meeting God, the Holy Prophet met Adam, Abraham, Moses, Jesus and some other prophets who preceded him. The purpose of this spiritual ascent was to confirm the status of the Prophet of Islam, a position that all Muslims believe is impossible to attain by any other human being. It is related that even Gabriel (Jabril), the Angel who was accompanying the Prophet, remarked at one stage:

*I am forced to stop here. I cannot go any further but you, O Messenger of Peace and friend of the Master of the World, continue your glorious ascent.*

It is also related that the Holy Prophet continued his journey until he was very close to the throne of God and attained the utmost nearness to him. After having drunk fully at the divine fountain of spiritual knowledge, he came down to impart that knowledge to mankind.

According to popular belief, Miraj, or spiritual ascension, took place on the 27th day of Rajab. Muslims celebrate the occasion by holding prayers and reminding themselves of the high morals taught during this night's journey. In some Muslim countries, the houses, streets – and especially the mosques – are decorated with colourful pennants and bunting, and at night, they are brightly illuminated by means of electric lights, candles or even oil lamps. In the evening, worshippers assemble in the mosques, and there often is a speaker to address the pious crowd at this holy event. After the ceremony is over, sweets are distributed to all. Most of this holy night is spent in prayer, and many wealthy Muslims share some of their wealth by distributing money and food among the poor and destitute.

## Shab-e-Barat

This day falls about a fortnight before Ramadhan, and is traditionally celebrated in anticipation and preparation for the month of Ramadhan. Muslims fast and spend the night in prayer, as God is said to make a record of all the good and bad actions of man and to dispose their fate according to their actions.

Originally intended by the Prophet of Islam as an occasion for vigils and fasting, this has developed into a joyous festival celebrated in many parts of the world, when sweets, *halva* (sweetmeats made of sesame seeds and honey) and bread are specially prepared and distributed to friends and to the poor.

## Ramadhan

Fasting is one of the five pillars of Islam, and the month of Ramadhan is the ninth month of the Muslim calendar, which the Prophet Mohammed chose to be spent restfully in prayer and meditation.

Muslims do not worship Mohammed, but they do regard him as the greatest Prophet of God, as he was the last to descend to earth and he was the one who actually completed the message of the earlier prophets. The encounter with the Angels is reserved only for the chosen ones and the messengers of God. They received their messages mainly through the Archangel Gabriel, who is described as powerful and honest, and is named in the Qur'an as the Holy Spirit who carried God's messages to His blessed prophets including Noah, Ibrahim, Lot, Ismail, Ishak, Yakoub, Yousuf, Musa (Moses), Haroun, El-Azer, Zakariya, Yahya (John) and Isa (Jesus).

Ramadhan is a very special month, as it is the month in which the Qur'an was first revealed as God's guidance to mankind. To mark their celebration and their gratitude, Muslims sacrifice some of their material pleasures, including food and drink, as an offering to the merciful God.

Fasting enables the rich to enter the experience of poverty and it teaches the value of self-discipline.

The Qur'an states:

*O ye who believe fasting is prescribed for you as it was prescribed for those before you, so that you may guard against evil.*
(The Qur'an 2:184)

The fast is obligatory for every healthy adult Muslim, male or female, but there are certain exemptions: for a sick person, a person who is travelling, a pregnant woman or one who is breastfeeding her child, and those who find the severity of the fast hard to bear on account of age or other infirmity. When the reason for exemption is only temporary, as with an illness from which the person recovers, the number of days missed are later made up. Should the cause of exemption continue over a lengthy period of time or become permanent, as in the case of the infirm and elderly, the exemption is absolute, but the person concerned, if he or she can afford to, should arrange to provide food for a poor person for the whole month or give the equivalent amount in charity known as *fidya*.

Fasting during this month is to make man realise his many blessings and is a means of showing his thanksgiving and gratitude to God.

Whereas the reward for every good action is prescribed by God and is written down by the recording angels, the reward for fasting is awarded and recorded by God himself. It is a month of communal worship when the Qur'an is read often, as it is believed that it was revealed around the 27th day of Ramadhan.

## Lailat-ul-Qadr – 27th of Ramadhan (The Night of Decrees)

This occasion falls on the eve of the 26th fast during the month of Ramadhan. It was on this night that the Qur'an was revealed to the Prophet Mohammed by the Archangel Gabriel, thus it is so important that it is known as The Night of Power which in Arabic is Lailat-ul-Qadr.

The Qur'an states:

*This month of Ramadhan is the month in which the Qur'an began to be revealed, the Book which comprises guidance and divine signs which discriminate between truth and falsehood*

...
(The Qur'an 2:186)

Prophet Mohammed was 40 years of age when he first received a revelation in a small cave on Mount Hira, which is a short distance away from Mecca. The Muslims believe that it is during this night that the earth was filled with angels, led by the Archangel Gabriel, to reveal the first verses of the Qur'an to Mohammed and signal the start of his mission:

*Read in the name of God, who created man from clinging cells, read for your God is the most generous, who taught man with the pen, taught man what he knew not.*
(The Qur'an 96:1–5)

It was significant that the first verses called for people to learn God's knowledge, and that it was Mohammed who was chosen to carry the Qur'an to mankind. The revelation continued until his death, for a period of about 23 years.

The whole month of Ramadhan is a period of spiritual training when believers devote much of their time to fasting, praying and reciting the Qur'an and remembering God (Allah), as well as giving charity and good will. The last ten nights, especially, are spent in worship and meditation, and the more devout Muslims retreat to the mosque and spend their time solely in the remembrance of Allah. They join the congregation at prayer times and for Taraweeh (special prayers recited with Isha Salat in the evenings).

Devoting their time so fully to the remembrance of Allah, they hope to receive the divine favours and blessings connected with this blessed night. It is related that when the last ten days of Ramadhan began, Mohammed used to stay awake the whole night and was most diligent in worship. Thus Muslims spend this night in remembrance of Allah, asking forgiveness for their shortcomings. They have a firm belief that God accepts the prayers of the supplicant readily during this night.

## Jumat-ul-Wida

This is the last Friday of the month in Ramadhan, the holy month of devotional celebration that is eagerly awaited by Muslims and missed when it ends. It is also a month of brotherhood and communal worship, as well as great spirituality, charity, peace and happiness. The last Friday marks the end of Ramadhan and, in the same way as a respected visitor is treated, Ramadhan is given a great welcome and likewise a special farewell.

Otherwise, Friday is the Muslim's holy day or Day of Assembly. At midday, Muslims gather at a mosque to pray together and listen to the imam preach his sermon. Work is carried out as normal before and after Friday prayers. Before performing the actual prayer, or handling the Qur'an, shoes are removed and one performs a Wu'zu (holy wash) whereby one cleanses oneself before touching the Qur'an or doing any pious act. Friday sermons are about Muslims' responsibilities and obligations, and strengthen the spiritual bond between the believers.

The Qur'an says:

*O ye who believe, when the call is made for Prayer on Friday, hasten to the remembrance of God and leave off all business, that is better for you, if you only knew.'*
(The Qur'an 62:10)

Muslims gather at the mosque to pray together and listen to the imam preach his sermon (khutba) at noon every Friday. But this particular Friday is significant as it is the last Friday of the holy month, and a feeling of both sadness and happiness is experienced, as all the excitement of the month comes to an end, and the people look forward to its return after a year.

## Eid-ul-Fitr

Eid is an Arabic word which means a day which returns often. There are two days in the year that are declared public holidays in Muslim countries. One is Eid-ul-Fitr (at the end of Ramadhan) and the other is Eid-ul-Adha, which comes about ten weeks after the first Eid.

Eid-ul-Fitr is celebrated at the end of a period of fasting (the holy month of Ramadhan). There is a great deal of excitement when the moon is sighted: a joyous surge runs through the hearts of all Muslims, young and old, in anticipation of one of the happiest of occasions. Friends and relatives exchange good wishes and blessings with each other. All the necessary preparations are made – shops are opened till late, streets and homes are decorated, and the preparations for the next day get under way.

On the day after the festival, after rising early and having a bath, people wear new clothes (or their best clothes) and a special non-alcoholic perfume called *athar*. They are treated to a special breakfast which includes a sweet dish of *sheer-kurma*, vermicelli cooked in milk with dried dates, raisins, almonds and other nuts.

Eagerly they proceed towards the Eidgah, which is the central mosque of the city, or to a specified open space that will accommodate the congregation. Separate enclosures are provided for women, because Islam does not permit the free intermingling of men and women. As was the practice of the Holy Prophet Mohammed, they go to the Eidgah generally by one route and return by another.

Eid prayer and Friday prayer is always offered in congregation, but no Adhan or Iqamat (introductory announcement of the prayer or exhortation) is called out for this service.

The prayer commences with the imam calling out 'Allah-o-Akbar' (Allah is the Greatest) aloud. When the prayer is over, a sermon is delivered by the imam, which generally includes the historical background and spiritual significance of the festival. After the service the worshippers greet each other by saying 'Eid Mubarak' and hug each other or just shake hands. The spirit of Eid is one of peace, forgiveness and of brotherhood, so after performing their duty they return home happy and contented. The women prepare exotic dishes, as this is a big day of celebration. They have friends and relations to join them for meals. Gifts and greetings are exchanged. Although it is an occasion for joy and happiness, it is certainly not an occasion to indulge in frivolity, over-eating and mere pursuit of pleasure. The main purpose is always to seek the pleasure of God by glorifying him and rendering thanks to him for having enabled them to perform their duties.

It is a family day in the smaller as well as the wider sense, when Muslims visit friends and relatives to exchange greetings and good wishes. The joy and happiness of the occasion originate mainly from managing to complete the Ramadhan fasting and in being nearer to God.

## Hajj – Pilgrimage

Hajj is one of the five pillars of Islam. Hajj is performed during the period from the eighth to thirteenth day of Zul-Hijja. During this time, pilgrims from all over the globe flock to Mecca in Saudi Arabia, and one of the finest examples of true brotherhood of man is shown to a world torn by political, economic, religious and cultural strife. A Muslim makes every effort to perform this pilgrimage at least once in a lifetime, whenever he finds the means to do so.

These are the important rituals associated with the ceremony.

1   Putting on Ihram. A male pilgrim has to discard his usual clothes and dress himself in two white sheets of seamless cloth. One sheet is wrapped round the waist covering the lower abdomen, while the other is slung over the left shoulder. The head remains bare. Women may dress themselves in simple clothes and are not required to cover their faces.

2   Performing seven circuits of the Kaaba, the pilgrims enter the great mosque. The Muslims' spirituality reaches a peak as they leave their worldly cares behind, clothe themselves in simple, humble, white sheets of cloth, and stand, rich and poor, master and servant, shoulder to shoulder, in concentric rings of prayer around the Kaaba, all raising their prayers to the One God who is unseen, but whose presence is felt everywhere. They walk round in an anti-clockwise direction, and all say the same phrase that the Prophet Abraham said four thousand years ago, which is translated as follows:

*Here I am, my Lord, here I am,*
*Here I am. There is no associate with thee.*
*Thine is the kingdom,*
*There is no associate with thee.*

The Kaaba is a very simple, stone structure, cubic-shaped, laying no claim to grandeur of size or beauty of architecture. It impresses by its very simplicity.

3   Performing the Sa'ee, which is going seven times between the two nearby mountains of Safa and Marwah, in commemoration of Hagar, the Egyptian wife of Ibrahim and mother of Ismael, in her attempts to look for water for her thirsty infant Ismael. The pilgrim then goes to drink water from the blessed well of Zam-Zam, that sprang out from underneath the feet of Ismael, in answer to his mother's prayer, and is still flowing to this day.

4   Visiting Mina, Arafat and Muzdalifah. On the eighth of Zul-Hijja, the pilgrims leave Mecca for Mina and spend the night there in prayer and meditation. On the ninth day, they go to Mount Arafat, the 'Mountain of Mercy', where God forgave Adam and Eve and led them back to each other. Being there with a repentant heart on the appointed date is all that is required to earn total forgiveness, yet another example of God's mercy and compassion. They arrive there after midday, offer Zuhr and Asr prayers, and remain at Arafat until sunset.

To stay at Arafat from post-meridian until sunset is regarded as an important ritual of Hajj, as it is on this plain that man seeks pardon for his sins and returns from Hajj as sinless as the day he was born. Pilgrims then proceed to Muzdalifah where Maghrib and Isha prayers are combined and the night is spent in praising God and in meditation. Some small stones are taken from here on the journey back to Mina after the morning prayer the next day. At Mina, the pilgrim stones the three places where Satan appeared to the prophet Abraham, trying to dissuade him from obeying God, as he was on his way to sacrifice his only son, Ismael. The stoning of the three places is to symbolise the Muslims' obedience to God, and their rejection of the devil.

5   On the tenth day of Zul-Hijja, the pilgrim sacrifices an animal that he can afford, such as a goat, sheep, cow or camel. This is known as the Feast of Sacrifice, thus commemorating the prophet Abraham's success in his test, demonstrating that he loved God more than he loved his son; when God stopped him sacrificing his son and offered him a fat ram to slaughter instead. The purpose of the sacrifice is to feed the poor, as well as one's friends, neighbours and oneself.

6   After staying at Mina for the three days of the feast, the pilgrims return to Mecca for Tawaaf al Widaa, the farewell visit before departure.

7   Pilgrims have their heads shaved or cut their hair short.

Pilgrimage is a time when Islam's history comes alive, especially when one remembers the Prophet Mohammed's glorious struggle, resolve, tolerance and wisdom in fulfilling his message. Thus the pilgrims pay their respects by visiting him in the mosque at Medina where he is buried. They return with holy water, dates, and blessings for everybody.

## Eid-ul-Adha (Bakra Eid) – The Festival of Sacrifice

The Eid is celebrated with great solemnity and reverence everywhere. Preparations commence several days before the festival. The animals to be sacrificed are bought well before the Eid day by those who can afford to do so and are well looked after. These animals should be free from all physical defects and should be fully grown. In the case of a sheep or goat, one animal suffices for one household, whereas a cow or camel can be shared by seven.

The details of these events are mentioned in the Bible and in the Qur'an. It is narrated that Abraham saw a vision that he was slaying his only son Ismael. He mentioned the dream to his son Ismael and asked, 'What do you think of it?' Ismael replied, 'Father, do that which you have been commanded. You will find me God-willing and steadfast.' Being thus convinced that God demanded the sacrifice of his son, who was bestowed to him in his old age, he began to make the necessary preparations. Then Abraham received the revelation that he had indeed fulfilled his covenant, and on God's command, the angels brought a ram instead and put it in place of Ismael. Thus the animal was sacrificed, and this festival of sacrifices therefore urges all Muslims to follow the examples of Abraham, Hagar and Ismael and show perfect submission to God's commands.

Therefore Muslims – especially adults who have performed their pilgrimage – make this sacrifice.

A third of the meat is kept for the use of the household, and the remainder is distributed uncooked among the poor and sent as gifts to friends and relatives.

Many families get together and cook exotic dishes, both savoury and sweet, and rejoice with relations and friends. They wear new clothes and attend prayers at the big mosque or Eid Gah.

# SIKHISM

## AN INTRODUCTION TO SIKHISM

The latter half of the fifteenth century witnessed the emergence of a vigorous new religious movement in northwest India. The founder of Sikhism, Guru Nanak, born in 1469, was according to some historians the first popular leader of the Punjab in recorded history, and the doctrines he preached (which his followers refer to simply as the *gurmat* or the teachings of the guru) are closely bound up with a language and culture that is essentially Punjabi. The twentieth century saw the rapid growth of Sikh settlements outside India. However, there is a strong affinity between Sikhism and its place of origin, and Punjab continues to be a powerful emotive symbol of faith and community for Sikhs all over the world.

Elements from both Hinduism and Islam influenced the doctrinal base of Sikhism as laid down by Guru Nanak and developed by the continuous line of nine spiritual leaders who followed him. During the 'Age of the Gurus' (1469–1708), the religious movement consolidated and acquired an identity of its own, symbolised by its distinctive rites of passage, its sacred literature, places of worship and the shared history of its followers.

## THE FUNDAMENTAL BELIEFS OF SIKHISM

The essence of Sikh belief is contained in the opening lines (*mul mantar*) of Guru Nanak's celebrated morning prayer – *Japji Sahib* – which is recited daily by devout Sikhs.

> *There is One God*
> *He is the Supreme Truth*
> *He, the Creator*
> *Is without fear and without hate.*
> *He the Omnipresent*
> *Pervades the universe.*
> *He is not born*
> *Nor does He die to be born again.*

The monotheistic creed preached by Guru Nanak, is symbolised by the numeral 1 which precedes the first composition recorded in the Sikh Holy Book, Guru Granth Sahib. God is described as formless (*nirankar*), eternal (*akal*) and ineffable (*alakh*). He is also *sarab vyapak* or inherent in all creation. Everything in creation, according to Guru Nanak, exists by God's will and is in accordance with the divine order (*hukam*). The revelation in creation is significant, for it is the way in which man can establish communion with the divine presence.

Guru Nanak's teachings incorporate the Hindu concept of *samsara* or the cycle of birth, death and rebirth, and the law of *karma*, whereby the nature of a person's life is conditioned by actions in a previous birth. Human beings in their unenlightened state, are self-centred and slaves to desire, anger, greed, materialism and pride. Their immersion in the material world and its false values traps them within the cycle of birth and death.

Those who seek salvation must, according to Guru Nanak, submit to a strict spiritual discipline and persist on that path until they have comprehended the divine order and brought themselves into harmony with it. This discipline involves focusing the mind inwards and meditating upon the divine name.

Sikhism is often described as *nama marga* because it emphasises constant repetition (*jap*) of the name of God as a way of cleansing the soul and disciplining the wandering mind, thereby inducing a heightened consciousness of the ultimate truth or divine reality. Spiritual development, according to Guru Nanak, proceeds in a series of stages (*khand*) experienced internally. The fifth and last of these (*sachkhand*) is the state of final awareness, wherein the individual attains mystical union with God, and the chains of transmigration are broken forever.

Sikhism does not advocate asceticism as a means for achieving awareness of the eternal truth and union with God. On the contrary, Guru Nanak exhorted his followers to shoulder their family responsibilities and to earn their living by honest means. Great importance was attached to congregational worship and *seva* (service to the community).

The concept of the guru is central to Sikh belief. The term refers to God (Sat Guru), Guru Nanak and the line of nine spiritual teachers who followed him in providing leadership and guidance to the Sikh community, the holy scriptures (Guru Granth Sahib) and the community itself.

*To have access to God's name, the Guru is the ladder,*
*the boat, the raft … The Guru is my ship to cross sin's lake*
*and the world ocean … The Guru is my place of pilgrimage*
*and sacred stream.*
(Adi Granth)

# THE SIKH GURUS

The history of Sikhism can be largely understood as the gradual institutionalisation of a religious truth as revealed to its founder, Guru Nanak. The *Janam Sakhis* (birth stories) state that he was born in 1469 in the village of Talwandi (renamed later as Nankana Sahib) near Lahore. Even as a child he had strong spiritual leanings, although he is believed to have had his first mystical experience at the age of 30. After this, Nanak is said to have disappeared for three days and nights. He reappeared on the fourth day, declaring that 'There is no Hindu, there is no Mussalman', and preached his message of 'one God for the universe and the equality of all human beings' throughout the Punjab and beyond. In the course of his travels, he is credited with having performed several miracles. Guru Nanak is believed to have died in the early hours of 22 September 1539.

Guru Angad Dev guided the Sikh community for 13 years, from 1539 to 1552. He collated all the hymns of Guru Nanak so that scattered congregations could have a focal point of piety and doctrine, and also developed the Gurmukhi script. This paved the way for a distinctive Sikh scripture as well as secular Punjabi literature.

Guru Amar Das (1552–74) responded to the need for greater cohesion within the Sikh community by instituting a system of pastoral supervision. The Hindu festival days of Diwali, Baisakhi and Magha were also designated as Sikh festivals, and it became customary for Sikhs to gather before their guru on these occasions. The tradition of the *langar*, where people of all castes ate together, first started by Guru Nanak, was carried on by Guru Amar Das, as it symbolised the Sikh ideal of equality of all mankind.

Guru Ram Das (1547–81) is best known for founding the holy city of Amritsar on land given to the Sikhs by the Mughal emperor, Akbar. He also composed the Sikh wedding hymn (*Lavan*) and initiated important social reforms particularly aimed at improving the status of women in society.

Guru Arjan Dev (1581–1606) was groomed for succession by his father, Guru Ram Das. He was the first guru to have been born a Sikh. Under his leadership, the Sikh community consolidated itself in the Punjab and began to exert considerable influence in the politics of the region. The guru compiled the first version of the Adi Granth – the most sacred scripture of the Sikhs and also commissioned the construction of the Harimandir Sahib (the Golden

Temple) at Amritsar. Guru Arjan Dev was a prolific poet and composer and contributed the largest number of hymns to the Adi Granth. His best-known composition is the *Sukhmani* or hymn of peace sung at Sikh funerals.

Guru Arjan Dev's execution by the Mughal emperor, Jahangir, had a profound impact on the course of Sikh history. His successor, Guru Hargobind (1606–44) embarked upon a policy of armed confrontation with the Mughal Empire. He is credited with having conceived the two-sword symbol of Sikhism – *Piri* and *Miri* – representing spiritual and temporal concerns respectively. Guru Hargobind also constructed the Akal Takh, the seat of Sikh temporal authority, within the complex of the Golden Temple. The pennant he provided for his army, the *Nishan Sahib,* became the flag of Sikhism, and to this day can be seen flying from the rooftop of every Sikh temple (*gurdwara*).

The seventh guru, Har Rai (1644–61) is chiefly remembered for his love of animals and his great interest in Ayurveda, the traditional medical system of India. His son, Har Kishan (1661–64) succeeded him at the age of five but died in childhood as a captive of the Mughal Emperor Aurangzeb.

Guru Tegh Bahadur (1664–75), the youngest son of Guru Hargobind, assumed leadership at a critical juncture in Sikh history. The fundamentalist policies and fanaticism of the Mughal emperor, Aurangzeb, were fiercely resisted by the Sikhs and the Hindus, and the guru rallied the community as they confronted the might of the Mughal empire. He was summoned to Aurangzeb's court and following a period of imprisonment, was publicly executed in Delhi. Guru Tegh Bahadur, like his predecessors, was also a great poet, and his compositions were added to the Adi Granth by his son who succeeded him as the tenth guru.

Guru Gobind Singh (1675-1708) formalised the process whereby a pacifist, inner-directed faith was forced to accommodate within its belief structure a strong component of disciplined militancy. His creation of the brotherhood of pure Sikhs (Khalsa), bound by their allegiance to their guru and five external symbols, helped to establish a clear-cut identity for the Sikh community in the Punjab.

The line of human gurus came to an end with the assassination of Guru Gobind Singh, the saint-soldier. In accordance with the guru's instructions, supreme spiritual authority was vested in the Adi Granth and in the corporate unity of the Khalsa.

## THE KHALSA

According to Sikh tradition, the Khalsa or the community of pure Sikhs, came into being on the day of the spring harvest festival, Baisakhi, in 1699. The tenth guru, Gobind Singh is believed to have summoned his followers to the town of Anandpur Sahib to celebrate the festival. After the morning service, the guru appeared before the congregation and asked for one Sikh who was prepared to sacrifice his life for the faith. After some hesitation, one man arose. He was taken into a tent and a few minutes later the guru appeared with a sword dripping with blood. Four more Sikhs, all belonging to different castes, stood up and offered their lives to the guru.

As the fifth Sikh was taken to be sacrificed, the doorway into the tent was flung open and the guru reappeared followed by the five men who were completely unscathed. He then declared that they, the *panj piyare* (five beloved ones) were to be the nucleus of a new casteless fraternity of Sikhs, the Khalsa.

The panj piyare – Daya Ram, Bharam Das, Bhai Sahib, Mohkam Chand and Bhai Himmat Rai – were initiated into the Khalsa in a special baptism ceremony. Water, sweetened with sugar crystals (*amrit*) was stirred in a bowl with a double-edged sword (*khanda*). The five men were made to drink out of the same bowl, thus signifying their absorption into a casteless community. Their Hindu names were discarded and they all adopted the surname of *Singh* or lion. The guru in turn accepted amrit from the baptised Sikhs and replaced his surname of Rai with that of Singh.

Many more members of the congregation stepped forward to receive *amrit*. The women initiates assumed the title of *Kaur* or princess.

Members of the Khalsa also came to be distinguished by five external symbols (*Panj Kakke,* the five 'K's). These were unshorn hair and beards (*Kesh*), a comb (*Kanga*), knee-length shorts (*Kaccha*), an iron bangle worn on the right hand (*Kara*) and a sword (*Kirpan*).

Long hair and beards were the mark of holy men in India from time immemorial. The comb was necessary to keep the hair tidy. The other three 'K's have militaristic connotations. The shorts were the uniform of soldiers of the period. They also symbolise purity and restraint. The iron bangle may have been an adoption of the Hindu custom of tying charms on the wrists of soldiers before they set out to war. It also protected the hand that wielded the Kirpan.

Baptised Sikhs were expected to refrain from alcohol, tobacco and meat and to lead a pure, righteous life. The assembled gathering of Sikhs were also exhorted to renounce their caste affiliations and to follow a strict monotheistic creed.

The names of the panj piyare are repeated in the *Ardas* (supplication made at the end of every prayer service). Mata Jitoji, the woman who assisted Guru Gobind at the first baptism ceremony at Anandpur Sahib, also occupies a place of honour in the annals of Sikh history.

# THE GURDWARA

In the early Sikh scriptures, there are many references to special rooms or buildings called *dharamshala*, which served as centres for worship. A local community of Sikhs (*sangat*) would gather there to listen to a pious discourse and to participate in devotional singing (*kirtan*). The dharamshala was also referred to as *gurdwara*, literally meaning the guru's door and, by strict definition, any place where the Sikh Holy Book, the Adi Granth or Guru Granth Sahib, is installed. In the course of time, the term 'gurdwara' came to be more generally used for the Sikh place of worship. The change in terminology could be associated with a developing belief among Sikhs that the guru is always present in spirit wherever members of the community gather to worship.

## Architecture of a Gurdwara

Gurdwaras range from the architectural splendours of the Golden Temple in Amritsar to simple, converted houses in suburban streets where the Guru Granth Sahib is installed and the faithful gather together to pray. The only external feature that identifies a gurdwara is the *Nishan Sahib* or saffron-coloured flag flying from the rooftop.

The flag, triangular in shape, flies at full mast throughout the year on a tall flagpole, which is also draped in saffron-coloured cloth. The Sikh emblem, the khanda, which is made of black material, is placed in the centre of the flag. This is a two-edged sword symbolising freedom and justice and the Sikh belief in one God. It is flanked by two crossed swords, the right-hand one symbolising spiritual authority (*Piri*) and the left-hand one signifying temporal power (*Miri*). A circle in the middle (*chakkar*) symbolises the balance between the two and also serves as a reminder of the timeless, infinite nature of the divine reality. The flag is replaced every year with a new one at the festival of Baisakhi, the Sikh New Year.

Gurdwaras usually have a special room where prayer services are held and another where the Guru Granth Sahib is stored at night. The focal point of the prayer room is a raised platform under a richly decorated canopy. The floor of the platform is covered with a soft quilt (*manji*) over which are placed two pieces of white cloth. The Guru Granth Sahib rests on three small cushions. The Holy Book, when not being read, is covered with a cloth (*rumala*) to prevent it from getting soiled. The rumala is usually gifted by a member of the congregation. By the side of the Holy Book is a fan made of yak hair embedded in a wooden or silver handle. While the Book is being read, an attendant stands behind the reader and waves the fan as a mark of respect for the Guru Granth Sahib.

Large white sheets are spread on the floor of the prayer room on which the congregation sit. Men and women sit on either side of a centre aisle but worship together.

## Iconography

The simplicity and absence of visual representation in the main prayer hall of a gurdwara is highly significant, as the Sikhs believe that worship requires only the presence of the Guru Granth Sahib and the congregation. However, as a result of influences, probably emanating from Hinduism, an iconographic tradition has developed to depict the gurus and incidents from Sikh history in popular prints, paintings and murals.

Guru Nanak is typically painted as seated on a pink lotus, with a halo encircling his head, rosary beads worn around his turban, his eyes half closed in contemplation and his right hand raised in the gesture of teaching. Beside his head, the numeral one is usually shown as a symbol of the monotheistic creed he preached.

## Daily Worship in the Gurdwara

Daily worship commences at dawn when the morning prayer – the *Japji Sahib* is recited. It was composed by Guru Nanak and consists of 38 verses in praise of God. The Guru Granth Sahib is brought into the prayer room, borne on the head of a *granthi* (an official of the gurdwara who is skilled in reciting and explaining the scriptures), and it remains there until night.

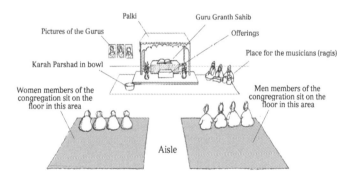

Pictures of the Gurus
Palki
Guru Granth Sahib
Offerings
Place for the musicians (ragis)
Karah Parshad in bowl
Women members of the congregation sit on the floor in this area
Men members of the congregation sit on the floor in this area
Aisle

After it is installed in its customary place under the canopy, the Holy Book is opened at random and the first complete verse (*shabad*) on the left-hand page is read. This random reading is known as *Vak* or *Hukamnamah* and it serves as a lesson or thought for the day. In some of the larger gurdwaras, the wordings of the Vak may be displayed on a notice board near the main entrance.

Around sunset, the evening prayer, *Rehras Sahib* is recited. This is a collection of hymns composed by Guru Nanak, Guru Amardas, Guru Ramdas, Guru Arjan Dev and Guru Gobind Singh. Finally at night, *Kirtan Sohilla* is recited and the Guru Granth Sahib is put to rest. The rumala is removed and the Book is wrapped in the two pieces of white cloth kept under the three cushions on the platform. It is carried on the granthi's head to the store room to rest all night on a quilt under a rumala. Whenever the Guru Granth Sahib is taken away or brought into the main prayer room, all those present stand up as a mark of respect.

At the end of each of the main prayers of the day, a special prayer *Ardas* is offered. It reminds the congregation of the teachings of the gurus, the sacrifices of the Sikh martyrs and of the bounty of God. Ardas is offered at the end of services to mark happy or sad events and the wording is altered to suit the occasion. At the conclusion of the Ardas, the entire congregation calls out the words:

*Waheguruji ka Khalsa, waheguruji ki fateh.*

which means:

'The Khalsa belongs to God, victory belongs to God.'

The service ends with the distribution of *karah parshad*, a sweet pudding made from wheat flour, sugar, clarified butter (ghee) and water. The devotee accepts it in both hands cupped together, and it is eaten straight away.

Sikhs do not have a special day for worship in the gurdwara. People may visit the gurdwara for private prayers and meditation at any time of the day as well as join in the congregational worship. The singing of hymns from the Guru Granth Sahib to the accompaniment of musical instruments (*kirtan*) is a popular form of worship.

Before going to the gurdwara it is customary to cleanse and purify the body. Footwear is left outside the gurdwara or in a special room set aside for this purpose, and men and women cover their heads as a mark of respect. The devotee usually bows to the flag before entering the gurdwara

Inside the prayer room, a Sikh will approach the platform upon which the Guru Granth Sahib rests, and bow or prostrate fully before it and make an offering of money or food, which will be used in the community kitchen. Careful not to turn their back on the Book, the worshipper will then sit on the floor with the rest of the congregation.

After the religious service, members of the congregation may partake of a meal cooked in the kitchen (*guru ke langar*) of the gurdwara. The Sikh tradition of the langar goes back to the time of Guru Nanak, who encouraged everyone who came to see him to sit down and eat together. The langar symbolises the equality and the unity of all mankind. Paying for the langar, cooking and serving it are considered to be some of the greatest acts of charity or service (*seva*) to the community. Any visitor to the gurdwara, Sikh or non-Sikh, may participate in the langar, as the Sikhs pride themselves on their hospitality.

## Karah Parshad

Karah parshad is a sweet pudding made of wheat flour, sugar, clarified butter (ghee) and water. It is cooked in the kitchen of the gurdwara by men and women who have cleansed themselves, the kitchen and the pots and pans before preparations commence. The ingredients are usually donated by devotees and, while the parshad is being cooked, hymns from the Guru Granth Sahib are sung.

After it is cooked, the pan is covered with a clean white cloth and taken to the prayer room. It is preceded by a person who sprinkles water all the way from the kitchen to the prayer room to ritually cleanse the path. The parshad is placed on a table near the Guru Granth Sahib and during Ardas it is marked with a sword by way of a blessing.

Karah parshad is distributed among all members of the congregation at the end of a religious service to symbolise the unity of the worshipping community and the sharing of God's grace.

## Akhand Path

Sikhs regard the Guru Granth Sahib as their living guru, and all-important ceremonies are conducted in the presence of the Holy Book. Practising Sikhs may read a few pages from it every day. On the occasion of a birth, wedding or death in the family or any other important occasion such as the start of a new business venture, the entire Book is read, without any break, over 48 hours. This is known as *Akhand Path* and it is believed that grace is conferred on all those who take part in reading, listening and arranging such an important event.

## The Five Takhats

There are five gurdwaras in India that have a special significance for Sikhs. They are known as *Takhats* or seats of moral, spiritual and political authority. The heads of these gurdwaras, the *Jathedar,* form a committee which legislates on all important matters, both sacred and secular, which concern the Sikh community across the world.

Akal Takhat is the oldest and the largest of the five most sacred gurdwaras. It was founded by Guru Hargobind and is situated opposite Harimandir Sahib, the Golden Temple, in Amritsar. Decisions taken here have come to be regarded as the cornerstone of Sikh religious life and polity.

Takhat Sri Patna Sahib is the birthplace of Guru Gobind Singh. It received formal recognition as an important centre of Sikhism, when the guru gifted to it one of the four copies of his revised version of the Guru Granth Sahib.

Takhat Sri Keshgarh Sahib is the birthplace of the Khalsa. It is located in Anandpur in Punjab.

Takhat Sri Damdama Sahib is the place where Guru Gobind Singh compiled the second (and final) version of the Guru Granth Sahib, during a period of rest between his campaigns against the Mughal Empire.

Takhat Sri Hazur Sahib is located in Nanded in the southern Indian state of Andhra Pradesh. Guru Gobind Singh spent his last days here and, before his death, sanctified the Guru Granth Sahib as the Guru incarnate, thus putting an end to the tradition of living gurus.

# SIKH RITUALS

## Nam Karan Ceremony

The birth of a child is always regarded as a happy event, and great importance is attached by Sikh families to choosing an auspicious name. *Nam karan* (naming ceremony) is conducted in the presence of the Guru Granth Sahib. A name is chosen beginning with the first letter of the Vak on the day of the child's birth. The baby's first visit to the gurdwara usually takes place on the tenth day after birth.

## Initiation Ceremonies

Young Sikhs are enjoined by the scriptures to formally declare their commitment to the faith and follow the tenets as laid down by the gurus. Initiation or baptism ceremonies are usually conducted when the young person reaches adolescence. The date of *Amrit Sanchar* (baptism) is normally announced in the gurdwara and all those who wish to become *Amrit Dhari* (baptised Sikhs) inform the granthis. The initiates are required to wash themselves, clean their long uncut hair and wear the five 'K's when they present themselves at the gurdwara on the appointed day.

Five baptised Sikhs (*Panj Pyaare*) prepare *amrit* (sugar candy dissolved in water) in an iron bowl in the presence of the Guru Granth Sahib. The ceremony is reminiscent of the first baptism rituals conducted by Guru Gobind Singh at Anandpur on the day of the Baisakhi festival in 1699. The initiates are called one by one to take amrit and each of them is asked to say the words:

*Waheguruji ka Khalsa, waheguruji ki fateh*
(The Khalsa belongs to God, victory belongs to God)

while they are given five sips of amrit to purify the body. Amrit is sprinkled into the eyes five times to purify the vision so that the initiate can receive a clear picture of God and His creation. Drops of amrit are then sprinkled on the hair five times to purify the intellect.

When all the initiates have gone through the same ritual, they are made to stand in a semi-circle and the bowl containing amrit is brought to them by the Panj Pyaare. The person at the extreme left of the semicircle is asked to take a sip of amrit and pass the bowl to the next person. When the last person has taken a sip, the bowl is then passed among all those present at the ceremony. This ritual is symbolic of the Sikh belief in social equality and the unity of the Khalsa or community of baptised Sikhs. All Amrit Dhari Sikhs are required to live their lives henceforth according to the *Sikh Rahat Maryada*, which is the Sikh Code of Conduct.

# SIKH WEDDING RITUAL

The Sikhs believe that the teachings of the gurus can best be followed in the householder state. Hence every Sikh is expected to marry and establish a family in the manner prescribed by the fundamental tenets of the faith.

Marriage is regarded as an alliance between two families and is traditionally arranged by the parents or senior members of the family. Nowadays it is usual for the young people concerned to meet before a decision is made.

As soon as a young person reaches marriageable age (this is usually 20+ for girls and 25+ for boys), word is passed around by their families. Intermediary kin may help to arrange introductions between families and to initiate discussions. Marriage negotiations are usually handled with a great deal of discretion and tact.

## The Rules of Marriage

Although the gurus advocated a casteless society, in practice the boundaries of caste define the universe within which all meaningful social relationships are conducted. Endogamy is believed to be the minimum criterion for the maintenance of caste identity, and great care is taken to ensure that marriages are arranged within the caste.

Sikhs also observe the rule of *gotra* exogamy. The gotra is a group of people claiming descent from a common ancestor, and marriage is prohibited between the members of such a group.

Sikh women were traditionally expected to marry outside their own villages, and a bride moved to her husband's village after marriage. A village is referred to as a *pind* and the practice of village exogamy is usually explained with reference to the fictive kin ties existing between the boys and girls born and brought up within the same village, who are regarded as brothers and sisters even though they are not related by blood.

Within the general framework of customary marriage rules, great variation may exist in the individual standards by which marriage partners are selected. Family background, socio-economic status, educational qualifications as well as personality and social skills are factors that influence the choice of a spouse.

## Sikh Marriage Customs

Sikh marriage ceremonies include compulsory rituals (*gur riti*), which take place in the presence of the Guru Granth Sahib and with the help of a granthi, as well as others that are both optional and more flexible. The former category of obligatory rituals include the kurmai (engagement) and the *Anand Karaj* (wedding ceremony).

The latter category includes the dinners and receptions that are hosted by both the bride's and bridegroom's families, as well as ceremonies such as the *Maiyan* and Chura, which usually take place at home in the presence of close family and which do not require the services of a religious specialist.

## The Prenuptial Ceremonies

The first ceremony is the *rokna* when the relatives of the girl literally reserve the bridegroom-to-be so that no other proposal may be considered by his family. Relatives of the girl take sweetmeats, dried and fresh fruit to the boy's house. At this stage in the proceedings, a potential alliance could be called off if a flaw or scandal is discovered on either side. The rokna may take place from six months to two years before the wedding.

Engagement ceremonies are often very grand occasions and may take place any time from a week to a few months before the wedding. On this occasion, the bride's relatives take fruit and sweetmeats (on a larger scale than for the rokna) to the boy's family, along with a gold ring, turbans for the groom and his immediate male relatives, as well as gifts of cash.

The groom is given a dried date to eat by the bride's father to signify that the marriage proposal has been accepted by his family and that wedding arrangements can now be made without fear of having to be cancelled.

The *Chunni* ceremony is another ritual that takes place either on the engagement day or on the following day. The bride is sent a sari or Punjabi suit, a gold ring and an elaborately embroidered *dupatta* (scarf) by her prospective mother-in-law. This is an exclusive women's function during which there is feasting and music.

Registry marriages usually take place after the engagement. This event is devoid of any religious content and merely complies with the legal requirement in countries outside India that the marriage is registered with the civil authorities.

## Anand Karaj

Preparations for a wedding commence several months in advance and they usually involve the co-operation of the extended kin network. The wedding day ceremonies are preceded by various colourful rituals, which have both symbolic and social significance.

On the day before the wedding, the bride's body is rubbed with a mixture of flour, oil and turmeric. This mixture, called *maiyan,* is supposed to cleanse and purify the girl for the wedding day. She is not allowed to have a bath or wash her hair after the Maiyan ceremony until the wedding day.

Maiyan is also performed for the bridegroom. Female relatives apply the turmeric paste to the bride, and male relatives attend to the groom, and the entire ritual takes place in a convivial atmosphere.

Another important ritual is the *Chura* ceremony in which the bride receives a set of red bangles from her maternal uncle. These bangles are worn long after the wedding, and are replaced with new ones when they break.

A week before the wedding, the female relatives of the bride get together for singing and dancing. One evening is also reserved for viewing the *daaj* or trousseau consisting of clothes, jewellery, household linen and other items, which are gifts for the bride from her parents and maternal grandparents.

## The *Viah* or Wedding

The wedding day commences with a reception of the *baraat* the bridegroom's entourage at the gurdwara. The bridegroom traditionally arrived at the venue of the wedding seated on horseback with a little boy perched behind him as a fertility symbol. The reception provides the setting for the *Milni* ceremony when the relatives of the bride and groom exchange garlands and gifts are presented from the bride's family to members of the bridegroom's family. The most important people who must meet at the Milni are the fathers and maternal uncles of both bride and groom.

Women also have a similar set of Milnis, which take place after the marriage ceremony and which are more private occasions. The gifts tend to be more expensive than those for men.

Sikh marriage rituals usually last for two to four hours and may be celebrated either in a gudwara or at the bride's house in the presence the Guru Granth Sahib.

Weddings are usually celebrated in the mornings and, once the guests assemble, the groom is seated in front of the *Guru Granth Sahib*. The bride, accompanied by a female relative such as a sister or sister-in-law, then joins the congregation and is seated to the left of the groom.

### The Bride's Costume

Brides usually wear the traditional Punjabi dress – the *salwar kameez*, which consists of a long tunic worn over trousers that are tight at the ankles. A *dupatta* (long scarf) is draped over the head. The wedding dress is usually red, as this is considered to be an auspicious colour for women, and is made of silk with intricate gold embroidery. Accessories include gold jewellery as well as the red bangles presented by her maternal uncle.

The traditional dress for the bridegroom is the *churidar-achkan*, which consists of a long jacket with a high collar worn over tight trousers. Nowadays, however, the bridegroom is usually dressed in a Western-style suit and carries the ceremonial sword.

The person conducting the service then asks the couple and their parents to stand. A short hymn is sung followed by a sermon (*sikhiya*), preached by an older member of the bride's party, which advises the couple on the meaning of the Sikh way of life and the marriage ceremony itself.

The bride and groom signify their assent to the marriage by bowing their heads towards the Guru Granth Sahib. When they sit down again, the bride's father comes forward to garland the Holy Book, his daughter and the groom, and to tie the end of the bride's dupatta to the muslin scarf that is draped around the groom's shoulders. Another hymn is then sung by the *ragis* (singers) and the granthi opens the

Guru Granth Sahib at the *Lavan* of Guru Ram Das, a hymn composed by the fourth guru for his daughter's wedding.

As the first verse is read and sung by the ragis, the couple, with the groom leading, go around the Guru Granth Sahib. They return to their places and sit down when the second verse is read, and then the circumambulation is repeated. On the fourth and final circumambulation (*laam*), flower petals or confetti are showered on the couple.

The religious service concludes with the singing of the first five and the last verses of the hymn *Anand* followed by the *Ardas*. The guru's counsel (*Vak*) is taken by opening the Holy Book at random and *karah parshad* is distributed to the guests.

The religious service is followed by lunch. Close relatives of the bridegroom then go to the bride's house for the *Doli* ceremony at which the bride is ceremoniously sent off to the groom's house. Gifts for the bride, the groom and for some of his relatives are also dispatched at this time.

The final ceremony is the *Muklawa*, which takes place the day after the wedding, when the bridegroom's relatives return to the bride's home for lunch. Earlier, when pre-pubertal marriages were quite common, the bride stayed on in her parental home for a few years after the marriage ceremony. It was only after the Muklawa ceremony that the bride shifted her residence permanently to her husband's home.

## SIKH FUNERAL RITES

Birth into the Sikh faith is believed to be the result of good *karma*, and death is considered to be the last obstacle to union with God. When a Sikh dies, the body is washed and dressed by relatives of the same sex as the deceased, and the five 'K's are placed beside it. The dead body is cremated as soon as possible, and close relatives of the deceased participate in the rituals. The grandeur and scale of the ceremonies usually vary according to the age and social status of the dead person.

In villages in the Punjab, the dead body is taken to the cremation grounds (which are usually situated outside the village) in a solemn procession of relatives chanting hymns. The funeral pyre is lit by a close male relative, usually the eldest son of the deceased person, and the evening hymn (*sohilla*) is sung. Prayers are also offered. The ashes are collected the next day and then thrown into a river.

In Britain, the funeral procession usually starts from the funeral director's premises. However, it is customary to make a stop at the house of the deceased en route to the crematorium.

After the funeral, the mourners are expected to have a bath and cleanse themselves of the pollution attached to death and the funeral. An *Akhand Path* is arranged at the home of the deceased and all adult members of the close kin circle usually participate in the complete reading of the Holy Book. On this occasion, however, the reading is likely to be spaced over a period of ten days instead of the customary 48 hours. Before taking leave of the bereaved family, mourners receive *karah parshad*.

# SIKH FESTIVALS

The birth and death anniversaries of Guru Nanak and the nine gurus who succeeded him are important events in the Sikh calendar and are marked by both religious and secular ceremonies. The celebrations start with the three-day Akhand Path, in which the Guru Granth Sahib is read continuously from the beginning to end without a break. The conclusion of the reading coincides with the day of the festival. Sikhs visit gurdwaras where special programmes are arranged and *kirtans* sung. Free sweets and *langar* are also offered to everyone who visits the gurdwara, irrespective of religious faith. Volunteers serve it with a spirit of *seva* (service) and *bhakti* (devotion).

The spring festival of Baisakhi commemorates the creation of the Khalsa. In recent years the elaborate religious celebration of the festival in the Golden Temple, Amritsar, can be seen by Sikhs (and non-Sikhs) throughout the world, courtesy of satellite television.

After the assassination of Guru Gobind Singh in 1708, the line of human gurus came to an end and the spiritual leadership of the Sikh community came to be vested in the holy scriptures – the Guru Granth Sahib. Sikh worship takes place in its presence, and on important occasions the Guru Granth Sahib is read from beginning to end, over 48 hours, without a break.

## Lohri

Lohri is the winter festival of Punjab and is celebrated by Hindus and Sikhs. The night of Lohri is usually one of the coldest nights of the year, and the festivities usually take place around bonfires. For many days before this festival, children go around people's houses singing folk songs, in return for which they are given either money or special items of food.

Lohri has particular significance in families with a new-born baby or a newly married son. Dried fruits, nuts, sesame snaps, popcorn and rice flakes are eaten and also distributed to relatives, friends and neighbours. It is customary to throw rice flakes, sesame seeds and popcorn into the bonfire for luck. A young bride is encouraged to throw black sesame seeds (which are rare), into the fire because it is believed she will have as many sons as the seeds she throws.

On the next day, which marks the beginning of the month of Magh (Maghi or Magha are vernacular versions of the name), Sikhs go to the gurdwara to join in the celebrations commemorating the new month. The town of Muktsar in the Punjab is the scene of a big fair held every year in memory of the tenth guru, Gobind Singh, and 40 Sikh martyrs.

## Basant Panchami

This is the festival heralding the arrival of spring. It falls on the fifth day after Magh in the Vikram calendar. Fields turn yellow with mustard flowers and people dress themselves in yellow clothes. The Namdhari Sikhs celebrate this day as the birthday of their founder, Guru Ram Singh Ji.

## Holla Mohalla

In 1680 at Anandpur, India, Guru Gobind Singh, the tenth guru of the Sikhs, introduced the festival of Holla Mohalla as an alternative to the Hindu festival of Holi. There are displays of swordsmanship, horsemanship, archery, wrestling competitions, display of weapons and poetic symposia, making it a very colourful festival in the Sikh calendar.

## Baisakhi/Vaisakhi

Baisakhi is the north Indian harvest festival celebrated in the spring season. At that time wheat, the staple crop of the area, is ready for harvest and the farmer celebrates the fruit of his hard work with celebrations involving songs and bhangra (harvest folk dance). It is also New Year's Day in the State of the Punjab and it usually falls on 13 April (occasionally on 14 April as in 1999 and 2002).

The founder of the Sikh faith, Guru Nanak Dev, started his missionary travels on this day, and later the third guru, Guru Amar Das, asked his disciples to gather on this day to celebrate it as a special festival, distinct from other faiths, to give the Sikhs a separate and individual identity. It continued in much the same way until the time of Guru Gobind Singh, the tenth guru who, in 1699, chose the festival as the birthday of the Sikh Khalsa.

Guru Gobind Singh had earlier commanded his followers, spread across various parts of India, to gather together on Baisakhi Day 1699. They came from far and wide and, on the actual day, over a hundred thousand had assembled for the morning prayer at Anandpur (literally 'the town of bliss'). This had been founded by Guru Gobind Singh's father, the ninth guru, Guru Teg Bahadur.

After the early morning prayers, the guru addressed the congregation, then drew out his sword in a flash and demanded the head of a Sikh who would be willing to die for (dharam) his faith. This was a strange demand coming from a guru who had won the hearts of his followers by helping the needy, the oppressed and the downtrodden. In setting up a democratic mechanism for leading mankind, Guru Gobind Rai wanted to select five people who were liberated from the bondage of the physical body.

Some people panicked and left the congregation; others stayed. But the silence was such that one could hear a pin drop. Then one man, Daya Ram, offered his head to the guru. He was taken inside a tent/marquee, which was erected near the platform from where the guru was addressing the huge gathering. The congregation heard the strike of the sword. The next moment the guru was back

before the congregation with the same sword dripping with blood, and demanded another head. There was consternation in the audience. Yet another man mustered courage and offered his head to the guru. It happened five times in all. Then the guru brought all five men back to the congregation adorned in identical attire and, it is said, there was a certain aura around them.

Another remarkable fact was that the men's names symbolised kindness, righteousness, courage, steadfastness and leadership – values that all Sikhs are encouraged to believe in and to uphold.

Guru Gobind Singh then baptised the five chosen men with a special nectar called *amrit* which he prepared in an iron bowl and to which his wife (Mata Sahib Kaur) added sugar crystals. The guru recited *Gurbani* (holy scriptures) throughout this process, while stirring the mixture with the Kirpan (the double-edged sword). Subsequently the guru asked the already baptised Sikhs to baptise him. Thus the brotherhood of the Sikhs was born, known as the Khalsa, a democratic arrangement in which the guru and his Sikh followers became equal participants.

After the initiation ceremony, the guru asked them to follow a code of conduct (the Sikh Rahit Maryada), which consisted of the taking of the second name *Singh* (which means lion) for men and *Kaur* (meaning princess) for women. Gender and social equality were enshrined in the very formalisation of Sikhism. The five symbols, all commencing with the letter 'K' in the original Punjabi, were given at the same time.

For the Sikhs, Baisakhi is an important festival, but the Baisakhi of 1919 is especially remembered as the Jallianwala Bagh massacre. General Dyer, the Commissioner of Amritsar, considering it to be a political meeting, fired on a large crowd of people including many children who had congregated in the walled park to celebrate this historic day. Nowadays it is celebrated among the Punjabis all over the world as a religious, social and political occasion.

For some years now, the Sikh community in England has contributed funds to the Golden Temple Broadcasting Appeal, to make it possible for Sikhs in England to participate in the festivities conducted at the Golden Temple.

## Guru Arjan Dev's Martyrdom Day

Guru Arjan Dev, the fifth guru of the Sikhs, was the first Sikh martyr. By the time of his leadership, the Sikh faith had developed into a well-organised and established religion, with missionary centres in all the major towns and districts in the north-west of India, particularly in the State of Punjab. Towns such as Kartarpur, Goindwal and Amritsar, which had been established by the previous gurus, were flourishing trading and commercial centres, and a strong Sikh community was taking shape.

Guru Arjan Dev was a man of the masses and wielded great influence. His growing power and prestige roused the jealousy of the emperor, Jahangir. It is said that a plot was hatched, as a result of which Guru Arjan Dev was suspected of supporting the dissident Prince Khusrau against the Mughal Jahangir. Guru Arjan Dev was asked to change the text of Guru Granth Sahib and also to pay a fine of 2,000,000 rupees.

Guru Arjan Dev refused to pay the fine or to change the Guru Granth Sahib. The guru was incarcerated at Lahore in the custody of Chandal Lal, a Hindu minister at Lahore Court and was sentenced to be tortured to death. Guru Arjan was starved for three days. On the fourth day he was taken out and forced to sit on a red-hot iron plate. Then burning hot sand was poured over the guru's body. Burnt and blistered, the guru was taken to the River Ravi under armed escort. The guru plunged into the water and was never seen again.

Guru Arjan Dev is celebrated in Sikh history as an apostle of peace and learning and the day of his martyrdom is celebrated as the victory of good over evil.

## The First Presentation of Adi Granth

Adi Granth was presented to the Sikh congregation for the first time by the fifth Guru, Arjan Dev, in 1604. Before that, *Gurbani* (word of God revealed through Sikh gurus) of the first four gurus was written in four different parts. Guru Arjan Dev collected together not only the Gurbani or spiritual teachings of the earlier gurus, but also the poetry of Hindu and Muslim saints who believed in one God and the equality of all humans, thus making it the 'Bible of the universal religion'. The total collection comprises 6,204 *shabads* (hymns) compiled in 31 different *ragas* (musical modes).

The first presentation of the Adi Granth was made in Harmandir Sahib, which was built by the fifth guru in the town of Amritsar. *Hari* means God, and *mandir* means house. Hence Harmandir is the House of God. There is an interesting universality about the Harmandir Sahib itself. The foundation stone was laid by a Muslim divine, Saint Main Mir. It has four entrances in four directions, offering a welcome to all irrespective of caste, colour, creed, country or sex.

The first *granthi* (a priest who is a specialist in sacred texts) appointed by Guru Arjan Dev was Baba Budha Jee.

## Guru Ram Das

Guru Ram Das was born on 24 September 1534 in Chuna Mandi, Lahore. As the first son of the family, he was called Jetha. His father, Hari Das, who belonged to the Sodhi caste, was a petty trader and, even as a child, Jetha had to supplement his family's income by selling boiled *grams* (black chickpeas).

He lost his mother at an early age and, when he was seven, his father died too. His maternal grandmother took him away to live with her, where he had to spend his days in poverty. When he was twelve, his grandmother decided to leave her village and move to Goindwal, a city founded by Guru Amar Das (the third guru) on the banks of the River Beas, and they settled there.

At Goindwal, Ram Das began to live a life dedicated to the guru's cause and would do any job for the guru. He was privileged to meet Guru Angad Dev, the second guru. He studied music, poetry, mythology and the sacred compositions of the gurus.

In 1552, Guru Angad Dev passed on his guruship to Amar Das and, in 1553, struck by the manifold qualities of Ram Das, Guru Amar Das decided to give to him the hand of his daughter, Bibi Bhani, in marriage. Ram Das stayed with his father-in-law and was closely associated with his ministry.

He commanded the full confidence of the guru, and for this reason he deputised for the guru in the court of King Akbar and accompanied him on a long journey to Hardwar to acquaint the people with his religion. Guru Amar Das was so impressed by him that in 1574 he got down from his seat, seated Ram Das there, and placed five paises (coins) and one coconut before him as a mark of handing over to him the *Gurgadhi,* or succession.

Soon after the marriage of his daughter to Ram Das, Guru Amar Das had asked him to start a new settlement on wasteland near the village of Sultanwind, which was then named Guru Ka Chak. A low-lying area with a small pond in the east of this settlement was also excavated into a bigger pool. Later, both the settlement and the pool were further developed by Guru Arjan who renamed them 'Ramdas Pur' and 'Amritsar' (*amrit* meaning nectar and *sar*, pool). The settlement around this pool of nectar, which developed into a thriving town, became known as Amritsar.

Guru Ram Das also composed the Sikh wedding hymns, which form a very important part of the Sikh marriage ceremony.

## Sikh Diwali

The Sikhs celebrate Diwali in honour of the sixth guru, Guru Hargobind. He was the son of Guru Arjan, the fifth Guru. Guru Hargobind became the sixth guru, after his father was assassinated in 1606 by the Mughals for refusing to change his faith.

Guru Hargobind was only eleven at that time. He decided to defend himself and his people by wearing the two swords of *Miri* and *Piri* – symbols of political and religious leadership. He also refused to pay the fine imposed on his father for preaching his religion.

On these grounds, the officers of the Mughal emperor, Jehangir, imprisoned him at the fort of Gwalior, where he stayed for about five years. Eventually, Jehangir examined the case personally and ordered the guru's release.

Sharing his prison were 52 Hindu princes, who were not offered their liberty. Guru Hargobind said that he would only accept his release if the princes were also allowed to leave the prison with him. The reply of the prison officers was that as many princes as could pass through the narrow passage of the prison, holding on to the guru's clothes, could go free.

The guru ordered a cloak to be made, which had long tassel-like ends. All the princes walked to freedom holding on to his train. That is why the Sikhs call Guru Hargobind 'Bandi-Chor' – the releaser of prisoners.

When the guru returned to Amritsar in 1620, the Sikhs illuminated the Golden Temple in honour of his release. Thus Diwali has a special meaning. It symbolises freedom of conscience, freedom to practise one's own faith, to respect another person's faith and to fight persecution. Later, his grandson, Guru Gobind Singh, said, 'There is only one race – the human race.' Everybody is invited to share in the celebrations.

On Diwali day, Sikhs from far and wide gather in the precincts of the Golden Temple from early morning. At night the temple and the surrounding buildings are illuminated with candles, lamps and electric bulbs.

The reflections of illuminations in the pool surrounding the Golden Temple add to the beauty and grandeur of the temple. There are also firework displays. Treasures accumulated during the Sikh rule are put on show, and a gala atmosphere pervades the town. In Britain, too, people decorate their homes and use candles and coloured light bulbs to illuminate them. Sweets and presents are exchanged. People go to worship at the gurdwaras and other holy places, which are specially decorated for the occasion.

## Succession of Guru Granth Sahib

It is said that three days before his passing away, Guru Gobind Singh ended the human succession to Guruship and installed the Adi Granth as Sri Guru Granth Sahib in 1708. The word guru means a guide or a teacher, a dispeller of the darkness of ignorance by sharing the light of spiritual knowledge with the world. The 1,430-page Holy Book contains writings of the gurus and Hindu and Muslim saints, thereby making it a universal book of prayer. It occupies the central place in a Sikh gurdwara.

## Guru Nanak's Birthday

Guru Nanak was born in the fifteenth century in the plains of the Punjab. He was born on 20 October 1469 (15 April according to some scholars) in Rai Bhoe ki Talwandi, now known as Nankana Sahib in the Sheikupur district of West Pakistan. His father, Mehta Kalu, was a patwari, an official in the revenue department. His mother's name was Tripta and he had an elder sister named Nanki, four years his senior.

Guru Nanak was the founder of the Sikh religion and first guru of the Sikhs. He was followed by nine successive gurus.

When he was five years old, like many other children he was sent to an elementary school for two years, he also attended a school run by a Hindu and was introduced to the Vedas (ancient scriptures) and philosophy. He was then sent to a Muslim teacher to learn Persian and Arabic to get a good post in a department of the government. He made himself familiar with the popular creeds of the Muslims and the Hindus, and gained a good knowledge of the Qur'an and the Brahmanic shastras (sacred writings). He displayed a remarkable grasp of the Upanishads (philosophical writings), the Qur'an, and other religious literature.

At nine, he was required by custom to invest himself with the sacred thread *Janaeu,* as the Hindus call it, but he refused to do so, saying that he would rather have a thread that would neither break nor get soiled nor be burnt or lost. (The ceremony of investing with the sacred thread is, strictly speaking, a Brahmin custom of confirmation in which a cotton cord is placed on an 8 to 10-year-old male. It is worn over the shoulder and across the chest. The twisted cotton thread is slightly thinner than a pencil.) The guru's view of the custom was:

*Out of the cotton of compassion spin the thread of contentment. Tie ends of continence, give it the twist of truth. Make such a sacred thread for the mind. Such a thread once worn will never break nor get soiled, burnt or lost. The man who weareth such a thread is blessed.*

His mind was so fixed on God that he would constantly sing his praise and meditate on his name. To take him out of this mood, his father tried him in various professions. He was sent to a neighbouring town with 20 rupees to buy goods of common use and sell them at a profit. On the way he came across a group of faqirs (saints), who had been hungry for several days. Guru Nanak spent his money feeding them. He felt that he had struck a real bargain in doing so, as he understood that it was more profitable to feed mankind in need than to make purely monetary profit. His father did not understand the guru's reasoning and flew into a rage and slapped his son.

At the age of sixteen he married and had two sons. In the meantime he was sent to Sultanpur to his sister's village and was there put in charge of the state granary. His inward struggle reached a crisis when he was charged with recklessly giving away the grain. An inquiry was conducted, accounts were scrutinised and the grain was re-weighed. It showed a balance in favour of the guru. Vindicated, he tendered his resignation and decided to commit himself fully to spreading the message of God.

The first utterance of Nanak as he embarked on his mission was that there is no Hindu and no Muslim. He also preached the concept of one God (Ek Onkar).

His message was a simple one. He preached universal brotherhood under the fatherhood of God. He laid stress on the performance of duty. One must work for the good of all, and all must work and secure the good of each member of society. He sought to bring man back to the path of true and purified religion. He preached that: 'Truth is the highest virtue, but higher still is truthful living.'

To spread his message he undertook arduous and extensive tours in the north, south, east and west and visited important centres of Hindu, Muslim, Buddhist, Jain, Sufi and other religions, and met people of different races, tribes and diverse cultures.

Guru Nanak's life can be divided into three periods on the basis of his activities. The first period covers his childhood and early manhood, mostly spent in meditation; the second period was spent in travelling; and the last period was that of relatively settled life at Kartarpur (Kartar = God, pur = place), where he lived the life of an ordinary farmer.

The network of centres that Guru Nanak founded contained communities of inspired disciples, which in turn became the body of the Sikh faith, which he called Sangat. He established Sikh communities all over India and outside India in Ceylon, Tibet and the Middle East.

He emphasised the need for religious and social discipline. The Japji, Rehras and Kirtan Sohila were fixed as morning, evening and night prayers. He himself worked in his fields, and his disciples were advised and encouraged to have regular daily labour, to have normal relationships with their families and to give some of their income to good causes. His three golden rules are:

1 *Naam Japo,* meditate on God's name
2 *Kirt karo,* earn an honest living
3 *Wand Chhako,* share your earnings with the needy.

He also laid the foundation for *guru ke langar* (community kitchen). All worked for their living and gave a part of their earnings for the community kitchen. Everyone, Muslim or Hindu, king or pauper, Brahmin or low caste, had to sit together in the langar as they ate their meals.

The birthday of Guru Nanak is one of the most important festivals in the Sikh calendar.

## Martyrdom of Guru Teg Bahadur

Guru Teg Bahadur was the ninth guru of the Sikhs and son of Guru Hargobind, the sixth guru. He toured the whole of the Punjab, Delhi, Eastern India and Assam, preaching the message of the fatherhood of God and the brotherhood of man, as it was preached by Guru Nanak. The Mughal ruler of the time was Aurangzeb. who was actively using the machinery of state to quicken the process of Islamisation among his subjects, who were mainly Hindus. Many Hindu schools were closed, temples demolished, and mosques built on the sites. Taxes were imposed on non-Muslims when visiting their own holy places, and *Jazia,* another tax, was imposed on all non-Muslims. Those who could not pay were forcibly converted.

A group of Hindu Brahmins under the leadership of Kirpa Ram came from Kashmir with the news that the ruler of that place was forcibly converting people by breaking their sacred threads and wiping their marks off their foreheads – two important signs of the high-caste Hindu. They said that they had heard about Guru Teg Bahadur as their only saviour and had come to seek his help.

When the guru heard this tale of oppression, he is said to have remarked that this situation could only be relieved through the sacrifice of a holy person. His nine-year-old son, Gobind Rai, who later became the tenth guru, remarked, 'Who is holier than you to make this sacrifice, Father?' At this point, Guru Teg Bahadur told the Kashmiri Brahmins to return and tell the ruler that they would change their faith only if Guru Teg Bahadur became a convert.

Guru Teg Bahadur's martyrdom is seen by the Sikhs not only as the act of a man accepting death for his own beliefs, but also on behalf of another religion and for the promotion of religious liberty as a principle.

Guru Gobind Singh composed these verses about his father's sacrifice:

*To preserve their caste marks and sacred threads,*
*Did he in the dark age perform the supreme sacrifice.*
*He went to the utmost limit to help the saintly,*
*He gave his head but never cried in pain.*

The Sikhs have now built a gurdwara at the place of execution. This martyrdom day is celebrated with great fervour and enthusiasm in Delhi, with a procession taking place one day before the event. Celebrations are held in the gurdwaras, on the actual day in India and on the nearest Sunday in the West, with hymn-singing, discourses, lectures and the distribution of sacred food.

## Guru Gobind Singh

Guru Gobind Singh was the tenth guru of the Sikhs. He was born at Patna in the Bihar state of India on 22 December 1666. The language of the area had a great impact upon his poetry, although he also studied Sanskrit, Persian and Arabic.

As a child he used to have mock battles with other children on the banks of the Ganges and was noted as a great marksman whose arrows never missed the target. At the age of seven he went to Anandpur in Punjab, where arrangements were made for further study of languages. He also learnt archery and swordsmanship.

He became guru at the age of nine after the martyrdom of Guru Teg Bahadur, and began to consolidate his position as the spiritual head of the community. He lived at Patna on the banks of the Yamuna from 1682 to 1686 and engaged in literary pursuits. There he composed the Jaap Sahib and other compositions. He directed the translation of several Sanskrit and Persian classics into Brij Bhasha. Brij Bhasha is a vernacular form of Hindi in which a number of devotional hymns were composed for the benefit of the masses who had no knowledge of classical Sanskrit or Persian. He had 52 court poets and most of them helped in the translations. He composed poetry, which is compiled in the Dasam Granth.

On Baisakhi Day 1699, he created the Khalsa on a famous occasion when five beloved ones presented themselves at his command. The sacred ceremony is described in the Baisakhi festival entry on page 113.

Guru Gobind Singh revolutionised the passive resistance movement and introduced the concept of Saint Soldier. He stressed common worship, common place of pilgrimage, common baptism for all classes, and common external appearance. In this way he brought unity among his followers and created the slogan 'The Khalsa belongs to God, victory belongs to God'.

On 7 October 1708, he called his followers together, placed five paises (coins) and a coconut before the Guru Granth Sahib, the Holy Book, and bowed to it as his successor. He told the congregation to behold Guru Granth Sahib as the living Guru and spiritual guide. He instructed the Sikhs to:

1   Worship only one God
2   Study Guru Granth Sahib as the spirit of the Guru
3   Regard the Khalsa as the visible body of the Guru.

'Where there is five,' he said, 'the Guru will be present.' Guru Granth Sahib is the everlasting Guru of the Sikhs.

Guru Gobind Singh's birthday is celebrated throughout the world, wherever there is a Sikh community. On this day, his life story is told to the congregation and hymns are sung in his memory.

# BUDDHISM

## AN INTRODUCTION TO BUDDHISM

Buddhism is the great oriental religion founded in India in the sixth century BCE by Siddharta Gautama, who is generally known as the Buddha or 'Enlightened One'.

In his first sermon – 'The Turning of the Wheel of Law' – the Buddha expounded the fundamental ideas on which his teaching is based. These are the Four Noble Truths, namely:

- The Noble Truth of Suffering
- The Noble Truth of the Cause of Suffering
- The Noble Truth of the Cessation of Suffering
- The Noble Truth of the Path that leads to the Cessation of Suffering.

The cessation of suffering is nirvana. For Buddhists, nirvana is the final goal of all human endeavour. It refers to a state of being in which lust, ignorance, hatred and egoism become extinct, and all human qualities are perfected.

Nirvana can be reached by following the Middle Way, which lies between the two extremes of hedonism and ascetic austerities. It is also known as the Noble Eightfold Path and consists of Right View, Right Thought, Right Speech, Right Action, Right Livelihood, Right Effort, Right Mindfulness and Right Concentration.

Traditionally, Buddhists have expressed their faith by taking refuge in the Buddha, his teachings (*dhamma*) and in the Sangha (assembly of Buddhists) who, from the very early times, helped to preserve the teachings of Buddha.

Buddhism in the modern world survives in three major forms. The early Theravada form is practised in Sri Lanka, Burma, Thailand, Laos and Cambodia. The later Mahayana form prevails in China, Vietnam, Japan, Korea and Mongolia. The form of Buddhism that developed in Tibet is often referred to as Vajrayana or Mantrayana.

Buddhism in the Theravada tradition is primarily a spiritual philosophy and a system of ethics. The goal of the faithful is to achieve nirvana and this state of spiritual perfection can be achieved through practice of humility, generosity, mercy, abstention from violence, and self-control.

In the Theravada tradition, each individual is expected to work out his own salvation. Religion, in Theravada countries, plays an important role in the critical stages of an individual's life cycle, such as birth, initiation, marriage and death. Monastic institutions are well established and play an integral part in the life of the community.

Mahayanists regard Gautama Buddha as one manifestation of an eternal, cosmic Buddha who appears at different times in order to make known the *dhamma* or liberating law.

In the Mahayana tradition, the ideal person is the Bodhisattva who achieves times in order to make known the dhamma or liberating law.enlightenment after great striving but defers entering nirvana in order to serve and save other suffering mortals. As the Bodhisattva ideal developed, so did the pantheon of Buddhas and Bodhisattvas who became the objects of faith and devotion. One of the most important Bodhisattvas is Avalokiteswara – the embodiment of compassion, who is believed to reincarnate in the Dalai Lama of Tibet.

The form of Buddhism introduced into Tibet was a synthesis of the Theravada, Mahayana and Hindu Tantric ideas and practices. It became even more complex by absorbing elements of the indigenous Bon religion, which was a form of nature worship. Tibetan Buddhism is associated with a voluminous body of scriptures, esoteric teachings, ritual and ceremonial. Great importance was given to the role of the teacher or lama.

# Rites of Passage

Buddhism has tended to merge into the everyday life of the countries where it has taken root. Consequently, there are no universal Buddhist birth, marriage and death ceremonies. Each country and sect has its own traditions and customs and the extent to which the monks and nuns are involved in the conduct of these ceremonies also varies.

## Coming of age

There are no specific ceremonies that mark the transition from childhood to adult status, although in Thailand young men often spend a short period of time in a monastery.

## Ordination

Ordination as a Buddhist monk (bhikhu) involves submission to the monastic rules derived from the teachings of the Buddha. When a new monk is ordained, he becomes a member of a distinctive lineage that can very often be traced back to the Buddha himself.

In Theravada Buddhist countries, the monks are easily recognised, because they wear the characteristic orange robe, shave their heads and walk barefoot. A newly ordained monk is given a new name and robe and is required to abide by the *Vinaya,* or code of 227 rules.

The bhikhu live a strict and simple life of meditation, study and work. They engage in the important tasks of teaching and assisting lay people and conducting ceremonies. They do not earn money and own few possessions. They are enjoined to work hard, have short hours of sleep, and eat only one meal a day. They are not, however, required to take the vow of remaining in a monastery for the rest of their lives.

In Mahayana Buddhist countries, there are two main branches: the Tibetan, with monks wearing the characteristic maroon robes; and the Far East, which also has an unbroken line of nuns, in which the monks' robes are black or grey.

## Wedding Ceremonies

Weddings are generally conducted as secular events in Buddhist countries. It is, however, customary to obtain blessings from monks at a local temple after the civil registration formalities have been completed.

Traditionally, marriages are solemnised before a specially erected shrine, complete with an image of the Buddha, candles, incense sticks and flowers. The bridal couple and their friends and relatives recite the Vandana, Tisarana and Panchsila, Buddhist prayers, in English or Pali (the ancient language of the Buddhist scriptures). The couple then light the candles and incense sticks and offer flowers to the Buddha image. The bride and groom in turn recite the traditional undertakings expected of them.

The marriage vows taken by the husband are as follows:

*Towards my wife I undertake to love and respect her, be kind and considerate, be faithful, delegate domestic management, provide gifts to please her.*

The bride is expected to respond as follows:

*Towards my husband I undertake to perform my household duties efficiently, be hospitable to my in-laws and friends of my husband, be faithful, protect and invest our earnings, discharge my responsibilities lovingly and conscientiously.*

Finally, all those gathered at the wedding recite the Mangala Sutta, a special prayer or hymn to sanctify the marriage, and Jayamangala Gatha as a blessing.

## Funeral Rites

One of the basic teachings of Buddhism is that existence is suffering, whether birth, daily living, old age or dying. Funeral rites are the most elaborate of all the lifecycle ceremonies and the ones entered into most fully by the followers of Buddhism.

Lay people rely upon monks to chant the sutras – religious discourses and instruction traditionally believed to have come from the Buddha – that will benefit the deceased and to conduct all funeral rites and memorial services. The idea that death is suffering, relieved only by the knowledge that it is universal, gives an underlying mood of resignation to funerals. Only a select few can hope for nirvana. For the vast majority, there is the expectation of rebirth either in this world or in some other plane of existence. Over the basic mood of gloom, beliefs that meritorious acts can aid the condition of the departed soul have arisen.

In Thailand and other south-east Asian countries, when a person is dying, an effort is made to fix his mind upon the Buddhist scriptures or one of the names of the Buddha. It is hoped that the fruit of this meritorious act will bring good to the deceased in their new existence.

When death occurs, the relatives may set up a wailing, to express sorrow and to notify the neighbours, who then come to help.

The dead body is bathed and then placed in a coffin and surrounded with wreaths, candles and incense sticks. Sometimes a photograph of the deceased is also placed alongside, and coloured lights are suspended about the coffin.

Theravada Buddhists follow the Hindu custom of cremation. In northern Thailand, cremation takes place within three days. Before the funeral procession begins, monks chant a prayer at the home of the deceased and then precede the coffin out of the house. There is a belief that the dead person should not leave the house by the usual exit. Consequently, the coffin is either removed through a hole in the wall or floor or the front entrance to the house is carpeted with green leaves to make it appear different from the usual.

A man carrying a white banner on a long pole often leads the procession to the crematorium grounds. He is followed by elderly males carrying flowers in silver bowls and then by a group of monks holding a broad ribbon (*bhusa yong*), which extends to the coffin. Portions from the *Abhidharma* are recited en route. The coffin may be carried by pall bearers or conveyed in a funeral car drawn by a large number of friends and relatives who, in doing so, are performing their last service for the deceased and engaging in a meritorious act as well.

The *Abhidharma* or *Abhidamma-pitaka* is the third part of the Pali canon known as the *Tripitaka*. The first part, the *Vinaya-pitaka*, describes the life of the Buddha and the origin of the monastic order, as well as the rules of discipline for the monks. The second part, known as the *Sutta-pitaka*, deals with the teachings of the Buddha and the monks and also contains 547 legends and stories from previous existences of the Buddha. The seven books of the *Abhidharma* deal with complex philosophical and doctrinal issues. It is intended for the monks rather than for lay followers of Buddhism.

After the chanting, the coffin is placed on a pyre made of brick. Lighted torches, candles, incense sticks and fragrant wood are tossed beneath the coffin to set light to it. Later, the ashes are collected and kept in an urn.

Occasionally, the cremation may be deferred for a week to allow distant relatives to attend the ceremony. The bodies of wealthy or prominent people may be kept for a year or more in a special building at a temple. In such cases, a series of memorial services are held on the seventh, fiftieth and hundredth days after the death. These services provide an opportunity for the relatives and friends to show respect to the deceased, as well as to perform religious rites that will benefit the departed soul.

Tibetan Buddhists believe that as soon as death has occurred, the personality goes into a state of trance for four days. During this period, known as the First Bardo, the lamas recite special prayers to reach the person. It is believed that towards the end of this time the dead person will see a brilliant light. If the radiance does not terrify, then the person will not be born again.

The Second Bardo begins at the point when the person becomes conscious that death has occurred. The actions and thoughts of a lifetime pass in front of them. Then comes the Third Bardo, which is the state of seeking another birth. All previous thoughts and actions direct the person to choose new parents who will give them their next body.

In the Mahayana tradition of Buddhism, to which most Chinese Buddhists subscribe, it is believed that between death and rebirth there is an intermediate period that is critical in determining the form that the rebirth shall take. If the family ensures that proper assistance in the form of prayer and remembrance ceremonies are duly performed, the departed is better able to take a favourable rebirth.

## Pilgrimage

The Buddhist scriptures mention four holy places to which pilgrimages may be undertaken as a meritorious act. These are the Buddha's birthplace (Lumbini Gardens), the place where he found enlightenment (Bodh Gaya), the place where he preached his first sermon (Sarnath) and the place where he died (Kusingara). In China, there are four sacred mountains, each one associated with a particular Bodhisattva.

Mount Kailash in Tibet is another important destination for pilgrims. Legend has it that Milarepa, Tibet's most prominent Buddhist sage, challenged a representative of the Bon religion to a race to the top of this mountain. By virtue of winning the contest through the use of his spiritual powers, he succeeded in establishing the pre-eminence of Buddhism in Tibet.

# BUDDHIST FESTIVALS

There are many special or holy days observed throughout the year by Buddhists. Many of these days celebrate the birthdays of the Boddhisattvas in the Mahayana tradition or significant events in the life of the Buddha. The most important celebrations take place on the night of the full moon in May, when Buddhists all over the world commemorate the birth, enlightenment and death of the Buddha. This is known as Buddha Day, Vesak or Vaisakhapuja.

With the exception of the Japanese, most Buddhists use the lunar calendar, and the dates of Buddhist festivals vary from country to country as well between the various Buddhist traditions. Thus, for instance, the Buddhist New Year is celebrated in the Theravada countries of Thailand, Burma, Sri Lanka, Cambodia and Laos for three days from the first full moon day in April. The Chinese, Koreans and Vietnamese celebrate the New Year in late January or early February, according to the lunar calendar; whereas the Tibetan Buddhist New Year begins a month later.

Buddhist festivals are always joyful occasions. People usually go to the local temple or monastery and offer food to the monks, participate in congregational prayers and chanting, and listen to discourses on the Buddhist dharma.

## Theravada Festivals

Observance days are on new and full moon days, with a lesser observance on the eighth day half-moons. All festivals are on full moon days and are named after the ancient lunar months in which they fall. On observance days, Buddhists may visit their nearest monastery to make offerings and engage in intense religious activity.

Most Theravada festivals include the practice of *Paritta*, a chanting ceremony performed for protection from negative influences. This may be performed by monks on behalf of the laity and can range in duration from an hour to two days. The monks sit on chairs connected by threads, and pots of water are placed around the area. At the end of the chanting, the threads connecting the chairs are cut into short lengths and tied around the wrists and necks of the people who attend the ceremony, and the water from the pots is sprinkled over them.

## Mahayana Festivals

Every new moon is Shakyamuni Buddha Day. Every full moon the Amitabha Buddha and the Buddha's enlightenment and Parinirvana are celebrated. Amitabha is the Buddha of 'immeasurable light'. One of the five 'meditation Buddhas' or 'Dhyani Buddhas' of Mahayana Buddhism, he is regarded as the ruler of the Pure Land to which the setting sun carries the souls of the dying. Devotees worship Amitabha, reciting his name or his mantra and do meditation practices that include concentrating on him and his Pure Land, a world in which everything helps in the practice of the Buddha's teachings and in the attainment of enlightenment. In Japan, Amitabha is known as Amida. Chinese and Japanese Buddhists celebrate the Bodhisattva of Compassion (Kuan Yin) on the 19th of the 2nd, 6th and 9th full moons.

Tibetan Buddhist festivals are also governed by the lunar calendar.

The Zen calendar, which is fixed and does not depend on the lunar calendar, includes the following special dates:

| | |
|---|---|
| 15 February | The Buddha's Parinirvana (Passing) |
| 8 April | The Buddha's birthday |
| 3 October | Bodhidharma's Day |
| 8 December | The Buddha's enlightenment |

## Uposatha Observance Days

Uposatha days are times of renewed dedication to dharma practice, observed by both lay people and monastics throughout the world of Theravada Buddhism.

For monastics, these are often days of more intensive reflection and meditation. On new moon and full moon days, the fortnightly confession and recitation of the *Patimokkha* (monastic rules of conduct) takes place.

Lay people observe the eight precepts (Noble Eightfold Path) on Uposatha days, as a support for meditation practice and as a way to re-energise commitment to the dharma. Whenever possible, lay people would visit their local monastery, to make special offerings to the Sangha, to listen to dharma, and to practise meditation.

The calendar of Uposatha days is calculated using a complicated traditional formula that is loosely based on the astronomical (lunar) calendar, with the result that the dates do not always coincide with the actual astronomical dates. To further confuse matters, each sect within Theravada Buddhism tends to follow its own calendar.

## Maghapuja or Dharma Day

This festival, also called All Saints' Day, commemorates three events in the Buddha's life, namely: the occasion when he took his two chief disciples, the occasion when he recited the rules by which monks should live, and his announcement that he would die in three months' time. It is usually celebrated in a monastery in the presence of monks. It occurs on the full moon of the third lunar month.

## Mahayana Parinirvana

The anniversary of the Buddha's death or liberation (Mahayana Parinirvana) is commemorated in all Buddhist countries, although there are different interpretations of the date on which this event is believed to have occurred.

In the Theravada Buddhist tradition, the Buddha's birth, enlightenment and death are observed on the same day. (These events occur in May/June, although the actual date varies each year.)

A candlelit procession around the temple is the most usual way the laity observe the anniversary of the Buddha's death/liberation in Theravada Buddhist countries such as Thailand and Sri Lanka.

In Mahayana Buddhist countries such as Japan, the death anniversary of the Buddha is celebrated on the same day every year. In many Zen Buddhist temples, all lights in the great meditation hall are extinguished on this day (also known as Nehar).

The entire congregation meditates and chants from special Buddhist texts and scriptures, and finally the lamps are re-lit. This ritual expresses the hope that the teachings of the Buddha will endure for all time.

## Avalokitesvara's Birthday (Kuan Yin)

Celebrations are held on the full moon day in March on the birthday of the Bodhisattva Avalokitesvara. He represents the ideal of compassion in the Mahayana Buddhist tradition.

## Higan

The spring and autumn equinoxes are important days in the Japanese calendar. They not only mark the seasonal changes but also symbolise the spiritual transition from the world of suffering (samsara) to the world of enlightenment (nirvana). Dead friends and relatives are particularly remembered at these times and special ceremonies are held to transfer merit to the departed.

## Hana Matsuri

This festival commemorates the Buddha's birthday according to the Zen Buddhist tradition. In Japan, images of the infant Buddha are washed with a special sweet tea made from hydrangea leaves. In large temples great numbers of priests take part in these rituals.

## Vaisakhapuja or Vesak

This is the most important festival in the Theravada Buddhist tradition. It commemorates three important events in the Buddha's life – his birth, enlightenment and death.

This is a time when people try especially hard to live up to the teachings of the Buddha. Kindness and generosity are two virtues that are particularly emphasised.

In all Theravada Buddhist countries, the festival is marked by much colour and gaiety. Homes are cleaned and decorated for the occasion. People visit temples to make offerings, and statues of the Buddha are washed with scented water. Streets and homes are lit with lanterns and, in Sri Lanka, there are various street entertainments and pageants. In Thailand, the day's celebrations usually come to an end with joyous candlelit processions around the local temples.

## Poson

This festival marks the bringing of Buddhism to Sri Lanka by the missionary Mahinda. The main feature of the celebrations is the Mininda Perahara, when important events in the life of Mahinda are re-enacted.

## Kandy Perahara

Kandy Perahara or Asalha Perahara is probably the most spectacular festival day for Sri Lankan Buddhists. This ten-day festival, celebrated in the ancient highland capital of Kandy, has religious and national significance. From the Temple of the Tooth, a casket containing a sacred tooth relic of the Buddha is paraded in a colourful procession of elephants, dancers and musicians. It takes place some time in August.

## Asalhapuja or Dhammacakka

This festival falls on the full moon day of the month of Asalha. It celebrates the first sermon of Buddha and the setting of the Wheel of Truth (Dhammacakka) into the world.

## Rains Retreat

The Rains Retreat, which begins on the full moon day in July and extends until October, is observed in all Theravada Buddhist countries. This is the time of year when monks settle down in a monastery or sheltered place and spend the time in prayer and contemplation. At the end of the Rains Retreat, it is customary for the laity to present the monks with new robes.

Pavarana (Sangha Day) is observed on the last day of the Rains Retreat. This is the occasion when *bhikkhus* (monks) invite the Sangha (assembly of Buddhists) to inform them of their faults.

## Ulambana (Ancestor Day)

This is celebrated in the Mahayana tradition from the first to the fifteenth days of the eighth lunar month. It is believed that the gates of Hell are opened on the first day and the ghosts may visit the world for fifteen days. Food offerings are made during this time to relieve the sufferings of these ghosts. On the fifteenth day (Ulambana) people visit cemeteries to make offerings to departed ancestors. Many Theravada Buddhists in Cambodia, Laos and Thailand also observe this festival. The Japanese Buddhist festival, Obon, beginning on 13 July and lasting for three days, also celebrates the reunion of the living with their dead ancestors.

## Kathina

The Kathina ceremony is observed in Thailand during October/November every year. During the week-long celebrations, the king and members of the Thai royal family visit nine monasteries around the country. A Kathina robe is offered in each monastery to the monk nominated by the abbot as the most virtuous one.

The Kathina ceremony is the only calendrical Buddhist festival authorised in the earliest scriptures.

## Enlightenment of the Buddha

When Gautama left his palace in search of spiritual enlightenment, he spent the first six or seven years in intense and austere religious practices. The decisive turning point before he achieved enlighement was his realisation of the futility of such practices. Insead he focused on discipling the mind through meditation. it was while he was in deep contemplation under the bo tree (fig tree) that he finally found the enlightenment he had been seeking, namely the cause of human suffering and the way of salvation. From this point on, he came to be know as the Buddha, or Enlightened One.

# JAINISM

## AN INTRODUCTION TO JAINISM

Jainism is one of three major religions that developed in ancient India. It probably had its roots in a strand of the 'renouncer' tradition, which appeared in India around the eighth century BCE as a reaction against the highly ritualistic form of Brahmanical Hinduism. The beliefs that form the core of Jainism, however, were given shape in the sixth century BCE by Vardhamana Mahavira, a contemporary of the Buddha.

Legend has it that Mahavira, the son of a warrior chieftain, left his home at the age of thirty in search of salvation from the cycle of birth, death and rebirth. After twelve years of wandering, during which time he practised rigorous austerities, he found enlightenment and became 'a perfect soul' or 'conqueror' – *Jina*.

Mahavira gained royal patronage and popular support for his new doctrine of salvation and his followers came to be known as Jainas or 'followers of the conqueror'. He is believed to have died at the age of 72 by the rite of *sallekhana* (voluntary starvation).

Jainism is essentially an atheistic, ascetic discipline, which places great emphasis on physical austerities and self-inflicted pain as a means of freeing oneself from the cycle of birth and death. Intentions and actions in this life determine the nature and quality of the next. The cycle of birth and rebirth is broken only when perfection is reached.

According to Jain cosmography, the universe is eternal and moves through a continuous cycle of progress and decline. Sin and sorrow in their milder forms began to appear in the third period and the need for spiritual guidance was felt. Twenty-four *Tirthankaras* – 'ford builders' or 'enlightened souls' – appeared on earth to preach the Jain doctrines. The last of the Tirthankaras was Mahavira.

The Jains believe that the entire universe is full of life and that even the four elements – earth, water, air and fire – are animated by souls. The Jain code of ethics is directed towards the avoidance of injury to any living being.

The principle of *ahimsa* or the avoidance of violence or injury, expresses itself in various ways. Vegetarianism is one practice that continues to endure among Jains. Monks and ascetics cover their mouths with a small mask to preserve the life of the air itself and to avoid breathing in any of the small insects of the air.

Image worship was introduced at an early stage in the history of Jainism. The construction of shrines and temples came to be regarded as a pious act, and many of these temples are remarkable for their rich and intricate ornamentation.

Although Mahavira rejected the authority of the Hindu sacred texts, the efficacy of ritual sacrifice and the underlying rationale of the Hindu caste system, temple worship among the Jains has been greatly influenced by Hindu practices. Jain temples contain images of the Tirthankaras as well as many of the Hindu gods, and it is customary to chant hymns of praise and sacred formulae as well as to make offerings of fruits, flowers and grain.

Around 300 BCE, the Jaina monastic community was split into two main sects: the *Digambaras* or 'sky-clad' who believed in total reincarnation of all material things, including articles of clothing; and the *Swetambaras,* who are usually dressed in white cotton garments. A seventeenth-century offshoot of the Swetambaras, the *Sthanakvasis,* allow little compromise over the rigorous discipline laid down in the Jain scriptures and tend to reject image worship and other practices that have crept into the religion with the passage of time.

## JAIN FESTIVALS

Principal Jain festivals are linked to major events in the lives of the Tirthankaras, particularly Rishabha (the first Tirthankara), Mahavira and his immediate predecessor, Parshva. The birthdate and death/liberation date of Mahavira, in the months of Chaitra (March/April) and Kattika (October/November) respectively, are widely celebrated by all Jain communities.

Monthly fast dates are also observed, the most significant of these being Akshayatrtiya (the immortal third), celebrated in the month of Vaisakha (April/May) and commemorating the first giving of alms to Rishabha, the first Tirthankara.

## Paryushana

This is the most important Jain festival. It is celebrated for eight days by Swetambaras or ten days by Digambaras, in the month of Bhadrapada (August/September). During this period, lay persons perform austerities on the ascetic model. On Samvatsari, the final day of Paryushana, it is customary for individuals to confess their transgressions of the past year, and letters are written and visits paid for the purpose of asking and extending forgiveness.

## Mahamastak Abhishek

The grand anointing ceremony of Bahubali, the first of the Jain Tirthankaras, takes place once every twelve years in the town of Shravana Belagola in the state of Karnataka, India. The last annointing was on 19 December 1993, so the next date will be in 2005. The festivities begin at dawn with the placing of 1,008 small metal bowls containing water at the foot of an 18-metre-high statue of Bahubali or Gomateshwara which was installed in this town in 981 CE. Priests chanting sacred hymns arrange the pots in a traditional geometrical pattern. Devotees then lift these pots and climb up the 600 steps to the top of the statue and position themselves on the scaffolding.

The statue is bathed with milk, sugarcane juice and therapeutic herbal lotions, and anointed with sandalwood and saffron paste. Gold, silver and precious gemstones are offered in reverence. As the grand finale to this spectacular ceremony conducted to the accompaniment of drums, trumpets and clashing cymbals, flowers are showered on the statue from a helicopter and consecrated water is sprinkled on the congregation from the devotees on the scaffolding.

# THE BAHA'I FAITH

## AN INTRODUCTION TO THE BAHA'I FAITH

The Baha'i faith was founded in the late 1850s by Mirza Husayn Ali. He called himself Baha'ullah or 'Glory of God' and, after several mystical experiences, believed he was a manifestation of God, sent to interpret the divine message for a new era. The primary sources of Baha'i doctrine and practice are the writings of Baha'ullah and the authorised interpretations of these by his successors.

The Baha'i faith is founded upon a belief in an all-powerful omniscient being who created the entire universe. Man has always been aware of a mysterious power in the universe and has developed complex, abstract ideas about the first cause through which creation came into being. However, Baha'i teachings declare that the essential nature of God is beyond human comprehension except through the medium of 'manifestations' or highly spiritual individuals who appeared at various periods in human history, charged with a messianic mission. Baha'ullah is believed to be the manifestation of God for the present age. Previous manifestations include Abraham, Moses, Krishna, Zoroaster, the Buddha, Jesus Christ, Mohammed and the Bab, a powerful spiritual leader who inspired Baha'ullah. The Baha'is believe that Baha'ullah will be succeeded in future ages by other manifestations who build upon the teachings of their predecessors but adapt their mission to the circumstances.

The core of Baha'i theology is 'evolution in time and unity in the present hour'. All phenomena including the revelations of God, are subject to the process of evolution. World unity is the last stage in the evolution of mankind and the purpose of the Baha'i faith is to foster this unity.

Baha'ullah categorically rejected the notion of sin and evil. In Baha'i eschatology, Heaven and Hell are spiritual states rather than physical entities. Heaven is the state of perfection and harmony with God's will; Hell is the absence of such harmony.

The Baha'i religion is characterised by the total absence of public rituals or sacraments. However, followers of the faith are expected to observe certain rituals in the course of their daily lives. An important aspect of daily worship are the obligatory prayers, which must be recited at prescribed times during the day.

Practising Baha'is are also expected to read daily from the writings of the Bab and Baha'ullah. Time must also be set aside each day for meditation and quiet contemplation.

The religious duties of a Baha'i also include assembling on the first day of each month in the Baha'i calendar in the home of a member of the community to celebrate the Feast of the Nineteenth Day. The occasion is a form of social exchange where congregational worship and the sharing of food assume great symbolic significance.

The nineteenth month of the Baha'i calendar is particularly important. Followers of the faith are expected to fast from dawn to sunset throughout the month.

### Fasting

Fasting is undertaken from 2 to 20 March, with abstinence from food and drink between sunrise and sunset. This is a period of meditation, prayer, spiritual recuperation and a symbolic reminder of abstinence from selfish and carnal desires. Fasting is only undertaken by those of the age of maturity (15 years).

## Pilgrimage

Pilgrimage is to the Baha'i holy places in Haifa, Israel, and is obligatory for Baha'is if they can afford it and are physically able to do so.

## Feast of the Nineteenth Day

This marks the first day of the Baha'i month, bringing together the Baha'is community of the locality for worship, consultation and fellowship.

## Birth and Naming

There are no specific ceremonies or rituals for the birth or naming of a child.

## Marriage

Baha'is are free to choose their marriage partner, but must obtain the consent of their living parents or guardians, as marriage is seen as the union of two families as well as two individuals.

The Baha'i marriage ceremony is chosen by the couple and may take any desired form but must include the Baha'i marriage vows, which are repeated by the couple in front of witnesses.

## Death Customs and Funeral Rites

The body is the temple of the spirit and must be respected and treated with honour. Under Baha'i law, cremation is forbidden and the body must not be transported more than one hour's journey from the place of death. The body should be wrapped in a shroud of silk or cotton and a ring, bearing a specific inscription, should be placed on the deceased's finger. The body is placed in a coffin made of crystal, stone or hard fine wood.

A specific Prayer for the Dead is to be said before internment. Baha'is are instructed to write a will and are free to dispose of their wealth in any way they wish.

# IMPORTANT ANNIVERSARIES AND HOLY DAYS

There are no prescribed ceremonies for the commemoration of holy days, but many Baha'i communities combine a devotional programme with fellowship or appropriate social activities.

## Baha'i New Year

21 March is the first day of the Baha'i year and it is known as Naw-Ruz, which literally means 'new day'. It is a time for rejoicing, as it also signals the end of the month of fasting. It begins at sunset on 20 March, and can take any form, provided there are a few prayers, and then there can be dancing, a musical performance or other celebrations. It is a Baha'i holy day when no work is to be done.

## Festival of Ridvan

Ridvan is the twelve-day festival commemorating Baha'ullah's declaration of his mission to his companions and is celebrated annually from 21 April through to 2 May. Baha'ullah acclaimed Ridvan as the 'most great festival'. The first, ninth and twelfth days of Ridvan are celebrated as holy days on which work is suspended.

## The First Day of Ridvan

This is the most important day in the Baha'i year. After the death of the Bab (the Gate), his followers were known as the Babis, and they gradually came to look upon one of his followers, Baha'ullah, as their leader. The Muslim authorities decided to kill off the movement altogether by sending the leader into exile to a series of countries belonging to the Ottoman Empire. The first stage of his exile was in Baghdad, in what is now Iraq, but they gave no indication at that time as to his next destination.

Meanwhile, he camped in the open, in large tents in a public park, accompanied by an ever-growing crowd of Babis who wanted to be with him until the last possible moment. They were grieving at the imminent parting, but at some time during their stay in the park, he informed them that he was the one promised to them by the Bab, as 'Him whom God shall make manifest', and the weeping changed to ecstasy and joy, as everyone realised that they had been privileged to meet the Promised One, even if only briefly before they would lose him.

In their joy they called the park 'the garden of Paradise', which is equivalent to Rivdan, in the Persian language. This was the momentous birth of the Baha'i faith, the revelation given to Baha'ullah during his incarceration in a filthy dungeon some years previously, but which he kept secret until this time of the Ridvan festival. His advent is the culmination of all the promises of all religions, and there are many passages in all the holy books that relate to this time as being the time of the reconciliation of all faiths, and of universal peace as man comes to maturity. The time of prophecy is over, and the age of fulfilment begins. The founders of all previous faiths are revered as 'sitting on the same throne', and thus unity can become a reality.

On this day, throughout the world, the believers in every town, city or village meet to celebrate and to hold their annual elections for the nine members of their community to serve on the local spiritual assembly for one year. No canvassing is allowed, and the balloting is secret, resting solely upon the good character and spirituality of those who are elected.

## Ninth Day of Ridvan

On the ninth day of Ridvan, the family of Baha'ullah finished their preparations for the journey, and joined him. Prayers are said, and Baha'i history books may be read.

## Twelfth Day of Ridvan

On the twelfth day of Ridvan, Baha'ullah and his family left to go over the mountains, and through the winter snows, to the shores of the Black Sea, going on by boat and landing at Constantinople; then via Adrianople to Gallipoli, and by sea to Alexandria. Finally, they were shipped to Akka, where he was confined to the old prison barracks, in a room overlooking the sea, with not a green tree in sight. The Israelis have nowadays given this room to the Baha'is, where it is visited by Baha'i pilgrims from around the world, but nobody else may go there.

## Declaration of the Bab

A spiritual seeker, Mullah Husayn, arrived at the town of Shiraz, and was met by a young *siyyid* (a direct descendant of the prophet Mohammed) wearing a green turban; he seemed to have been expecting him, and invited the traveller to his home. They spent the evening in prayer, and eventually the host revealed to his guest that all the signs given to him by his teacher, and the conditions laid down, were fulfilled in the young siyyid, as being the one whose advent all the wise people of Islam awaited. He called himself the Bab (the Gate), and told Mullah Husayn that henceforth he would be known as the Bab-ul-Bab, which meant the Gate of the Gate.

The Bab further declared, 'This night, this very hour, shall, in the years to come, be regarded as one of the greatest festivals.' The very hour registered on the clock was two hours and eleven minutes after sunset on the evening of 23 May in the year 1844. The Bab cautioned his visitor to tell nobody about this meeting, for 17 other souls should spontaneously arise and find him, and together they would all constitute the 'Nineteen Letters of the Living', to bring the good news to all peoples. The Bab also said his sole purpose was to prepare the world for the Promised One of all faiths and the scriptural prophecies of the past, and he said, 'I am but a ring upon his finger.' The Baha'i era dates from that year, 1844 in the Western calendar. The Baha'is celebrate the day with joy, and send cards. Work is prohibited as it is a holy day.

## Ascension of Baha'ullah

After imprisonment in Akka for two years in the old barracks, from which he wrote letters to the ruling monarchs and leaders of the world, Baha'ullah, his son Abdu'l-Baha (Servant of the Glory) and his family were moved to various locations, and Baha'ullah was eventually given complete freedom, and enjoyed the great esteem of many people.

He died peacefully on the morning of 29 May 1892. He lies buried in a mansion in Bahji, surrounded by a beautiful garden, laid out in such a way as to symbolise the order in the world of the future.

Pilgrims to the Baha'i shrines in Israel visit the tomb to pray there. They come from all quarters of the globe. This solemn anniversary is often observed by reading or chanting from the scriptures. Work is suspended as it is a holy day.

## The Martyrdom of the Bab

During all the years of his brief ministry from the age of 25 to 31, the Bab was hounded and persecuted by the divines of the prevailing state religion, and consigned to bleak prisons in obscure parts of Iran, in the hope that he and his teachings would be forgotten. Eventually he was condemned to death, and the story of his execution is most extraordinary and worth telling.

One of his disciples begged to be allowed to share his fate, and this wish was granted. On the eve of his execution, the leader of the execution squad, a Christian, came to see the prisoner, and confessed to him that he did not personally harbour any grudge against him and did not want to kill him. The Bab said, 'If your intention be sincere, the Almighty is surely able to relieve you of your perplexity.'

When the hour came – 12 noon on 9 July 1850 – the Bab and his disciple were suspended (face to face, by ropes passing under their armpits) from a prominent pillar in the barrack square of Tabriz. Thousands of people stood on the walls, jeering. An Armenian firing squad lined up and fired and, when the smoke cleared, the Bab had gone, but his disciple was standing against the wall, unhurt. Only the ropes had been severed, and the Bab was found back in his cell, dictating notes to a secretary. The soldiers were so shaken by the 'miracle' that they all refused to try again. In due course, a new regiment was called in and the prisoners again tied up.

The Bab addressed the crowds: 'Had you believed in me, every one of you would have followed the example of this youth, who stood in rank above most of you, and would have willingly sacrificed himself in my path. The day will come when you will have recognised me; that day I shall have ceased to be with you.' And so they fired again and this time the bodies were riddled with bullets, but the faces little marred. The bodies were eventually rescued from a moat outside the town into which they had been thrown, and were hidden by faithful believers until, years later, the remains were interred on Mount Carmel in Israel, beneath the lovely golden-domed building known as the Queen of Carmel. The execution was at noon, and at that time all over the world the Baha'is read special prayers for the occasion, turning to stand in the direction of Haifa. This is a 'no-work' day.

## The Birthday of the Bab

The Bab was born on 20 October 1819 in Shiras, Persia. As his father died when he was still a baby, he was brought up by a maternal uncle. One day he was sent home from school because his teacher considered that there was nothing more he could teach him. The uncle thought the child must have behaved badly, but the teacher said that the pupil knew more than he did – the fact being that he had innate knowledge.

The Bab was a direct descendant of the Prophet Mohammed, and therefore was entitled to wear the traditional green turban. He has been described as being sweet and gentle mannered, of noble character, and great personal beauty. He was trained in commerce, and was known for his fair dealings.

The believers celebrate this event with reverence and joy, in community gatherings.

## The Birthday of Baha'ullah

Baha'ullah was born Mirza Husayn before sunrise on 12 November 1817, of a wealthy family, and his father was a minister of state at the court of the Shah of Persia (Iran). Upon his death when his son was 22 years old, the post was offered to the young man, who turned it down, and the prime minister said, 'But I am convinced that he is destined for some lofty career …' Baha'ullah accepted the mission of the Bab and accordingly suffered the fate of thousands of those who thought as he did, and was imprisoned under awful conditions. However, it was in the dungeon that he experienced his revelation.

His birthday is celebrated with parties as well as the community gathering. Gifts are given, and cards sent to friends overseas. Work is suspended on this day.

## Day of the Covenant

This is an anniversary, not a holy day. When Baha'ullah died, he left a will and testament decreeing that the believers should turn to his eldest son, whom he referred to as the 'Most Great Branch', the 'Branch from the Ancient Root', 'The Master', and the 'Centre of the Covenant'. It ensured that there should be no divergence of opinion among the believers and no split in the community, as all turned to

Abdu'l-Baha for guidance. In his turn, Abdu'l-Baha appointed his eldest grandson to be the sole interpreter of his words and those of Baha'ullah. 'The Guardian', as he was called, left provision for the election of the Universal House of Justice, which Abdu'l-Baha had outlined and said, 'Whatever they say is of God. Whoever obeys them has obeyed God, and whoever has disobeyed them has disobeyed God.' Abdu'l-Baha is known as the 'Centre of the Covenant', and as the perfect exemplar of the faith.

This is celebrated on 26 November. It is not essential to avoid work as it is not a holy day.

## Ascension of Abdu'l-Baha

In 1921, in Haifa, Israel (then Palestine), Abdu'l-Baha suffered years of imprisonment, before being set free by the Young Turks Rising, after which he travelled to the West, including Britain, where he met with many important people who flocked to see him and discuss various problems with him. At home in Palestine he was known as the 'father of the poor'. He was knighted by the British Government for saving the people from famine during the First World War, by having saved up grain in anticipation of such an event. Many thousands of mourners came together for his funeral, representing all levels of society, including the High Commissioner, Sir Herbert Samuel, the Governor of Jerusalem; the consuls of various countries; the heads of the various religious communities, Jews, Christians, Muslims, Druzes, Egyptians, Greeks. The representatives of the Jews, Christians and Muslims raised their voices in eulogy and regret.

*So united were they in their acclamation of him as the wise educator and reconciler of the human race in this perplexed and sorrowful age, that there seemed to be nothing left for the Baha'is to say.*
Lady Blomfield

His funeral was truly the uniting of many peoples of all races, creeds and colours. He was interred in the shrine on Mount Carmel. The believers commemorate the event at about 1.30 a.m. on 28 November.

# National, Secular and Folk Festivals

### Ganjitsu – Japanese New Year

New Year's Day is celebrated with a morning visit to a shrine or temple. A family dinner, *the Osechi,* is eaten. This is cooked on New Year's Eve and placed in the *jyubaker* (special box). Included with the dinner is a traditional Japanese rice cake.

An ancient game, called hajoita, is played for Japanese pennies. The bats used for the game have colourful paintings on one side.

Parents 'spoil' their children a little on this day with cash gifts (otoshidama).

### Setsubon – Japanese Spring Festival

Special rituals are conducted to drive out evil spirits. A wooden rice measure containing beans is placed on the shrine by the head of the family household. As darkness falls, the beans are scattered around all the entrances of the house and in the dark corners. A small charm is then placed over each entrance to prevent the evil spirits from sneaking into the house.

### Tu B'Shevat

This marks the end of the heavy rain season in Israel and commemorates the 'New Year for Trees'. This minor festival has received new significance with the establishment of the modern state of Israel, where young children are encouraged to plant trees in celebration. Jewish children may attend school on this day.

### Chinese New Year

New Year's Day is the most important event in the Chinese calendar and marks the beginning of the first lunar month, which falls at the end of January or the beginning of February. The festivities generally last for two or three weeks, though the first week tends to be the most important.

A week before the New Year, the family will honour the kitchen god, and he then reports to Heaven on their conduct. While he is away the house must be thoroughly cleaned, debts should be paid, all food should be prepared, and the home decorated with flowers such as peach blossoms or jonquils. The kitchen god returns on New Year's Eve and firecrackers are let off.

For the New Year, people wear new clothes to represent the discarding of the old year and its misfortunes. Visits are made to relatives and friends with gifts of food and drink. Traditional foods include cakes made from rice flour or sesame seeds, and kumquats, which signify prosperity. The usual greeting to be heard at New Year is, in Cantonese (the most widely spoken Chinese dialect in Britain), 'Kung hay fat choy' (pronounced 'Goong hay fut choy') meaning 'May you prosper'. Another important custom at this time is the giving of money in red paper packets by married couples to unmarried relatives, friends and children. In Cantonese these are called *laisee* or *hungpow* and are believed to bring the recipient good luck.

The Lantern Festival on the first full moon of the New Year marks the end of the festivities. It celebrates the return of light, the coming of spring and the beginning of the growing season. Strings of lanterns of all shapes, sizes and colours are hung out to decorate homes and public places. Besides the family celebrations, there are also colourful community events, of which the most important are the dragon and lion dances.

A lion dance can be seen at New Year in London's Chinatown. The 'two-man' pantomime lion dances through the streets to the sound of gongs and drums and reaches up to take money in red packets hung outside shops. It is believed that to give the lion money and food, such as kumquats and lettuce, will bring the establishment good fortune during the year.

Each year is associated with an animal from Chinese astrology: 2001 is the year of the Snake; 2002 is the year of the Horse; 2003 is the year of the Goat; 2004 is the year of the Monkey; 2005 is the year of the Rooster; 2006 is the year of the Dog.

## Losar – Tibetan New Year

Losar is a three-day festival. On the first day, celebrations are restricted mainly to the family. On the second and third days, visits and gifts are exchanged with friends and relatives.

Houses are whitewashed and thoroughly cleaned, people wear new clothes, and special food is prepared. Good luck symbols such as dried ears of corn are placed in the house, and dishes of water and dough models called *torna* are placed in household shrines along with other offerings.

People visit monasteries to make offerings, and Buddhist monks conduct special religious ceremonies. A number of rituals are performed to drive away evil spirits, and alms are given to the poor. There is also much merrymaking with feasts, dancing and archery competitions.

2001 is the year 2128 in the Tibetan Buddhist calendar; 2005 is the year 2132.

## Holocaust Memorial Day

Holocaust Day on 27 January was instigated in 2001. It commemorates the millions of people who have died in mass atrocities around the world. The date is symbolic since it is the anniversary of the liberation of the Auschwitz concentration camp in Krakow, Poland, which was used by the Nazis during the Second World War to exterminate Jews and other minorities.

Civic as well as religious services are held throughout the world to remember the genocide of six million Jews in Nazi Germany, the slaughter of Armenians by the Turkish Ottoman Empire during the First World War as well as those massacred in more recent ethnic conflicts such as in Cambodia, Rwanda and the Balkans.

## Monlam Chenmo

Monlam Chenmo, the Great Prayer Festival, is celebrated in Tibet from the fourth day of the New Year until the twenty-fifth day. The fifteenth day Chonga Chopa is particularly spectacular. Scenes from the Buddha's life are sculpted in butter and coloured with vegetable dyes. The visual displays are accompanied by puppet shows and other street celebrations.

## Hina Matsuri

Hina Matsuri, the Japanese Dolls' Festival, was originally celebrated as the Girls' Festival. A display of beautiful dolls is the main feature of the celebrations. The ceremonial dolls are usually handed from generation to generation within a family, and are placed on display in the best room of the house. In addition to the dolls, exquisitely crafted miniature household articles are also displayed. The dolls most highly valued are the Daini-sana, which represent the emperor and empress, both dressed in elaborate court attire. When the festival (3 March) is over, the articles are carefully packed away and stored until the next year.

## April Fools' Day

All Fools' Day – the 'fun' day when people are tricked by others or sent on silly errands – is observed in many countries in Europe and Asia.

The origin of these practices is obscure. One explanation as to why it is so widespread is that 1 April marked the end of the spring equinox, when celebrations were held to mark the period when the sun's rays fall vertically on the equator, and day and night are of equal length all over the earth.

According to some British historians, 1 April marks the end of the New Year celebrations in the old calendar when New Year's Day was 25 March. Yet another explanation offered is that it is a remnant of an old Celtic rite.

## Qingming Festival

Qingming (pronounced 'Chingming'), or the Chinese Tomb-sweeping Festival, is not fixed by the lunar calendar, but occurs on the day the sun's longitude passes fifteen degrees at the start of one of the twenty-four sections of the solar year.

From early in the morning, people visit their ancestors' shrines and tombs, carrying with them offerings of incense, joss paper and food cooked specially for the dead. Family members sweep the tombs of their loved ones, clear the ground of weeds, plant a new tree and repaint faded inscriptions on the tombstone. Joss paper is distributed around the tombs as a mark of their visit. Imitation paper money and paper clothes may be burnt as sacrificial gifts for the ancestors.

The festival is not usually celebrated in Britain, though many overseas Chinese return home sometimes for New Year and Qingming.

## Sinhala and Tamil New Year's Day

This is a time of great merrymaking, and it is customary for people to be lavish in their hospitality on this day. Special sweetmeats and delicacies are prepared, and people dress in their finery to participate in the various celebrations.

In Sri Lanka, New Year's Eve is also celebrated as a public holiday.

## Songkrar Day

This is also celebrated as the Thai New Year. The main feature of the celebrations is the water festival. Many colourful spectacles – such as boat races, parades, pageants and the appearance of the Songkrar princess on a splendidly caparisoned wooden horse – are also associated with this festival.

On the last day of the festival, a drum and bell are simultaneously sounded three times in temples all over the land. As the vibrations die away, the festivities come to an end for another year.

For the past 50 years or so, Thai New Year has been celebrated on 31 December, although there remains a historic link with old April celebrations.

## May Day

May Day is an old folk festival, which later acquired religious significance, but like many other festivals its origins are disputed. According to one legend, it stems from the Roman Festival to Maia, the mother of Mercury, in whose honour sacrifices were made on the first day of her month, accompanied by considerable merrymaking.

May Day celebrations are also associated with the beneficent qualities ascribed to tree spirits. This explanation suggests that May Day festivities are relics of the ancient custom of tree worship.

In medieval England, May Day was a public holiday, when most villages arranged processions, with all those participating carrying green boughs of sycamore and hawthorn. The most conspicuous element in the procession would be the Maypole, a young tall tree, stripped of its branches and decorated with garlands of flowers and ribbons.

May Day celebrations did not find favour with the Church and devout Christians for a long time and, when Oliver Cromwell came to power, all festivities were forbidden. It was only later when Charles II came to the throne that the customary merrymaking associated with this folk festival was revived.

Towards the end of the nineteenth century, 1 May became known as Labour Day, and is commemorated in many parts of the world with military parades and political rallies.

## Boys' Festival

Since the Second World War, 5 May has been designated a national holiday in Japan and is known as Kodomono Hi or Children's Day.

Paper or cloth streamers in the shape of a carp are hoisted on a wooden pole in the yard or garden. Several legends account for the choice of the carp, the most popular being based on the fact that this fish has great energy, power and determination to overcome obstacles and is therefore a fitting example for young boys.

This day is as much a day of festivity for small boys as 3 March, Hina Matsuri, is for girls in Japan.

## Dragon Boat Festival

Duan Yang, the Dragon Boat Festival, is celebrated on the fifth day of the fifth lunar month. It commemorates the suicide by drowning in 279 BCE of Qu Yuan, a famous poet and high-ranking official. Legend has it that the peasants took out their dragon boats and rushed to save him, but in vain. In order to prevent the fish eating his body, they threw rice dumplings wrapped in bamboo leaves into the river. These dumplings are made and eaten during the festival.

It also became the custom to hold races between dragon boats. These are very long, narrow, rowing boats, brightly painted like dragons with plenty of red and gold and with a dragon's head at the prow. They are usually manned by rival crews from neighbouring villages. The races take place accompanied by men waving flags and the noise of beating gongs. Later, in the evening, the boats parade along the water, bedecked with colourful lanterns.

Some races are held in Britain, but one of the most spectacular international races is held in Hong Kong.

## Obon

Obon is a four-day festival celebrated in Japan to pay respect to the spirits of dead ancestors. Legend has it that the Buddha rescued the mother of one of his disciples on this day after she had been sent to one of the hells. Graves are cleaned and decorated with flowers. Incense is lit and prayers offered. The spirits of the dead are invited to return home, and hemp reeds are burned to light the way. Special food is prepared for the honoured guests.

At the end of Obon, the Bon-Odori dances take place. This is a simple folk dance performed to the accompaniment of songs and drumbeats.

## Onam

Onam is celebrated as a harvest festival by people of all faiths in Kerala – the state at the south-western tip of India.

According to legend, Kerala was once ruled by the benevolent King Mahabali. The gods, jealous of his popularity, determined to teach him a lesson. Thus Vishnu – one of the Holy Trinity in the Hindu pantheon – appeared in the guise of a dwarf Brahmin and begged the king for as much land as he could cover in three paces. The king immediately agreed, and in fact begged the Brahmin to take more land. Vishnu, however, could not be tempted and started to measure out the three paces. The first step he took covered the heavens and the second the entire earth. For the third step, he placed his foot on the bowed head of the king, who had by this time realised the true identity of the dwarf Brahmin, and pushed him into the earth, first granting him the wish of being allowed to return once a year to visit his subjects.

On this day, therefore, people dress up in new clothes and decorate their homes with beautiful flower arrangements. A grand feast is prepared and food is distributed to the Brahmins and to the poor and needy.

The festivities in the state are also marked by boat races. The normally quiet backwaters of Kerala are transformed, as people line the banks along the route to cheer their favourite team. The celebrations are brought to an end with firework displays.

The festival is held in August/September. The exact date is available, near to the time, on a year-by-year basis.

## Mid-autumn Festival

Zhong Qiu, the Chinese Mid-autumn or Moon Festival, is held on the fifteenth day of the eighth month, which in a lunar month is the day of, or day before, the full moon. It is one of the major festivals, and traditionally incense is burned, and offerings of fruit such as melons, pomegranates, grapes and peaches together with mooncakes are made to the moon goddess and to the hare that lives in the moon.

The mooncakes commemorate an uprising against the Mongols in the fourteenth century when the call to revolt was written on pieces of paper embedded in the cakes. They are made of a pastry filled with bean paste or lotus seeds, and often contain solid duck egg yolks to represent the moon.

The festivities may include lion dances, and in the evening children form parades carrying multi-coloured lanterns. These may be made in many shape, from cars and planes to traditional animals such as the symbolic carp or mandarin ducks.

Mooncakes and lanterns are sold around this time in London's Chinatown, and there is usually a lion dance.

## Chong Yang Festival

Chong Yang, the ninth day of the ninth moon, also called Double Nine, is a Chinese festival commemorating an incident that is believed to have taken place on this day.

According to the legend, there were two friends who travelled together for many years pursuing their studies. One day one of them had a premonition that on the ninth day of the ninth moon the household of his friend would meet with a grave disaster. It could be avoided if the family left their home for the day and took refuge in the hills.

The friend did as he was advised and did not return home with his family until nightfall. On their return, they discovered that during their absence all the domestic animals had perished mysteriously. The same fate would have overtaken the family had they not fled to the hills. Since then, it has become customary for Chinese people to climb hills, towers and pagodas on Double Nine, which is also called the Day of Ascending Heights.

## Hallowe'en

Hallowe'en is an ancient Celtic celebration, which is a mixture of pagan ideas, folklore and religion, celebrating the end of the Celtic year. Witches and evil spirits have to be driven away before the beginning of the New Year. Bonfires and the ceremonial extinguishing of fire and lights symbolise the end of the year. Many games and superstitions are associated with it.

## Guy Fawkes Day

Guy Fawkes Day is celebrated all over Britain on 5 November. On this day in 1605, a conspirator called Guy Fawkes, with a group of others, tried to blow up the Catholic King James I of England and his Parliament but they were discovered and arrested.

The nationwide celebrations feature fireworks and bonfires on which effigies of Guy Fawkes are burnt. These effigies are usually made by children who beg passers-by on the streets for 'a penny for the guy'.

Since the abortive plot of 1605, the vaults of the House of Lords are always searched by the sovereign's bodyguard – the Yeomen of the Guard – before the State Opening of Parliament.

The Guy Fawkes celebrations might have faded out had not William of Orange landed at Torbay on the anniversary of the day the plot was discovered, rekindling Protestant emotions. Both events were commemorated in a state service bound up with the Church of England Prayer Book until the services were abrogated by Queen Victoria in 1859.

## Thanksgiving

Thanksgiving Day was first celebrated in America by the Pilgrim Fathers to mark their gratitude for a good harvest in their first year of settlement in a new land. The American celebration is an adaptation of Lammas Day (Loaf Mass, 1 August), which was celebrated in Britain only if there was an abundant harvest. Loaves of bread made from the successful wheat crop were brought to Mass as a token of thanksgiving.

Abraham Lincoln was the first US president to declare Thanksgiving as a national festival, and he set the date as the last Thursday in November. This was later changed by President Roosevelt to the fourth Thursday in November. Roast turkey and pumpkin pie are the main elements of the traditional Thanksgiving meal. The latter has close links with the native American Indians, who cultivated the vegetable and which they, in all probability, shared with the English settlers.

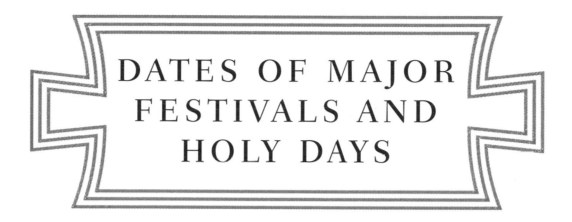

# DATES OF MAJOR FESTIVALS AND HOLY DAYS

## Hindu Festival Dates

|  | 2001 | 2002 | 2003 | 2004 | 2005 |
|---|---|---|---|---|---|
| Lohri | 12 Jan | 13 Jan | 13 Jan | 13 Jan | 13 Jan |
| Makara Sankrant/Pongal | 14 Jan | 14 Jan | 14 Jan | 14 Jan | 14 Jan |
| Vasanta/Basant Panchami | 29 Jan | 17 Feb | 6 Feb | 26 Jan | 3 Feb |
| Mahasivaratri | 21 Feb | 13 Mar | 1 Mar | 18 Feb | 8 Mar |
| Navaratri | 26 Mar | 13 Apr | 2 Apr | 21 Mar | 9 Apr |
| Holi | 10 Mar | 29 Mar | 19 Mar | 7 Mar | 26 Mar |
| Ramnavami | 2 Apr | 21 Apr | 11 Apr | 30 Mar | 18 Apr |
| Vaisakhi/Baisakhi | 13 Apr | 13 Apr | 14 Apr | 13 Apr | 13 Apr |
| Tamil New Year/Sinhala New Year | 13 Apr | 13 Apr | 13 Apr | 13 Apr | 13 Apr |
| Vishu | 14 Apr | 14 Apr | 14 Apr | 14 Apr | 14 Apr |
| Rakshabandhan | 4 Aug | 22 Aug | 12 Aug | 30 Aug | 19 Aug |
| Janmashtami | 12 Aug | 31 Aug | 20 Aug | 7 Sep | 27 Aug |
| Ganesh Chaturthi | 22 Aug | 10 Sep | 31 Aug | 18 Sep | 7 Sep |
| Dassera (Vijayadashami) | 26 Oct | 13 Oct | 3 Oct | 22 Oct | 12 Oct |
| Karva Chauth | 4 Nov | 25 Oct | 14 Oct | 31 Oct | 20 Oct |
| Diwali/Deepawali | 14 Nov | 4 Nov | 25 Oct | 12 Nov | 1 Nov |

# JEWISH HOLY DAY DATES

| | 2001 | 2002 | 2003 | 2004 | 2005 |
|---|---|---|---|---|---|
| Passover (Pesach) | | | | | |
| 1st Day | 8 Apr | 28 Mar | 17 Apr | 6 Apr | 24 Apr |
| 2nd Day | 9 Apr | 29 Mar | 18 Apr | 7 Apr | 25 Apr |
| 7th Day | 14 Apr | 3 Apr | 23 Apr | 12 Apr | 30 Apr |
| 8th Day | 15 Apr | 4 Apr | 24 Apr | 13 Apr | 1 May |
| Pentecost (Shavuot) | | | | | |
| 1st Day | 28 May | 17 May | 6 Jun | 26 May | 13 Jun |
| 2nd Day | 29 May | 18 May | 7 Jun | 27 May | 14 Jun |
| Tish B'av | 28 Jul | 17 Jul | 6 Aug | 26 July | |
| New Year (Rosh Hashanah) | | | | | |
| 1st Day | 18 Sep | 7 Sep | 27 Sep | 16 Sep | 4 Oct |
| 2nd Day | 19 Sep | 8 Sep | 28 Sep | 17 Sep | 5 Oct |
| Day of Atonement (Yom Kippur) | 27 Sep | 16 Sep | 6 Oct | 25 Sep | 13 Oct |
| Tabernacles (Succoth) | | | | | |
| 1st Day | 2 Oct | 21 Sep | 11 Oct | 30 Sep | 18 Oct |
| 2nd Day | 3 Oct | 22 Sep | 12 Oct | 1 Oct | 19 Oct |
| 8th Day | 9 Oct | 28 Sep | 18 Oct | 7 Oct | 25 Oct |
| 9th Day (Simchath Torah) | 10 Oct | 29 Sep | 19 Oct | 8 Oct | 26 Oct |

## Other Jewish Festival Dates

| | | | | | |
|---|---|---|---|---|---|
| Tu B'Shevat | 7 Feb | 27 Jan | 17 Jan | 6 Feb | 25 Jan |
| Lag B'Omer | 10 May | 29 Apr | 19 May | 8 May | 27 May |
| Chanucah | 9 Dec | 29 Nov | 19 Dec | 8 Dec | 26 Dec |
| Purim | 8 Mar | 25 Feb | 6 Mar | 6 Mar | 25 Mar |

# CHRISTIAN FESTIVAL DATES

| | 2001 | 2002 | 2003 | 2004 | 2005 |
|---|---|---|---|---|---|
| New Year's Day | 1 Jan | 1 Jan | 1 Jan | 1 Jan | 1 Jan |
| Epiphany | 6 Jan | 6 Jan | 6 Jan | 6 Jan | 6 Jan |
| Christian Unity Week | 19–25 Jan | 18–24 Jan | 17–23 Jan | 16–22 Jan | 21–27 Jan |
| St Brigid's Day | 1 Feb | 1 Feb | 1 Feb | 1 Feb | 1 Feb |
| Candlemas | 2 Feb | 2 Feb | 2 Feb | 2 Feb | 2 Feb |
| Shrove Tuesday | 27 Feb | 12 Feb | 4 Mar | 24 Feb | 8 Feb |
| Ash Wednesday | 28 Feb | 13 Feb | 5 Mar | 25 Feb | 9 Feb |
| St David's Day | 1 Mar | 1 Mar | 1 Mar | 1 Mar | 1 Mar |
| St Patrick's Day | 17 Mar | 17 Mar | 17 Mar | 17 Mar | 17 Mar |
| Mothering Sunday | 9 Mar | 10 Mar | 30 Mar | 21 Mar | 6 Mar |
| Palm Sunday | 23 Mar | 24 Mar | 13 Apr | 4 Apr | 20 Mar |
| Maundy Thursday | 12 Apr | 28 Mar | 17 Apr | 8 Apr | 24 Mar |
| Good Friday | 13 Apr | 29 Mar | 18 Apr | 9 Apr | 25 Mar |
| Holy Saturday | 14 Apr | 30 Mar | 19 Apr | 10 Apr | 26 Mar |
| Easter Sunday | 15 Apr | 31 Mar | 20 Apr | 11 Apr | 27 Mar |
| St George's Day | 23 Apr | 23 Apr | 23 Apr | 23 Apr | 23 Apr |
| Christian Aid Week | 13–19 May | 12–18 May | 11–17 May | 9–15 May | 8–13 May |
| Ascension Day | 24 May | 9 May | 29 May | 20 May | 5 May |
| Pentecost Day (Whit Sunday) | 3 Jun | 19 May | 8 Jun | 30 May | 15 May |
| Corpus Christi | 14 Jun | 30 May | 19 Jun | 10 Jun | 26 May |
| Feast of St Peter and St Paul | 29 Jun | 29 Jun | 29 Jun | 29 Jun | 29 Jun |
| Assumption of the Blessed Virgin | 15 Aug | 15 Aug | 15 Aug | 15 Aug | 15 Aug |
| Harvest Festival | 28 Sep | 27 Sep | 26 Sep | 24 Sep | 23 Sep |
| All Saints' Day | 1 Nov | 1 Nov | 1 Nov | 1 Nov | 1 Nov |
| All Souls' Day | 2 Nov | 2 Nov | 2 Nov | 2 Nov | 2 Nov |
| First Sunday of Advent | 30 Nov | 1 Dec | 30 Nov | 28 Nov | 27 Nov |
| St Andrew's Day | 30 Nov | 30 Nov | 30 Nov | 30 Nov | 30 Nov |
| Feast of the Immaculate Conception | 8 Dec | 8 Dec | 8 Dec | 8 Dec | 8 Dec |
| Christmas Day | 25 Dec | 25 Dec | 25 Dec | 25 Dec | 25 Dec |
| St Stephen's Day | 26 Dec | 26 Dec | 26 Dec | 26 Dec | 26 Dec |

# MUSLIM FESTIVAL DATES

|                   | 2001   | 2002   | 2003   | 2004   | 2005   |
| ----------------- | ------ | ------ | ------ | ------ | ------ |
| Lailat-ul-Qadr    | 13 Dec | 2 Dec  | 22 Nov | 10 Nov | 30 Oct |
| Eid-ul-Fitr       | 17 Dec | 6 Dec  | 26 Nov | 14 Nov | 3 Nov  |
| Eid-ul-Adha       | 6 Mar  | 23 Feb | 12 Feb | 2 Feb  | 21 Jan |
| Hijrat (New Year) | 26 Mar | 15 Mar | 5 Mar  | 22 Feb | 10 Feb |
| Ashuraa           | 4 Apr  | 24 Mar | 14 Mar | 2 Mar  | 19 Feb |
| Eid Milad-un-Nabi | 4 Jun  | 24 May | 14 May | 2 May  | 21 Apr |
| Shab-e-Miraj      | 15 Oct | 4 Oct  | 24 Sep | 12 Sep | 1 Sep  |
| Shab-e-Barat      | 2 Nov  | 22 Oct | 12 Oct | 30 Sep | 19 Sep |
| Ramadhan 1st Day  | 17 Nov | 6 Nov  | 27 Oct | 15 Oct | 4 Oct  |

# SIKH FESTIVAL DATES

|                   | 2001   | 2002   | 2003   | 2004   | 2005   |
| ----------------- | ------ | ------ | ------ | ------ | ------ |
| Lohri             | 13 Jan | 13 Jan | 13 Jan | 13 Jan | 13 Jan |
| Basant Panchami   | 29 Jan | 17 Feb | 6 Feb  | 26 Jan | 3 Feb  |
| Baisakhi/Vaisakhi | 13 Apr | 13 Apr | 13 Apr | 13 Apr | 13 Apr |
| Diwali            | 30 Oct | 19 Oct | 7 Nov  |        |        |

**Birthdays, accession to guruship and deaths of the ten sikh gurus**
These dates are fixed as they are according to the Nankshahi calendar.

| Guru              | Birthday           | Accession | Death  |
| ----------------- | ------------------ | --------- | ------ |
| Guru Nanak Dev    | Katik Poornamashi  |           | 22 Sep |
| Guru Angad Dev    | 18 Apr             | 18 Sep    | 16 Apr |
| Guru Amar Das     | 23 May             | 16 Apr    | 16 Sep |
| Guru Ram Das      | 9 Oct              | 16 Sep    | 16 Sep |
| Guru Arjan Dev    | 2 May              | 16 Sep    | 16 Jun |
| Guru Hargobind    | 5 Jul              | 11 Jun    | 19 Mar |
| Guru Har Rai      | 31 Jan             | 14 Mar    | 20 Oct |
| Guru Harkrishan   | 23 Jul             | 20 Oct    | 16 Apr |
| Guru Tegh Bahadur | 18 Apr             | 16 Apr    | 24 Nov |
| Guru Gobind Singh | 5 Jan              | 24 Nov    | 21 Oct |

# BUDDHIST FESTIVAL DATES

All variable dates are approximate only and should be verified each year. Contact the publisher on 01753 526769.

| | 2002 | 2003 | 2004 | 2005 |
|---|---|---|---|---|
| New Year (Mahayana) | First full moon in January | | | |
| | 28 Jan | 18 Jan | 7 Jan | 25 Jan |
| Tibetan New Year (Losar) | First full moon in February | | | |
| | 27 Feb | 16 Feb | 6 Feb | 24 Feb |
| Maghapuja | Full moon day of 3rd lunar month | | | |
| Parinirvana (Mahayana/Zen) | 15 Feb | 15 Feb | 15 Feb | 15 Feb |
| Avalokitesvara's Birthday | Full moon day in March | | | |
| | 28 Mar | 18 Mar | 6 Mar | 25 Mar |
| Birthday of the Buddha (Mahayana/Zen) | 8 Apr | | | |
| New Year (Theravada) | First full moon in April | | | |
| | 27 Apr | 16 Apr | 5 Apr | 24 Apr |
| Vaisakhapuja/Vesak (Theravada) | First full moon in May (or June in leap years) | | | |
| | 26 May | 16 May | 4 May | 23 May |
| Poson | Jun | | | |
| Asalhapuja/Dhammacakka | Jun | | | |
| Ulambana | 13–16 Jul | | | |
| Asalha Puja | Full moon day of 8th lunar month | | | |
| | 24 Jul | 13 Jul | 2 Jul | 21 Jul |
| Kandy Perahara | Aug | | | |
| Rains Retreat | Jul–Oct | | | |
| Bodhidharma's Day (Zen) | 3 Oct | 3 Oct | 3 Oct | 3 Oct |
| Paravana Day | Marks the end of the Rains Retreat | | | |
| | 21 Oct | | | |
| Kathina | Within one month of the end of the Rains Retreat | | | |
| Enlightenment of the Buddha (Zen) | 8 Dec | 8 Dec | 8 Dec | 8 Dec |
| Enlightenment of the Buddha (Mahayana) | Dec | | | |

## JAIN FESTIVAL DATES

Variable dates are approximate only and should be verified each year. Contact the publisher on 01753 526769.

|  | **2002** |
| --- | --- |
| Paryushana | 22–23 Aug |

## BAHA'I HOLY DAY DATES

| Period of the Fast | 2–20 Mar |
| --- | --- |
| Feast of Naw-Ruz (Baha'i New Year) | 21 Mar |
| Feast of Ridvan (Declaration of Baha'ullah) | 21 Apr–2 May |
| First Day of Ridvan | 21 Apr |
| Ninth Day of Ridvan | 29 Apr |
| Twelfth Day of Ridvan | 2 May |
| Declaration of the Bab | 23 May |
| Ascension of Baha'ullah | 29 May |
| Martyrdom of the Bab | 9 Jul |
| Birthday of the Bab | 20 Oct |
| Birthday of Baha'ullah | 12 Nov |
| Day of the Covenant | 26 Nov |
| Ascension of Abdu'l-Baha | 28 Nov |

## CHINESE FESTIVAL DATES

|  | **2001** | **2002** | **2003** | **2004** | **2005** |
| --- | --- | --- | --- | --- | --- |
| New Year | 24 Jan | 12 Feb | 1 Feb | 22 Jan | 9 Feb |
| Lantern Festival | 7 Feb | 26 Feb | 15 Feb | 5 Feb | 23 Feb |
| Qingming | 5 Apr | 5 Apr | 5 Apr | 4 Apr | 5 Apr |
| Dragon Boat Festival | 25 Jun | 15 Jun | 4 Jun | 22 Jun | 11 Jun |
| Mid-autumn Festival | 1 Oct | 21 Sep | 11 Sep | 28 Sep | 18 Sep |
| Chong Yang | 25 Oct | 14 Oct | 4 Oct | 22 Oct | 11 Oct |
| Animal Signs | Snake | Horse | Goat | Monkey | Rooster |

## JAPANESE FESTIVAL DATES

| Ganjitsu | 1 Jan |
| --- | --- |
| Setsubon | 3 Feb |
| Dolls' Festival (Hina Matsuri) | 3 Mar |
| Boys' Festival (Kodomono Hi) | 5 May |
| Obon | 13–16 Aug |

# 2002 TO 2005
# CALENDARS

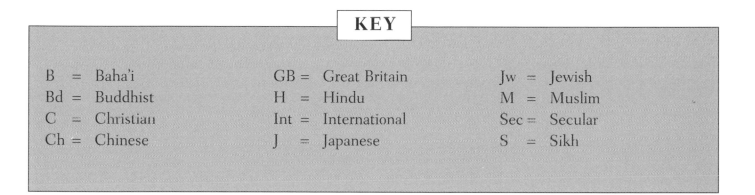

## KEY

| | | | | | | | | |
|---|---|---|---|---|---|---|---|---|
| B | = | Baha'i | GB | = | Great Britain | Jw | = | Jewish |
| Bd | = | Buddhist | H | = | Hindu | M | = | Muslim |
| C | = | Christian | Int | = | International | Sec | = | Secular |
| Ch | = | Chinese | J | = | Japanese | S | = | Sikh |

# 2002

## January

| | |
|---|---|
| 1 | New Year's Day (C) |
| | Ganjitsu (J) |
| 2 | |
| 3 | |
| 4 | |
| 5 | Birthday of Guru Gobind Singh (S) |
| 6 | Epiphany (C) |
| 7 | |
| 8 | |
| 9 | |
| 10 | |
| 11 | |
| 12 | |
| 13 | Lohri (H/S) |
| 14 | Makara Sankrant/Pongal (H) |
| 15 | |
| 16 | |
| 17 | |
| 18 | Christian Unity Week begins (C) |
| 19 | |
| 20 | |
| 21 | |
| 22 | |
| 23 | |
| 24 | |
| 25 | |
| 26 | |
| 27 | Tu B'Shevat (Jw) |
| | Holocaust Memorial Day (Int) |
| 28 | Mahayana New Year (Bd) |
| 29 | |
| 30 | |
| 31 | Birthday of Guru Har Rai (S) |

## February

| | |
|---|---|
| 1 | St Brigid's Day (C) |
| 2 | Candlemas (C) |
| 3 | Setsubon (J) |
| 4 | |
| 5 | |
| 6 | |
| 7 | |
| 8 | |
| 9 | |
| 10 | |
| 11 | |
| 12 | Shrove Tuesday (C) |
| | Chinese New Year (Ch) |
| 13 | Ash Wednesday (C) |
| 14 | |
| 15 | Piriniravana (Bd) |
| 16 | |
| 17 | Vasanta /Basant Panchami (H/S) |
| 18 | |
| 19 | |
| 20 | |
| 21 | |
| 22 | |
| 23 | Eid-ul-Adha (M) |
| 24 | |
| 25 | Purim (Jw) |
| 26 | |
| 27 | Tibetan New Year (Bd) |
| 28 | |

## March

| | |
|---|---|
| 1 | St David's Day(C) |
| 2 | 19 Day Fast begins (B) |
| 3 | |
| 4 | |
| 5 | |
| 6 | |
| 7 | |
| 8 | |
| 9 | |
| 10 | Mothering Sunday (C) |
| 11 | |
| 12 | |
| 13 | Mahasivaratri (H) |
| 14 | |
| 15 | Hijrat/New Year (M) |
| 16 | |
| 17 | St Patrick's Day (C) |
| 18 | |
| 19 | Martyrdom of Guru Hargobind (S) |
| 20 | |
| 21 | Baha'i New Year (B) |
| 22 | |
| 23 | |
| 24 | Ashuraa (M), Palm Sunday (C) |
| 25 | |
| 26 | |
| 27 | |
| 28 | Pesach 1st day (Jw) |
| | Maundy Thursday (C) |
| | Avalokitesvara's Birthday (Bd) |
| 29 | Pesach 2nd day (Jw) |
| | Holi (H) |
| | Good Friday (C) |
| 30 | Holy Saturday (C) |
| 31 | Easter Sunday (C) |

## April

| | |
|---|---|
| 1 | April Fools' Day (Sec) |
| 2 | |
| 3 | Pesach 7th day (Jw) |
| 4 | Pesach 8th day (Jw) |
| 5 | Qingming (Ch) |
| 6 | |
| 7 | |
| 8 | Birthday of the Buddha (Bd) |
| 9 | |
| 10 | |
| 11 | |
| 12 | |
| 13 | Navaratri (H) |
| | Baisakhi/Vaisakhi (S/H) |
| | Tamil/Sinhala New Year |
| 14 | Vishu (H) |
| 15 | |
| 16 | Martyrdom of Guru Angad Dev (S) |
| | Martyrdom of Guru Harkrishan (S) |
| 17 | |
| 18 | Birthday of Guru Angad Dev (S) |
| | Birthday of Guru Tegh Bahadur (S) |
| 19 | |
| 20 | |
| 21 | Ramnavami (H) |
| | Feast of Ridvan until 2 May (B) |
| 22 | |
| 23 | St George's Day (GB) |
| 24 | |
| 25 | |
| 26 | |
| 27 | Theravada New Year (Bd) |
| 28 | |
| 29 | Lag B'Omer (Jw) |
| | Ninth Day of Ridvan (B) |
| 30 | |

## May

| | |
|---|---|
| 1 | May Day (Int) |
| 2 | Birthday of Guru Arjan Dev (S) |
| | Twelfth Day of Ridvan (B) |
| 3 | |
| 4 | |
| 5 | Boys' Festival (J) |
| 6 | |
| 7 | |
| 8 | |
| 9 | Ascension Day (C) |
| 10 | |
| 11 | |
| 12 | Christian Aid Week begins (C) |
| 13 | |
| 14 | |
| 15 | |
| 16 | |
| 17 | Shavuot 1st day (Jw) |
| 18 | Shavuot 2nd day (Jw) |
| 19 | Pentecost/Whit Sunday (C) |
| 20 | |
| 21 | |
| 22 | |
| 23 | Declaration of the Bab (B) |
| | Birthday of Guru Amar Das (S) |
| 24 | Eid Milad-un-Nabi (M) |
| 25 | |
| 26 | Vaisakhapuja (Bd) |
| 27 | |
| 28 | |
| 29 | Ascension of Baha'ullah (B) |
| 30 | Corpus Christi (C) |
| 31 | |

## June

| | |
|---|---|
| 1 | |
| 2 | |
| 3 | |
| 4 | |
| 5 | |
| 6 | |
| 7 | |
| 8 | |
| 9 | |
| 10 | |
| 11 | |
| 12 | |
| 13 | |
| 14 | |
| 15 | Dragon Boat Festival (Ch) |
| 16 | Father's Day (Sec) |
| | Martyrdom of Guru Arjan Dev (S) |
| 17 | |
| 18 | |
| 19 | |
| 20 | |
| 21 | |
| 22 | |
| 23 | |
| 24 | |
| 25 | |
| 26 | |
| 27 | |
| 28 | |
| 29 | Feast of St Peter and St Paul (C) |
| 30 | |

# 2002

## July

1
2
3
4
5 Birthday of Guru Hargobind (S)
6
7
8
9 Martyrdom of the Bab (B)
10
11
12
13 Ulambana (Bd)
14
15
16
17 Tish B'av (Jw)
18
19
20
21
22
23 Birthday of Guru Harkrishan (S)
24 Asalha Puja (Bd)
25
26
27
28
29
30
31

## August

1
2
3
4
5
6
7
8
9
10
11
12
13 Obon (J)
14
15 Blessed Virgin (C)
16
17
18
19
20
21
22 Rakshabandhan (H)
23
24
25
26
27
28
29
30
31 Janmashtami (H)
   Onam 1st day (Sec)

## September

1
2
3
4
5
6
7 Rosh Hashanah 1st day (Jw)
8 Rosh Hashanah 2nd day (Jw)
9
10 Ganesh Chaturthi (H)
11
12
13
14
15
16 Yom Kippur (Jw)
   Martyrdom of Guru Amar Das (S)
   Martyrdom of Guru Ram Das (S)
17
18
19
20
21 Succoth 1st day (Jw)
   Mid-autumn Festival (Ch)
22 Succoth 2nd day (Jw)
   Martyrdom of Guru Nanak Dev (S)
23
24
25
26
27
28 Succoth 8th day Jw
29 Simchath Torah (Jw)
   Harvest Festival (C)
30

## October

1
2
3 Bodhidharma's Day (Bd)
4 Shab-e-Miraj (M)
5
6
7
8
9 Birthday of Guru Ram Das (S)
10
11
12
13 Dassera (H)
14 Chong Yang (Ch)
15
16
17
18
19 Diwali (S)
20 Birthday of the Bab (B)
   Martyrdom of Guru Har Rai (S)
21 Martyrdom of Guru Gobind Singh (S)
   Paravana Day (Bd)
22 Shab-e-Barat (M)
23
24
25 Karva Chauth (H)
26
27
28
29
30
31 Hallowe'en (Sec)

## November

1 All Saints' Day (C)
2 All Souls' Day (C)
3
4 Diwali (H)
5 Guy Fawkes Day (GB)
6 Ramadhan 1st day (M)
7
8
9
10 Remembrance Sunday (GB)
11 Birthday of Baha'u'llah (B)
12
13
14
15
16
17
18
19
20 Birthday of Guru Nanak (S)
21
22
23
24 Martyrdom of Guru Teg Bahadur (S)
25
26 Day of the Covenant (B)
27
28 Ascension of Abdu'l-Baha (B)
   Thanksgiving (Sec)
29 Chanucah (Jw)
30 St Andrew's Day (C)

## December

1 First Sunday of Advent (C)
2 Lailat-ul-Qadr (M)
3
4
5
6 Eid-ul-Fitr (M)
7
8 Immaculate Conception (C)
   Enlightenment of the Buddha (Bd)
9
10
11
12
13
14
15
16
17
18
19
20
21
22
23
24
25 Christmas Day (C)
26 St Stephen's Day (C)
   Boxing Day (GB)
27
28
29
30
31

# 2003

## January

| | |
|---|---|
| 1 | New Year's Day (C) |
| | Ganjitsu (J) |
| 2 | |
| 3 | |
| 4 | |
| 5 | Birthday of Guru Gobind Singh (S) |
| 6 | Epiphany (C) |
| 7 | |
| 8 | |
| 9 | |
| 10 | |
| 11 | |
| 12 | |
| 13 | Lohri (H/S) |
| 14 | Makara Sankrant/Pongal (H) |
| 15 | |
| 16 | |
| 17 | Tu B'Shevat (Jw) |
| | Christian Unity Week begins (C) |
| 18 | Mahayana New Year (Bd) |
| 19 | |
| 20 | |
| 21 | |
| 22 | |
| 23 | |
| 24 | |
| 25 | |
| 26 | |
| 27 | Holocaust Memorial Day (Int) |
| 28 | |
| 29 | |
| 30 | |
| 31 | Birthday of Guru Har Rai (S) |

## February

| | |
|---|---|
| 1 | St Brigid's Day (C) |
| | Chinese New Year (Ch) |
| 2 | Candlemas (C) |
| 3 | Setsubon (J) |
| 4 | |
| 5 | |
| 6 | Vasanta/Basant Panchami (H/S) |
| 7 | |
| 8 | |
| 9 | |
| 10 | |
| 11 | |
| 12 | Eid-ul-Adha (M) |
| 13 | |
| 14 | |
| 15 | Parinirvana (Bd) |
| 16 | Tibetan New Year (Bd) |
| 17 | |
| 18 | |
| 19 | |
| 20 | |
| 21 | |
| 22 | |
| 23 | |
| 24 | |
| 25 | |
| 26 | |
| 27 | |
| 28 | |

## March

| | |
|---|---|
| 1 | St David's Day (C) |
| | Mahasivaratri (H) |
| 2 | 19 Day Fast begins (B) |
| 3 | |
| 4 | Shrove Tuesday (C) |
| 5 | Ash Wednesday (C) |
| | Hijrat/New Year (M) |
| 6 | Purim (Jw) |
| 7 | |
| 8 | |
| 9 | |
| 10 | |
| 11 | |
| 12 | |
| 13 | |
| 14 | Ashuraa (M) |
| 15 | |
| 16 | |
| 17 | St Patrick's Day (C) |
| 18 | Avalokitesvara's Birthday (Bd) |
| 19 | Holi (H) |
| | Martyrdom of Guru Hargobind (S) |
| 20 | |
| 21 | Baha'i New Year (B) |
| 22 | |
| 23 | |
| 24 | |
| 25 | |
| 26 | |
| 27 | |
| 28 | |
| 29 | |
| 30 | Mothering Sunday (C) |
| 31 | |

## April

1 April Fool's Day (Sec)
2 Navaratri (H)
3
4
5 Qingming (Ch)
6
7
8
9
10
11 Ramnavami (H)
12
13 Vaisakhi/Baisakhi (H/S)
  Palm Sunday (C)
  Tamil/Sinhala New Year
14 Vishu (H)
15
16 Martyrdom of Guru Angad Dev (S)
  Martyrdom of Guru Harkrishan (S)
  Theravada New Year (Bd)
17 Pesach 1st day (Jw)
  Maundy Thursday (C)
18 Pesach 2nd day (Jw)
  Good Friday (C)
  Birthday of Guru Angad Dev (S)
  Birthday of Guru Tegh Bahadur (S)
19 Holy Saturday (C)
20 Easter Sunday (C)
21 Feast of Ridvan until 2 May (B)
22
23 St George's Day (C)
  Pesach 7th day (Jw)
24 Pesach 8th day (Jw)
25
26
27
28
29 Ninth Day of Ridvan (B)
30

## May

1 May Day (Int)
2 Birthday of Guru Arjan Dev (S)
  Twelfth Day of Ridvan (B)
3
4
5 Boys' Festival (J)
6
7
8
9
10
11 Christian Aid Week begins (C)
12
13
14 Eid Milad-un-Nabi (M)
15
16 Vaisakhapuja (Bd)
17
18
19 Lag B'Omer(Jw)
20
21
22
23 Declaration of the Bab (B)
  Birthday of Guru Amar Das (S)
24
25
26
27
28
29 Ascension of Baha'ullah (B)
  Ascension Day (C)
30
31

## June

1
2
3
4 Dragon Boat Festival (Ch)
5
6 Shavuot 1st day (Jw)
7 Shavuot 2nd day (Jw)
8 Pentecost/Whit Sunday (C)
9
10
11
12
13
14
15 Father's Day (Sec)
16 Martyrdom of Guru Arjan Dev (S)
17
18
19 Corpus Christi (C)
20
21
22
23
24
25
26
27
28
29 Feast of St Peter and St Paul (C)
30

## July

| | |
|---|---|
| 1 | |
| 2 | |
| 3 | |
| 4 | |
| 5 | Birthday of Guru Hargobind (S) |
| 6 | |
| 7 | |
| 8 | |
| 9 | Martyrdom of the Bab (B) |
| 10 | |
| 11 | |
| 12 | |
| 13 | Ulambana (Bd) |
| | Asalha Puja (Bd) |
| 14 | |
| 15 | |
| 16 | |
| 17 | |
| 18 | |
| 19 | |
| 20 | |
| 21 | |
| 22 | |
| 23 | Birthday of Guru Harkrishan (S) |
| 24 | |
| 25 | |
| 26 | |
| 27 | |
| 28 | |
| 29 | |
| 30 | |
| 31 | |

## August

| | |
|---|---|
| 1 | |
| 2 | |
| 3 | |
| 4 | |
| 5 | |
| 6 | Tish B'av (Jw) |
| 7 | |
| 8 | |
| 9 | |
| 10 | |
| 11 | |
| 12 | Rakshabandhan (H) |
| 13 | Obon (J) |
| 14 | |
| 15 | Blessed Virgin (C) |
| 16 | |
| 17 | |
| 18 | |
| 19 | |
| 20 | Janmashtami (H) |
| 21 | |
| 22 | |
| 23 | |
| 24 | |
| 25 | |
| 26 | |
| 27 | |
| 28 | |
| 29 | |
| 30 | |
| 31 | Ganesh Chaturthi (H) |

## September

| | |
|---|---|
| 1 | |
| 2 | |
| 3 | |
| 4 | |
| 5 | |
| 6 | |
| 7 | |
| 8 | |
| 9 | |
| 10 | |
| 11 | Mid-autumn Festival (Ch) |
| 12 | |
| 13 | |
| 14 | |
| 15 | |
| 16 | Martyrdom of Guru Amar Das (S) |
| | Martyrdom of Guru Ram Das (S) |
| 17 | |
| 18 | |
| 19 | |
| 20 | |
| 21 | |
| 22 | Martyrdom of Guru Nanak Dev (S) |
| 23 | |
| 24 | Shab-e-Miraj (M) |
| 25 | |
| 26 | |
| 27 | Rosh Hashanah 1st day (Jw) |
| 28 | Rosh Hashanah 2nd day (Jw) |
| | Harvest Festival (C) |
| 29 | |
| 30 | |

## October

1
2
3 Dassera (H)
  Bodhidharma's Day (Bd)
4 Chong Yan (Ch)
5
6 Yom Kippur (Jw)
7
8
9 Birthday of Guru Ram Das (S)
10
11 Succoth 1st day (Jw)
12 Succoth 2nd day (Jw)
   Shab-e-Barat (M)
13
14 Karva Chauth (H)
15
16
17
18 Succoth 8th day (Jw)
19 Simchath Torah (Jw)
20 Birthday of the Bab (B)
   Martyrdom of Guru Har Rai (S)
21
22
23
24 Martyrdom of Guru Gobind Singh (S)
25 Diwali (H)
26
27 Ramadhan 1st day (M)
28
29
20
31 Hallowe'en (Sec)

## November

1 All Saints' Day (C)
2 All Souls' Day (C)
3
4
5 Guy Fawkes Day (GB)
6
7 Diwali (S)
8 Birthday of Guru Nanak (S)
9 Remembrance Sunday (GB)
10
11
12 Birthday of Baha'u'llah (B)
13
14
15
16
17
18
19
20
21
22 Lailat –ul-Qadr (M)
23
24 Martyrdom of Guru Tegh Bahadur (S)
25
26 Day of the Covenant (B)
   Eid-ul-Fitr (M)
27 Thanksgiving (Sec)
28 Ascension of Abdu'l-Baha (B)
29
30 St Andrew's Day (C)
   First Sunday of Advent (C)

## December

1
2
3
4
5
6
7
8 Immaculate Conception (C)
  Enlightenment of the Buddha (Bd)
9
10
11
12
13
14
15
16
17
18
19 Chanuccah (Jw)
20
21
22
23
24
25 Christmas Day (C)
26 St Stephen's Day (C)
   Boxing Day (GB)
27
28
29
30
31

# 2004

## January

1  New Year's Day (C)
   Ganjitsu (J)
2
3
4
5  Birthday of Guru Gobind Singh (S)
6  Epiphany (C)
7  Mahayana New Year (Bd)
8
9
10
11
12
13  Lohri (H/S)
14  Makara Sankrant/Pongal (H)
15
16  Christian Unity Week begins
17
18
19
20
21
22  Chinese New Year (Ch)
23
24
25
26  Vasanta/Basant Panchami (H/S)
27  Holocaust Memorial Day (Int)
28
29
30
31  Birthday of Guru Har Rai (S)

## February

1  St Brigid's Day (C)
2  Candlemas (C)
   Eid-ul-Adha (M)
3  Setsubon (J)
4
5
6  Tu B'Shevat (Jw)
   Tibetan New Year (Bd)
7
8
9
10
11
12
13
14
15  Parinirvana (Bd)
16
17
18  Mahasivaratri (H)
19
20
21
22  Hijrat/New Year (M)
23
24  Shrove Tuesday (C)
25  Ash Wednesday (C)
26
27
28

## March

1  St David's Day
2  Ashuraa (M)
   19 Day Fast begins (B)
3
4
5
6  Purim (Jw)
   Avalokitesvara's Birthday (Bd)
7  Holi (H)
8
9
10
11
12
13
14
15
16
17  St Patrick's Day (C)
18
19  Martyrdom of Guru Hargobind (S)
20
21  Mothering Sunday (C)
   Navaratri (H)
   Baha'i New Year (B)
22
23
24
25
26
27
28
29
30  Ramnavami (H)
31

## April

| | |
|---|---|
| 1 | April Fools' Day (Sec) |
| 2 | |
| 3 | |
| 4 | Palm Sunday (C) |
| | Qingming (Ch) |
| 5 | Theravada New Year (Bd) |
| 6 | Pesach 1st day (Jw) |
| 7 | Pesach 2nd day (Jw) |
| 8 | Maundy Thursday (C) |
| 9 | Good Friday (C) |
| 10 | Holy Saturday (C) |
| 11 | Easter Sunday (C) |
| 12 | Pesach 7th day (Jw) |
| 13 | Vaisakhi/Baisakhi (H/S) |
| | Pesach 8th day(Jw) |
| | Tamil/Sinhala New Year |
| 14 | Vishu (H) |
| 15 | |
| 16 | Martyrdom of Guru Angad Dev (S) |
| | Martyrdom of Guru Harkrishan (S) |
| 17 | |
| 18 | Birthday of Guru Angad Dev (S) |
| | Birthday of Guru Tegh Bahadur (S) |
| 19 | |
| 20 | |
| 21 | Feast of Ridvan until 2nd May (B) |
| 22 | |
| 23 | St George's Day (C) |
| | Declaration of the Bab (B) |
| 24 | |
| 25 | |
| 26 | |
| 27 | |
| 28 | |
| 29 | Ninth Day of Ridvan (B) |
| 30 | |

## May

| | |
|---|---|
| 1 | May Day (Int) |
| 2 | Eid Milad-un-Nabi (M) |
| | Birthday of Guru Arjan Dev (S) |
| | Twelfth Day of Ridvan (B) |
| 3 | |
| 4 | Vaisakhapuja (Bd) |
| 5 | Boys' Festival (J) |
| 6 | |
| 7 | |
| 8 | Lag B'Omer (Jw) |
| 9 | Christian Aid Week begins (C) |
| 10 | |
| 11 | |
| 12 | |
| 13 | |
| 14 | |
| 15 | |
| 16 | |
| 17 | |
| 18 | |
| 19 | |
| 20 | Ascension Day (C) |
| 21 | |
| 22 | |
| 23 | Birthday of Guru Amar Das (S) |
| | Declaration of the Bab (B) |
| 24 | |
| 25 | |
| 26 | Shavuot 1st day (Jw) |
| 27 | Shavuot 2nd day (Jw) |
| 28 | |
| 29 | Ascension of Baha'ullah (B) |
| 30 | Pentecost/Whit Sunday (C) |
| 31 | |

## June

| | |
|---|---|
| 1 | |
| 2 | |
| 3 | |
| 4 | |
| 5 | |
| 6 | |
| 7 | |
| 8 | |
| 9 | |
| 10 | Corpus Christi (C) |
| 11 | |
| 12 | |
| 13 | |
| 14 | |
| 15 | |
| 16 | Martyrdom of Guru Arjan Dev (S) |
| 17 | |
| 18 | |
| 19 | |
| 20 | Father's Day (Sec) |
| 21 | |
| 22 | Dragon Boat Festival (Ch) |
| 23 | |
| 24 | |
| 25 | |
| 26 | |
| 27 | |
| 28 | |
| 29 | Feast of St Peter and St Paul (C) |
| 30 | |

## July

1
2 Asalha Puja (Bd)
3
4
5 Birthday of Guru Hargobind (S)
6
7
8
9 Martyrdom of the Bab (B)
10
11
12
13 Ulambana (Bd)
14
15
16
17
18
19
20
21
22
23 Birthday of Guru Harkrishan (S)
24
25
26 Tish B'av (Jw)
27
28
29
30
31

## August

1
2
3
4
5
6
7
8
9
10
11
12
13 Obon (J)
14
15 Blessed Virgin (C)
16
17
18
19
20
21
22
23
24
25
26
27
28
29
30 Rakshabandhan (H)
31

## September

1
2
3
4
5
6
7 Janmashtami (H)
8
9
10
11
12 Shab-e-Miraj(M)
13
14
15
16 Rosh Hashanah 1st day (Jw)
   Martyrdom of Guru Amar Das (S)
   Martyrdom of Guru Ram Das (S)
17 Rosh Hashanah 2nd day (Jw)
18 Ganesh Chaturthi (H)
29
20
21
22 Martyrdom of Guru Nanak Dev (S)
23
24
25 Yom Kippur (Jw)
26 Harvest festival (C)
27
28 Mid-autumn Festival (Ch)
29
30 Shab-e-Barat (M)
   Succoth 1st day (Jw)

## October

1 Succoth 2nd day (Jw)
2
3 Bodhidharma's Day (Bd)
4
5
6
7 Succoth 8th day (Jw)
8 Simchath Torah (Jw)
9 Birthday of Guru Ram Das (S)
10
11
12
13
14
15 Ramadhan 1st day (M)
16
17
18
19
20 Birthday of the Bab (B)
   Martyrdom of Guru Har Rai (S)
21 Martyrdom of Guru Gobind Singh (S)
22 Dassera (H)
   Chong Yang (Ch)
23
24
25
26
27
28
29
20
31 Hallowe'en (Sec)
   Karva Chauth (H)

## November

1 All Saints' Day (C)
2 All Souls' Day (C)
3
4
5 Guy Fawkes Day (GB)
6
7
8
9
10 Lailat-ul-Qadr (M)
11
12 Diwali (H)
   Birthday of Baha'ullah (B)
13
14 Remembrance Sunday (C)
   Eid-ul-Fitr (M)
15
16
17
18
19
20
21
22
23
24 Martyrdom of Guru Tegh Bahadur (S)
25 Thanksgiving (Sec)
26 Birthday of Guru Nanak (S)
   Day of the Covenant (B)
27
28 First Sunday of Advent (C)
   Ascension of Abdu'l-Baha (B)
29
30 St Andrew's Day (C)

## December

1
2
3
4
5
6
7
8 Imaculate Conception (C)
   Chanuccah (Jw)
   Enlightenment of the Buddha (Bd)
9
10
11
12
13
14
15
16
17
18
19
20
21
22
23
24
25 Christmas Day (C)
26 St Stephen's Day (C)
   Boxing Day (GB)
27
28
29
30
31

## January

| | |
|---|---|
| 1 | New Year's Day (C) |
| | Ganjitsu (J) |
| 2 | |
| 3 | |
| 4 | |
| 5 | Birthday of Guru Gobind Singh (S) |
| 6 | Epiphany (C) |
| 7 | |
| 8 | |
| 9 | |
| 10 | |
| 11 | |
| 12 | |
| 13 | Lohri (H/S) |
| 14 | Makara Sankrant/Pongal (H) |
| 15 | |
| 16 | |
| 17 | |
| 18 | |
| 19 | |
| 20 | |
| 21 | Christian Unity Week begins (C) |
| | Eid-ul-Adha (M) |
| 22 | |
| 23 | |
| 24 | |
| 25 | Tu B'Shevat (Jw) |
| | Mahayana New Year (Bd) |
| 26 | |
| 27 | Holocaust Memorial Day (Int) |
| 28 | |
| 29 | |
| 30 | |
| 31 | Birthday of Guru Har Rai (S) |

## February

| | |
|---|---|
| 1 | St Brigid's Day (C) |
| 2 | Candlemas (C) |
| 3 | Setsubon (J) |
| | Vasanta/Basant Panchami (H/S) |
| 4 | |
| 5 | |
| 6 | |
| 7 | |
| 8 | Shrove Tuesday (C) |
| 9 | Ash Wednesday (C) |
| | Chinese New Year (Ch) |
| 10 | Hijrat/New Year (M) |
| 11 | |
| 12 | |
| 13 | |
| 14 | |
| 15 | Parinirvana (Bd) |
| 16 | |
| 17 | |
| 18 | |
| 19 | Ashuraa (M) |
| 20 | |
| 21 | |
| 22 | |
| 23 | |
| 24 | Tibetan New Year (Bd) |
| 25 | |
| 26 | |
| 27 | |
| 28 | |

## March

| | |
|---|---|
| 1 | St David's Day (C) |
| 2 | 19 Day Fast begins (B) |
| 3 | |
| 4 | |
| 5 | |
| 6 | Mothering Sunday (C) |
| 7 | |
| 8 | Mahasivaratri (H) |
| 9 | |
| 10 | |
| 11 | |
| 12 | |
| 13 | |
| 14 | |
| 15 | |
| 16 | |
| 17 | St Patrick's Day (C) |
| 18 | |
| 19 | Martyrdom of Guru Hargobind (S) |
| 20 | Palm Sunday (C) |
| 21 | Baha'i New Year (B) |
| 22 | |
| 23 | |
| 24 | Maundy Thursday (C) |
| 25 | Good Friday (C) |
| | Purim (Jw) |
| | Avalokitesvara's Birthday (Bd) |
| 26 | Holy Saturday (C) |
| | Holi (H) |
| 27 | Easter Sunday (C) |
| 28 | |
| 29 | |
| 30 | |
| 31 | |

## April

1  April Fools' Day (Sec)
2
3
4
5  Qingming (Ch)
6
7
8
9  Navaratri (H)
10
11
12
13  Vaisakhi/Baisakhi (H/S)
    Tamil/Sinhala New Year
14  Vishu (H)
15
16  Martyrdom of Guru Angad Dev (S)
    Martyrdom of Guru Harkrishan (S)
17
18  Ramnavami (H)
    Birthday of Guru Angad Dev (S)
    Birthday of Guru Tegh Bahadur (S)
19
20
21  Eid Milad-un-Nabi (M)
    Feast of Ridvan until 2 May (B)
22
23  St George's Day (C)
24  Pesach 1st day (Jw)
    Theravada New Year (Bd)
25  Pesach 2nd day (Jw)
26
27
28
29  Ninth Day of Ridvan (B)
30  Pesach 7th day (Jw)

## May

1  May Day (Int)
   Pesach 8th day (Jw)
2  Birthday of Guru Arjan Dev (S)
   Twelfth Day of Ridvan (B)
3
4
5  Boys' Festival (J)
   Ascension Day (C)
6
7
8  Christian Aid Week begins
9
10
11
12
13
14
15  Pentecost/Whit Sunday (C)
16
17
18
19
20
21
22
23  Declaration of the Bab (B)
    Birthday of Guru Amar Das (S)
    Vaisakhapuja (Bd)
24
25
26  Corpus Christi (C)
27  Lag B'Omer (Jw)
28
29  Ascension of Baha'ullah (B)
30
31

## June

1
2
3
4
5
6
7
8
9
10
11  Dragon Boat Festival (Ch)
12
13  Shavuot 1st day (Jw)
14  Shavuot 2nd day (Jw)
15
16  Martyrdom of Guru Arjan Dev (S)
17
18
19  Father's Day (Sec)
20
21
22
23
24
25
26
27
28
29  Feast of St Peter and St Paul (C)
30

# July

1
2
3
4
5 Birthday of Guru Hargobind (S)
6
7
8
9 Martyrdom of the Bab (B)
10
11
12
13 Ulambana (Bd)
14
15
16
17
18
19
20
21 Asalha Puja (Bd)
22
23 Birthday of Guru Harkrishan (S)
24
25
26
27
28
29
30
31

# August

1
2
3
4
5
6
7
8
9
10
11
12
13 Obon (J)
14
15 Blessed Virgin (C)
16
17
18
19 Rakshabandhan (H)
20
21
22
23
24
25
26
27 Janmashtami (H)
28
29
30
31

# September

1 Shab-e-Miraj (M)
2
3
4
5
6
7 Ganesh Chaturthi (H)
8
9
10
11
12
13
14
15
16 Martyrdom of Guru Amar Das (S)
   Martyrdom of Guru Ram Das (S)
17
18 Mid-autumn Festival (Ch)
19 Shab-e-Barat (M)
20
21
22 Martyrdom of Guru Nanak Dev (S)
23 Harvest Festival (C)
24
25
26
27
28
29
30

## October

1
2
3 Bodhidharma's Day (Bd)
4 Ramadhan 1st day (M)
  Rosh Hashanah 1st day (Jw)
5 Rosh Hashanah 2nd day (Jw)
6
7
8
9 Birthday of Guru Ram Das (S)
10
11 Chong Yang (Ch)
12 Dassera (H)
13 Yom Kippur (Jw)
14
15
16
17
18 Succoth 1st day (Jw)
19 Succoth 2nd day (Jw)
20 Karva Chauth (H)
  Birthday of the Bab (B)
  Birthday of Guru Har Rai (S)
21 Martyrdom of Guru Gobind Singh (S)
22
23
24
25 Succoth 8th day (Jw)
26 Simchath Torah (Jw)
27
28
29
30 Lailat-ul-Qadr (M)
31 Hallowe'en (Sec)

## November

1 All Saints' Day (C), Diwali (H)
2 All Souls' Day (C)
3 Eid-ul-Fitr (M)
4
5 Guy Fawkes Day (GB)
6
7
8
9
10
11
12 Birthday of Baha'ullah (B)
13 Remembrance Sunday (C)
14
15 Birthday of Guru Nanak (S)
16
17
18
19
20
21
22
23
24 Martyrdom of Guru Tegh Bahadur (S)
  Thanksgiving (Sec)
25
26 Day of the Covenant (B)
27 First Sunday of Advent (C)
28 Ascension of Abdu'l-Baha (B)
29
30 St Andrew's Day (C)

## December

1
2
3
4
5
6
7
8 Immaculate Conception (C)
  Enlightenment of the Buddha (Bd)
9
10
11
12
13
14
15
16
17
18
19
20
21
22
23
24
25 Christmas Day (C)
26 St Stephen's Day (C)
  Chanuccah (Jw)
  Boxing Day (GB)
27
28
29
30
31

# INDEX OF RELIGIOUS FESTIVALS

B = Bahai
Bd = Buddhist
C = Christian
Ch = Chinese
GB = Great Britain
H = Hindu
Int = International
J = Japanese
Jai = Jain

Jw = Jewish
K = State of Kerala
M = Muslim
Sec = Secular
S = Sikh
T = Tibetan
Th = Thai
US = USA

Page numbers in **bold** indicate major references

# GENERAL INDEX

Page numbers in **bold** indicate major references